Ba

MW01119658

Business Intelligence

Business Intelligence

Evaluation and Impact on Performance

Corine Cohen

First published in France in 2004 by Hermes Science/Lavoisier entitled: *Veille et intelligence stratégiques*
© LAVOISIER, 2004
First published in Great Britain and the United States in 2009 by ISTE Ltd and John Wiley & Sons, Inc.

ISTE Ltd
27-37 St George's Road
London SW19 4EU
UK

www.iste.co.uk

John Wiley & Sons, Inc.
111 River Street
Hoboken, NJ 07030
USA

www.wiley.com

© ISTE Ltd, 2009

Library of Congress Cataloging-in-Publication Data

Cohen, Corine.
 [Veille et intelligence stratégiques. English]
 Business intelligence : the effectiveness of strategic intelligence and its impact on the performance of organizations / Corine Cohen.
   p. cm.
 Includes bibliographical references and index.
 ISBN 978-1-84821-114-8
 1. Business intelligence. 2. Strategic planning. 3. Information technology--Management. I. Title.
 HD38.7.C6413 2009
 658.4'72--dc22

                                                                                    2008054466

British Library Cataloguing-in-Publication Data
A CIP record for this book is available from the British Library
ISBN: 978-1-84821-114-8

Printed and bound in Great Britain by CPI Antony Rowe, Chippenham and Eastbourne.

Table of Contents

Introduction

The world in which we live has never been more troubled – recent years have seen wars, and attacks of several types – natural, economic, sanitary, social, political; industrial catastrophes, financial crises, technological revolution etc. People, companies and governments survive and change in an environment which is at a constant breaking point, with sometimes dramatic consequences. In every sector, a fundamental and recurring question should be raised: how can we predict the unpredictable?

To anticipate unexpected events and to avoid fatal surprises, governments and companies use specific strategic intelligence devices. Nations have always developed information services, whether they are military, political or economic. Organizations have always monitored their environment. Ever since the late 1960s, an increasing number of them have made this a formal activity. This movement progressed overseas in the 1980s, and in the 1990s in France, to cope with an unstable, complex and competitive environment. Surveillance has become Strategic Intelligence (SI).

However, looking at the harsh reality of international terrorism, demonstrated by the New York attacks in September 2001, the Moscow hostage crisis in October 2002 and others in increasing numbers all over the world, it is natural to question the usefulness of these government information agencies. Similarly, countless threat (or opportunity) examples are wrongly ignored by companies, and we can question the use of company Strategic Watch and SI systems. The unprecedented financial crisis governments and companies are facing today is more evidence of the weaknesses of existing Strategic Watch and Intelligence systems.

Unfortunately, monitoring and/or intelligence problems are always more visible than their advantages, and despite all poor performance demonstrations, nations and companies are still investing in this activity which is vital, as it represents a sort of "life insurance".

Government information devices and company SI systems are obviously interdependent, with areas in common, but their purposes are different. The parallel established exists in all intelligence-focused documentation. It describes the shortcomings, but also the absolute necessity of SI activities.

The usefulness of strategic intelligence services should not be in question, but their effectiveness should be:

1) Why and how do companies manage the monitoring of their environment?

2) How should strategic intelligence be defined? What are the effectiveness factors of SI?

3) How should we measure SI effectiveness and its impact on the performance of organizations?

This book attempts to answer these different questions. Its general goal is the result of these multiple questions: understanding the strategic intelligence activity in order to propose a model to measure its effectiveness and its impact on organizational performance.

In this new millennium, the importance and usefulness of monitoring the corporate environment are clearly recognized: the company with an efficient SI system has a major competitive advantage. Anticipation is not its only goal. Satisfying the need for information and knowledge and providing decision support are other central objectives of efficient SI. Before presenting the origins and challenges of SI for the organization, we must first explain the terminology and define what we will use.

The general surveillance field covers notions of watch, scanning, intelligence, competitive intelligence, vigilance, business intelligence, economic intelligence, economic and strategic intelligence, etc.

SI is defined here as a formalized process of research, collection, information processing and distribution of knowledge useful to strategic management. Beside its information function, the main goals of SI are to anticipate environmental threats and opportunities (anticipatory function), propose and/or engage in action (proactive function), help in strategic decision making and improve competitiveness and performance of the organization. It requires a organizational network structure, and human, technical and financial resources.

A distinction must therefore be made between Strategic Watch and SI. SI goes beyond Strategic Watch with its proactivity and its deeper involvement in the strategic decision process. Watch can (must) indicate the impacts of a detected event for example. However, it becomes intelligence when it produces recommendations and provides instructions to the recipient (all the more so when it implements them).

Now that this difference is explained, this book focuses on the most advanced level of SI.

By proposing a tool to measure SI effectiveness and its impact on the performance of the organization, this book is mainly aimed at SI users and managers. It can also be used by consultants for internal or external SI system audits.

Chapter 1

Scanning the Environment: A Vital Necessity for Companies

1.1. Getting informed: a very well-established and necessary requirement

The rapid evolution of the concept of scanning the corporate environment naturally leads to questioning its origin(s) and the reasons for its development within organizations. Is this concept really new? Where does it come from? Why do managers feel the need to monitor the environment of their companies?

Whether it is at the individual, government or company level, getting informed is a very well-established requirement.

1.1.1. *A fundamental need*

Getting informed is first and foremost a basic human need. In an often hostile natural environment, man had to acquire information to ensure his survival.

However, man is also curious by nature and eager to learn. He searches, interprets and constantly uses this information to improve his understanding of the world and to act in accordance with his environment. The discoveries of great explorers and the evolution of sciences are constant reminders. This natural curiosity seems to be different from one country to another. We observe for example that it is more prevalent in Asian cultures than in Western cultures.

1.1.2. *"To be beaten is excusable, but to be taken by surprise is unforgivable" (Napoleon Bonaparte)*

Obtaining information has always been vital in battlefields. All great commanders-in-chief were familiar with the strategic importance of information in armed combat. Obtaining strategic information was vital to better understand the enemy, avoid surprises and to be able to implement defensive and offensive actions. The military thus has long-standing knowledge of fact finding – intelligence – and companies find this expertise appealing. That is the main reason why we see so many military professionals go into the private sector. In addition to the necessity of finding new opportunities after the fall of the Eastern Bloc and the end of the Cold War, the defense department is now linked to economic defense. In fact, the activity of information collection and processing is also well-established in economic and political fields. It has often made it possible to ensure the supremacy of empires and continues to be a development lever for governments.

1.1.3. *Acquiring or maintaining economic and political power*

Numerous historical examples illustrate the enduring role of information in the power of countries. They show that colonial, industrial or commercial adventures always form the basis of contemporary intelligence systems (H. Martre).

There are pioneers such as the Republic of Venice, Sweden and Great Britain and modern intelligence systems from Japan, Germany, the USA or France.

The pioneers

THE EXAMPLE OF THE REPUBLIC OF VENICE

Founded in the 6th century, the Republic of Venice was part of the Byzantine Empire in the 9th century. From the 10th to the 12th centuries, its power was built on commercial maritime trade, particularly between the East and the West. Its ambassadors throughout Europe formed a network of informers. From the 12th to the 15th centuries, Venice became master of the seas and developed a true colonial empire.

THE CASE OF SWEDEN

In the 18th century, newspapers often reported European inventions described by Swedish merchants and travelers. This information then made it possible to introduce production methods in industries such as porcelain manufacture. From the middle of the 20th century, Sweden chose a winning internationalization strategy using education in language and strategic information management. The use and study of intelligence was a national affair, supported by the large network of businessmen and BISNES academics.

THE CASE OF GREAT BRITAIN

Great Britain was the leading international economic power during the Industrial Revolution. The first textile manufacturing plants were devised in Great Britain, along with numerous technical innovations such as the cotton spinning machine. Employees divulging information about these inventions were punished. In the petroleum field, the country used its own intelligence department to reinforce dominance, defend its colonial interests and to control its grounds and concessions. Large British corporations were the first to implement *Marketing Intelligence* services in the 1950s. Today, this intelligence activity is concentrated in the City, around banks, insurance companies and consulting firms.

Modern intelligence systems

THE JAPANESE MODEL

Japan has long been a model in this field. It built an impressive global information collection device which was at the heart of its exceptional growth in the 1980s, and its origin dates back to the Meiji era. Starting in 1868, this period marked the country's modernization and its opening up to the West. The search for information was made in the interest of protection, to maintain Japan's economic independence. The Japanese intelligence system is characterized by a collective and offensive information approach.

THE CASE OF GERMANY

In the 19th century, Bismarck's Germany developed its information system to take advantage of the Industrial Revolution, and to fight against the domination of Victorian Britain. During this period, a strong synergy developed between banks and large German manufacturers, building a centralized information management system which further empowered the young German state in 1870.

Today, the uniqueness of the German intelligence system lies in the strategic alliance between banks, insurance companies and the large manufacturing groups centralizing information flows. This central organization connects trading companies, small businesses, consulting firms, etc. in a single national interest.

THE CASE OF THE USA

Towards the end of the 1950s, large American corporations started putting internal competitive intelligence services in place. Personnel and financial resources for these structures are important: the budget for the scanning device implemented by General Motors equals the funds dedicated to France's foreign intelligence. However, because of their global economic dominance, the USA mostly focused on managing information about American competition and ignored foreign threats. For example, General Motors and Ford spied on each other for over 40 years.

Since the end of the 1970s and because of Japanese and then European competition, the USA developed a powerful global intelligence system. Greatly consolidated during the Clinton administration, it is supported by an undisputed leadership in information technology and computer and communication sciences. However, the effectiveness of the government's intelligence services was widely criticized during the September 11th 2001 attacks.

THE CASE OF FRANCE

France has also been using intelligence for a long time. French manufacturers were smuggling machine tools from Great Britain in order to compensate for not having kept up with the technical innovation of the first Industrial Revolution. Similarly, in order to beat the competition in high-precision clock making, then dominated by the British, manufacturing secrets were acquired from the leading expert in the field, allowing the supply of high quality chronometers to the Navy (Martre report).

Because of its policy of innovation, France had been a pioneer in technological watch since the early 1970s. It was, however, quickly left behind by other countries when the concept of intelligence was overcome by cultural barriers and prejudices: individualism, the notion of power connected to information, assimilation of industrial espionage, etc.

To make up for this setback, governments and corporations focused their energy on launching awareness and education campaigns in the 1990s. The contribution of the Martre report in 1994 then became significant.

The concept of research, processing and use of information is very old. It is inherent in humans and has always been practiced in the military, economic and political fields. Inquiring about the economic environment is also not a new activity for corporate players who have to make decisions on a daily basis. What is new, however, is that in this current period of uncertainty, it has become a necessity for most companies. The development of the surveillance concept in management sciences can be explained by different elements.

1.2. The corporation and its environment

The reasons why corporations use scanning are mainly linked to the nature and evolution of their circumstances in the post-War period.

1.2.1. *The corporation: an open system interacting with its environment*

After the Second World War, changes in the economic environment were observed, radically changing the concept of organization which went from being represented as a black box, or a closed system, to an open system in constant interaction with its environment. Understanding this environment and allowing better interaction with it seemed vital to the survival and competitiveness of corporations. The quality of information exchanges between the firm and its environment would influence the company's viability. From then on, the environment evolved into an increasingly complex and disruptive state.

Instability and complexity of the environment

The causes of the increasing instability and complexity of the environment are numerous and interdependent. Among these are globalization and the transformation of information and communication technologies, requiring new game rules and a very rapid response time for economic players.

The race to internationalization is unavoidable for all companies regardless of their size and market (national or regional):

– the slowdown in growth and saturation of national markets generates more intense competitiveness and drives corporations to gain new markets, to search for new opportunities beyond their borders;

– overcapacity caused by improvements in productivity generates important inventory levels that must be disposed of at all costs;

– companies are forced to reinforce their competitive positions and to improve their international competitiveness;

– they can seize the opportunity to extend product lifecycles: a mature or declining product in original markets can be exported to countries where it can be launched as a new product or be in the growth phase of the product's life;

– they can optimize the effects connected to size and benefit from economies of scale.

This inevitable movement toward globalization generates strong pressure from competition and complex economic problems. For example, liberalization was designed so that European companies could compete with foreign competition for services offered and economic performance. Liberalization first appeared in transportation, postal services, telecommunications and energy, resulting in the end of public service monopolies. In addition, other trading groups emerged. For example, the European Economic Community has become the largest domestic market in the world, with 340 million residents, and is the largest exporter. These economic zones resulted in a political union (European Union), an economic union (MERCOSUR) and free trade zones (NAFTA, ASEAN and MCCA). Moreover, the consumer has become more demanding and less loyal, forcing companies to become more aggressive toward their competitors in order to satisfy customers and make them more loyal. The increase in global production has led to significant overcapacity problems in all industrialized countries, resulting in severe social disruption. Finally, protection of the natural environment has become a major concern for many countries, imposing new norms and regulations on corporations.

The move toward globalization has considerably accelerated under the influence of New Information and Communication Technologies (NICTs). Flows between commercial blocs have accelerated. All sectors are involved and have undergone deep structural changes.

However, even NICTs, despite strong growth and the promise of exceeding all expectations, were unable to withstand environmental instability for long.

In fact, we have entered the era of the cyber-economy, information highways and the Internet. New players evolving in the world of new technology have become outstanding performers compared to the traditional economy heavyweights. According to a Boston Consulting Group study, at the end of the 1990s, 60 out of the 100 companies creating value for their shareholders were in the information technology field. This observation confirmed the outstanding vitality of this sector as the first names on the list belonged to e-business corporations, but the crash in early 2000 corrected, in a brutal way, this expansion and damaged the NICT sector.

In a context of permanent instability and complexity, uncertainty is at its highest. The company is much more vulnerable and decision-makers need ample, quality and instant – if not advance – information. Advance information is especially important because decreasing the uncertainty, which is a direct consequence of environment instability, and anticipating crises (or even better, managing them as they occur) are major concerns of economic players.

Uncertainty, anticipation and risk and crisis management

UNCERTAINTY

Since the late 1960s, the corporate environment has been turbulent, putting managers in an increasing state of uncertainty. In order to cope with this problem, the first step that the manager must take is to recognize the existence of uncertainty instead of ignoring it; according to Morin: "whereas ignorance of uncertainty leads to error, knowledge of uncertainty not only leads to doubt, but also to monitoring. Uncertainty is not only the cancer eroding knowledge, it is also the stimulus, it is pushing to investigate, verify, communicate, think, invent."

In 1975, in the same vein as Aguilar, Igor Ansoff recommended a scanning activity – radar surveillance – to detect low signals in order to anticipate threats and opportunities. However, when events are too new, it is impossible to predict the future. Later, authors proposed the organization of a more formalized and more proactive surveillance, going from scanning to intelligence.

In order to cope with this permanent state of uncertainty, CEOs felt the need to implement a scanning device for their environment, particularly to protect their corporation from risks and anticipate unexpected events such as crises.

PROTECTION AGAINST RISKS

Risk is a possible danger that can be predicted or is the possibility of a detrimental event. This notion is well known in the corporate world, especially in decision making where the risk of making a mistake is often important. It is at its highest when the decision maker has no information to use in an unknown situation or field. This position enhances the need for business intelligence, which can be viewed as risk insurance for preventing risk or protecting against it.

There are metaphors for this phenomenon in meteorology and volcanology. The scientific study of atmospheric phenomena such as weather forecasting or volcanic activity uses satellite devices with technical power capable of seeing and analyzing infinite data. Because of this finite vision, they help to prevent the risk of storms, eruptions, etc., days or even months or years in advance and thus may be able to avoid their multiple consequences.

Whereas the risk may be foreseeable, the crisis is sudden and violent, and is therefore much more difficult to predict and manage.

ANTICIPATION AND MANAGEMENT OF CRISES

Whether we talk about wars, oil, economic or food crises, economic consequences are such that corporations have learned the importance of having systematic scanning equipment to be able to foresee the unpredictable. Unfortunately, today, numerous examples highlight governmental and corporate deficiencies in this field.

First, armed conflicts, past war experience and their economic consequences (the Yom Kippur War, the Islamist Revolution, the Iran-Iraq War, etc.) have not kept governments and firms from being surprised by the invasion of Kuwait and the Gulf War, and more recently, by the September 11th attacks or by the third oil shock following those in 1973 and 1979.

Next, ecological crises occurred with the recent sinking of the *Erika* and the *Ievoli Sun* (only eight months apart) and the *Prestige* in November 2002. The massive dumping of the *Erika's* tanks on French shores led to the extinction of several bird species. The damage to marine life was just as important. The catastrophe ruined several industries such as tourism, salt production and oyster farming. Because of Brussels' inertia and an obvious lack of attention, the second shipwreck with a much more dangerous cargo was not avoided. Today, the Spanish shores of Galicia are damaged by tons of oil following the sinking of the *Prestige*.

Finally, we should mention crises in the food industry and public health sectors, the most dramatic example being "mad cow disease". This was thought to be limited to Britain's borders, but is a troubling reminder of the situation regarding contaminated blood. The emergence of an increasing number of cases in France, as well as a lack of information and communication, has thrown the country into an unprecedented panic. After a beef sales plunge of more than 50% in the first week after the announcement, the whole agricultural industry, the crown jewel of France, was affected. Fingers pointed to government organizations responsible for public health watch. Only a few months later, in this same field, foot-and-mouth disease cost over £9 billion or €14.3 billion to the British economy in an interim balance sheet.

Nations and firms with a powerful scanning system are the only ones who can protect themselves from risks, anticipate crises and avoid or limit their consequences.

The paradigm of need and the overabundance of information

To decrease the uncertainty resulting from a turbulent environment and to anticipate crises, decision makers encourage corporations to collect more information than is necessary. Nevertheless, they are conscious that the quantity of information available will never be enough to confirm that any decision is 100% perfect; there will always be a degree of uncertainty and doubt.

Once a decision is made, they still require more information for reassurance, in order to confirm their judgment, even if the information that comes after is not required by the company. Managers are constantly in need of information.

Paradoxically, the quantity of information and the power of information technology do not solve all the manager's problems. Besides the need for facts, the manager also needs assistance with the mass of data in order to make sense of often scattered, fragmented and inconsistent information.

With this over-information problem, the example of the September 11th attacks was enlightening. Soon after the tragedy, Americans found out that their intelligence systems had all the information necessary to predict this event. However, the government's intelligence devices could not extract the vital parts from the excessive amount of information provided.

A powerful scanning system must be able to measure this paradox between the need and the overabundance of information.

The uncertainty linked to an increasingly unstable and complex environment and the demands caused by overinformation are not the only explanation for the implementation of a monitoring system.

Two reasons in particular, which are interconnected, explain the fact that corporations have been using environment scanning practices: the absolute necessity to innovate and the example of the success in Japan.

1.3. Innovation and Japan

1.3.1. *Innovation: a vital imperative for the corporation*

Progress and innovation are at the heart of economic and social development. In order to be efficient and to survive pressures from the competition, the corporation must be constantly innovating.

Regardless of the nature of the innovation – technological, commercial or strategic – the scanning activity is the way to reach this major goal for the corporation.

Definitions and typology of innovation

DEFINITIONS

According to Barreyre, innovation is the original development and carrier of progress of a discovery, an invention or simply a concept. However, there are other definitions of innovation, such as that from Morin distinguishing between innovation as seen from the market or from the corporation:

– Innovation as seen from the market:

"For a given market, innovation is any product or service, or element from a product or service, offered for the first time to users or consumers, and which, compared to other products or services already filling the same types of needs, presents a new characteristic (performance, function, design, maintenance, access mode, etc.), or satisfies a new requirement" (Morin).

ABS and centralized door closing are innovations that improved the existing automobile product: braking performance for ABS, security and practicality for centralized door closing. Minitel, microwave ovens, debit cards and Walkmans are examples of innovations responding to new needs which did not exist in a formal or even latent form.

– Innovation as seen from the corporation:

"For a given corporation…, innovation is the result of a process focused on economic goals, and called development, during which the corporation implements, under new conditions, at least one combination, new or otherwise, that must work together toward the design of a product or service, its development, marketing, invoicing, management and organization of vital functions required for its activities" (Morin, 1992).

We frequently distinguish between product innovations and process innovations which are often dependent and inseparable.

However, new events in industry have corrected this vision of things.

– Disruptive technologies.

There are numerous examples where technological potential as well as commercial potential has been underestimated. Alcatel did not believe in the portable phone; similarly, the clock industry ignored the arrival of digital watches. In their article, *Disruptive Technologies: Catching the Wave*, Bower and Christensen analyze the many cases of well-established corporations who did not take advantage of opportunities offered by new technologies. They were too disruptive to their position as leaders. Nevertheless, they offered a potential of colossal proportions for the future of the corporation. That is how Goodyear and Firestone entered the radial tire market too late, how Xerox let Canon create the small photocopier market, and how Sears paved the way for Wal-Mart… In particular, they suggest that managers should not ignore new technologies which do not immediately meet consumer requirements.

– Typology of innovations.

The literature presents several typologies which are generally based on four criteria: the degree of novelty for the corporation, the intrinsic nature of the innovation (technological or commercial), the origin of the innovation (the corporation or market) and the degree of novelty for the consumer.

– The degree of novelty for the corporation.

The strategic risk is all the more important for the corporation as the market is new for it. There are four levels of risk:

1) Market and products are known; the risk is limited because the corporation relies on its distinctive skills.

2) The market is new but the product is known; the risk is mainly commercial and the corporation uses its marketing know-how.

3) The market is known but the product is new; the risk then is mainly technical and the corporation uses its technological knowledge.

4) The market and product are new, risks add up and the corporation must manage a diversification strategy.

– Nature of the innovation.

We generally distinguish between technological innovation and marketing innovation.

Technological innovation occurs in the physical characteristics of the product (manufacturing process, use of a new component, new raw products, new drug, new finished products or new complex systems, etc.).

The organizational or commercial innovation focuses on modes of organization, distribution or communication in the marketing process of a product or service (new design, new presentation, new publicity, new packaging, new payment method, etc.).

– The origin of the innovation: the corporation or the market.

We generally compare the new product led by demand (green products, Cash & Carry) to the product pushed by the corporation (CDs, Toys 'R' Us concept) – either responding to the demands of the market or creating a demand.

Previous studies show that an innovation strategy which starts with a needs analysis before going to the drawing board is more effective than the opposite (Lambin, 1998).

– Innovation and consumer behavior.

This fourth classification is based on the combination between the intensity of the product's technological change and the intensity of the behavioral change of the user who would use it. There are four types of innovation:

1) Technological improvements: technological change and behavioral change are low. They represent progressive improvements of a product (i.e. its development) but they have no impact on consumer behavior. This type of incremental innovation was the approach traditionally adopted in Japan. Three examples are Canon Libris combining the computer and printer function in a single product, the Gillette GII two blade razor and the fax using regular paper.

2) Technological breakthroughs, technological change is high but behavioral change is low. They combine important technological innovations which do not really lead to a change in consumer behavior (for example, CDs).

3) Organizational breakthroughs: technological change is low but behavioral change is high. Innovations do not lead to important technological change but result in modifications in consumer

behavior. For example, we can examine the case of product recycling (glass bottles, plastic, paper) or the collection of used batteries. We should also cite the concept of self-service, which was one of the major innovations of the 20th century.

4) Radical innovations: technological change and behavioral change are high. This type of innovation involves major technological modifications triggering strong changes in user behavior. Examples: the cell phone, Internet, microprocessor, chip card, DVDs, microwave ovens, etc.

Innovation research has recently focused more on the market, i.e. on the product and the consumer. The preference given to consumer perception leads to two categories of innovation: small innovation (perception of the innovative nature of a product by the consumer is low) and large innovation or breakthrough innovation (perception of a strong innovation). For the latter, management uses technological breakthrough innovation and social breakthrough innovation terms.

Technological breakthrough innovation: this is a major scientific advance which may involve one or more sectors. Computers and new information and communication technologies are current examples. The methodology associated with technological breakthrough innovation seems to come from an idea (discovery, invention, concept, etc.) oriented toward the market.

Commercial breakthrough innovation: the innovation is not always technological. A new concept, an original idea can also lead to an innovation. McDonald's, Ikea or Club Med concepts are innovations with no technological content. We should note however that even though the technological breakthrough innovation may result in a new and unknown product, the commercial innovation can lead to a product that is known but has acquired new value. It is then more incremental by nature. In this case, the methodology consists of starting with the market to arrive at the idea.

The innovation can therefore generate from the R&D or the Marketing Department of a corporation. These two departments collaborate more now than in the past.

Next to technological or commercial innovations, we find strategic innovation.

Strategic innovation: in his major book on strategic innovation, Gary Hamel presents corporations with totally different concepts. Revolution, the logical next step in conquering the future, is a strong call for strategic innovation. For the author, corporations wanting to reach and especially stay in a favorable position must continually reinvent strategies. By giving a fine analysis of the environment's sphere of influence and particularly competitor intentions and plans, intelligence may be a powerful lever in strategic innovation.

1.3.2. *Innovation: a mandatory strategic choice*

To ensure its continuity and competitive position, an innovation strategy has become mandatory for the corporation for at least four reasons.

The contribution of new products to revenue and corporate profits

The contribution of new products to corporate revenue is becoming more significant. In 1995, the sales figure proportion for products that did not exist five years previously was 45% on average. This percentage, which is much higher for high-tech sectors, went from 33% between 1976 and 1981 to 42% between 1986 and 1990.

New products also have an effect on the corporation's profits. In 1982, a study carried out by PDMA concluded that new products represented 23% of profit, a percentage that grew by 33% compared to the previous five years.

Since the innovations mostly originated in research, R&D expenditures are good indicators of the sector's activity and of corporate innovation strategies. In 1998, the R&D expenditures of some corporations in the fields of information technology (Microsoft, 16.9%, Intel, 9.4%), pharmaceuticals (Pfizer, 15.8%, Roche, 15.5%, Glaxo Welcome, 14.4%, Novartis, 11.8%) and telecommunications (Ericsson, 14.5%, Northern, 13.9%, Motorola, 9.2%) are noteworthy.

Consumer demands

Consumers have become more demanding and want greater variety. We have gone from a mass consumption society to one of individualized consumption. Innovation can then become a real competitive advantage for the corporation wanting to distance itself from its competitors by offering a wide range of products.

Market saturation

Market saturation encourages organizations to let their products lapse, to encourage re-buying or over-equipment. The CD, for example, re-launched the Hi-Fi market which had lost some of its dynamism because of the stagnating market for record players and long-playing records. Similarly, the mountain bike reactivated the bicycle market.

The shortening of a product lifecycle

Finally, the lifecycle of products has shortened significantly and the race for innovation gets faster. In 1990, Honda could launch a new model in less than two years, whereas the President of Peugeot maintained that they needed four years. New automobile models are currently launched every two years by most manufacturers.

Innovation is therefore an essential strategic choice for managers with a performance and competitive objective for their companies. For Bernard Arnault, President of LVMH, global leader in the luxury industry, the main axis of strategy is creativity, innovation and marketing of new products. For Daniel Bernard, President of Carrefour, European leader and number two worldwide for distribution, innovation is the group's key to success – winning and building customer loyalty means being able to innovate at all levels. To encourage innovation strategy and to provide them with the necessary means for their success, corporations have organized scanning activities for their environment.

1.3.3. *Scanning for innovation strategy*

The origin of innovation

As we have seen, innovation does not always begin in a research laboratory. It can be a new combination of existing technologies or the acquisition of new technologies. It can also come from marketing departments or from observing the competition. For Kirzner, it is imperative to be in a position of listening, looking and alertness toward the market, the economic and competitive environment of the corporation.

This scanning will lead to an idea or a concept which will be the basis of the innovation. Scientific and technical scanning (technological watch) of markets and competition (marketing, commercial and competitive intelligence) is therefore a vital activity to detect potential sources of innovation and to improve the flow of new products.

Better internal technological choices

In the context of general permanent change, the corporation has to be in constant innovation mode and to constantly renew itself. Innovation can occur externally by the marketing of new products, as well as internally by process and technology changes. In fact, choosing a technology at the right time may be vital for the survival of a corporation. An example of errors made by the *Le Monde* newspaper is one representation (see Fontaine, 1984).

In the 1980s, the daily newspaper was certain that its characteristic format was the main reason for its success. The newspaper was prospering, and a decision to replace an outdated piece of equipment had to be made. New presses bought in Switzerland were specially built to retain the characteristic dimensions of the newspaper. Unfortunately, the uniqueness of the format became a problem when the facsimile process – a technique making it possible to print a newspaper simultaneously in different areas – grew. Another mistake involved the acquisition of sophisticated rotary presses to replace the offset process which had become too slow for a newspaper with a large circulation. The newspaper did not predict the rapid evolution of the offset technique. The rotary presses were labor-intensive and quickly became obsolete. These unfortunate choices had a negative impact on the newspaper's results.

The performance of a corporation often depends on its own technological choices. It must constantly be in scanning mode in order to anticipate scientific and technical developments which may occur either in its own business or in another, sometimes completely different industry.

Decrease of risks linked to innovation strategies

These risks are important and occur at each step of the innovation process. They are linked to the length of the process, to R&D expenditures, to the newness of the product and market, etc.

Numerous industries such as oil, energy or pharmaceuticals depend on technologically long horizons. Research, development and launching processes for a new product (promotion, publicity, acceptance, etc.) are long, expensive and risky. A scanning activity must be able to achieve gains in time and money and to decrease risks.

Scanning makes it possible to avoid wasting resources, such as R&D expenditure for outdated products. In the pharmaceutical industry for example, the development process can last 15 years between fundamental research, clinical tests and the demand for marketing and publicity. If intelligence detects side-effects from the publishing of clinical tests of one of the components, the project can be quickly abandoned or redirected.

In any innovative project, uncertainty is large, as technological evolution, consumer and competitive reactions and trend phenomena are increasingly unpredictable elements. By providing the corporation with accurate information on markets, products, clients, providers, competitors, etc., the scanning activity can reduce the risk of failure linked to innovation strategies.

The absolute necessity to innovate partly explains the approach of corporations toward more formalized scanning systems, and the Japanese model was a powerful catalyst for this movement.

1.3.4. *The inevitable Japanese example*

Information and competitiveness

In the 1980s, Japan experienced an impressive period of economic growth, imposing its rhythm on the global competitive game. In 1984, of the 200 largest corporations who made it to the Forbes list, 61 were Japanese. Similarly, of the 500 largest manufacturing companies on Fortune's list, 146 were Japanese. Finally, looking at over 100 banks, 28 were Japanese, specifically the first four. Japanese corporations were among the first in all manufacturing sectors. In the automobile industry, Toyota and Nissan were number three and four after General Motors and Ford. In the steel industry, Nippon Steel outdistanced US Steel and in the electric industry, Hitachi and Matsushita Electric were second and third after General Electric, ahead of Philips and Siemens. The largest groups were threatened by Japanese competitors: Caterpillar by Komatsu, Kodak by Fuji Film, Texas Instrument by NEC, and IBM by Fujitsu and Hitachi (Abegglen and Stalk Jr.).

For many authors, the economic performance of Japan in the 1980s was mainly due to the effectiveness of its global information collection and analysis system and a systematic interest in its competitors' activities. In fact, systematic scanning of information published worldwide, in particular in industrialized countries, followed by rational use of this information was largely responsible for the Japanese success.

This made the country the real pioneer of watch and intelligence practices. In order to counter the emergence of new Japanese competitors and to imitate a powerful model, numerous corporations – and nations – organized their own intelligence systems.

To understand why and how information management was the main performance lever of Japan, we have to examine the country's culture and its evolution.

The origin of intelligence in Japan

THE WEST AND JAPAN: DIFFERENT PHILOSOPHIES AND CULTURES

The West is marked by the Socratic philosophy "know thyself", whereas for Japan, knowledge of the opponent is vital: "if you want to defeat the opponent, know him first" (*The Book of Five Rings*, Miyamoto Musashi, 1594-1645 and Sun Tzu).

For Japan, information is a strategic power: "the Japanese manage information as Westerners manage money: they exchange it between groups, buy it and negotiate for it" (M. Bayen, 1989). In addition, Japan has maintained a culture of information sharing. In contrast to Western countries, information is considered a collective resource. In the corporation, each employee is judged by his or her ability to transmit information within a group. Finally, for the 121 million Japanese, getting information is natural, it is a state of mind. In 1989, 68 million newspapers were sold each day.

The origin of the Japanese intelligence model

The Japanese interest in knowledge has grown since the Meiji empire. The 122nd Emperor of Japan, Mutsuhito (1852–1912), was the pioneer of modern Japan, opening his country to the world and to Western methods. In the 1868 Japanese constitution, one of the five oaths to the Emperor states: "We will look for knowledge throughout the world in order to reinforce the foundations of the Imperial rule."

The objective corresponding to this permanent approach to research into worldwide knowledge is first to protect Japan and to ensure economic independence from Western powers. The country has developed a strict industrial property policy for the protection of its inventions and markets.

After the Second World War, Japan started implementing an organized and sophisticated device for global scanning. After its defeat, it used the economic weapon of information as Americans had used the intelligence weapon during the War. In the 1970s, Japanese competitors emerged and destabilized the largest American corporations. The Director of Toshiba France Public Sector recognized that the Toshiba Group started functioning in 1985, but managers were already in place right after the War.

The main characteristics of the Japanese intelligence model

INNOVATION ABOVE ALL

The Japanese corporations and government quickly realized that innovation was absolutely necessary to reach a dominant competitive position. Attaining technological leadership was their main objective. R&D was therefore very important within the corporation, and information research practiced by the Japanese was first and foremost technological in nature. In order to reach their goal, the vital question in the post-War era was: should we reinvent or buy technology?

In fact, Japan reached its development level because of imported technology. From 1951 to March 1984, close to 42,000 foreign technology import contracts were signed.

We then witnessed a massive transfer of technologies from West to East. Up until early in the 1980s, the invariable approach of the Japanese consisted of searching outside for (mainly technological) knowledge and copying or drawing inspiration from it to create identical or improved products. R&D missions were the improvement of acquired processes and the appropriation of products emerging from these processes (M. Berger, CFCE, 1991).

As indicated in Figure 1.1, in 1978, only 5% of Japanese products came from a completely original technology.

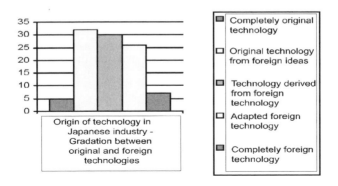

Figure 1.1. *Origin of technology in Japanese industry*
(source: Euroconsult)

At that time, Japan was also using the reverse engineering technique: by studying in detail, they dissected foreign products to get inspiration, or even copied them (Bayen, CPE, CFCE, 1991).

That is how the Japanese earned their reputation as imitators 40 years ago. They also bought foreign knowhow at a very high cost, notably in the fields of the steel industry and electronics from Germany and the USA respectively (A. Takahashi, 1990).

During the 1980s, however, acquisitions became more difficult, leading to an increase in R&D investment. In 1985, Japanese corporate R&D expenditure was higher than those of American corporations. In one year (from 1988 to 1989), the total research budget in Japan went from €65 to 73 billion, an increase of 11.23%. The R&D budget for the six largest electric equipment corporations (Hitachi, Nec, Fujitsu, etc.) was €10 billion (Berger).

This important R&D activity was consolidated by patents. The Japanese registered 320,000 patents a year compared to less than 2,000 in France. Hitachi, for example, registered as many patents as all the French corporations put together. Innovation was thus systematically protected. Japan became the premier patent registerer in the world, to such a degree that these patents appeared suspicious and were often seen as manipulation to divert competitors. In this way, the Japanese only depended on foreign technology for 10% of their innovations (Takahashi).

Among the information sources used by the Japanese, the patent was the most efficient tool for technological and marketing intelligence: it involved previous technology, advantages brought by the invention and its applications. In addition, 70% of the information contained in the patents did not appear anywhere else. A 1970 statistic already indicated that in over 314 Japanese corporations, 92.7% practiced patent intelligence.

Conversely, for foreign corporations wanting to monitor Japanese patents, language was an important barrier (only 25% of Japanese patents were translated into English). Geographic remoteness, insularity and culture reinforced Japanese economic protectionism. Besides these natural barriers, Japan erected artificial obstacles such as discretion, communication and protection (Board).

In fact, in addition to registering patents, the extraordinary protection of the Japanese domestic market and investments in capital was due to the supervision of government ministries (MITI, Transport, Health, Postal Service and Telecommunications, etc.). These departments are at the service of Japanese manufacturing and also play a central role in global information research and collection.

THE MAIN PLAYERS

– The role of government and civil service departments:

The MITI made important contributions to the development of the economic power of Japan. Created in 1925 by former Japanese intelligence agents, it was compared to the CIA by Americans. It centralizes information on foreign competitors from corporations, private companies, professional organizations and other government departments. For example, all Japanese corporate managers have to present a report when they come back from a foreign mission: they note everything that seems new or interesting for their corporation. This information is transmitted to MITI which integrates it in a database that is available to all manufacturers. In addition, manufacturing groups have long had the implicit obligation (administrative guidance) to divulge their commercial or technological negotiations. This established industrial protection of sorts against Japanese competition. A de facto monopoly arbitrated by MITI was then established.

Other departments reinforced its action. The following organizational chart shows the close links which exist between state entities and information research and process organizations.

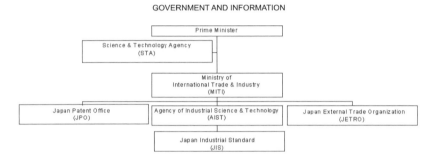

GOVERNMENT AND INFORMATION

Figure 1.2. *Government and information*

– The role of Shôshas:

These large Japanese trading houses (C. Itoh, Nichimen, Mitsui, Mitsubishi and Sumitomo for example) are conglomerates with revenues between $30 and 90 billion and a workforce between 3,000 and 12,000 people. There are a dozen of them, and each one has an impressive network because they have offices all over the world. The motto of MITSUI, one of the most important trading houses, is "information is the blood of the corporation". In this Shôsha, 84 people focus on foreign technologies. Shôshas are unique economic entities. In 1989, the first nine Japanese trading companies were responsible for half of import–export operations in Japan.

– Specialized organizations:

There are reputedly over 10,000 industrial information collection specialists in Japan (among them 350 private agencies for the city of Tokyo alone). These organizations are often linked to a government agency or to an important group. They sometimes use methods which are just short of being illegal (Bayen, IDT 1989). In 1983 for example,

Tadashi Kurihara, a former diplomat accompanied by military intelligence specialists, created a Private Institute for Industrial Property where industrial espionage and corporation protection methods were taught. An increasing number of corporations now take responsibility for information research and processing within internal services. According to a survey by Juro Nakagawa, 473 Japanese corporations have their own information department and managed 5.203 projects in 1991.

RESOURCES

– Financial resources:

Each year in Japan, a billion dollars of public money is dedicated to intelligence. In each year of the 1980s, the annual budget for information was between €1.5 and 1.85 billion. The annual budget for technological intelligence represents between €0.7 and 1 billion and 10 to 15% of the R&D budget. Corporations devote 1.5% of their revenue to mainly technological intelligence activities. For some Shôsha managers, expenditure devoted to technological intelligence represents a percentage of the Gross National Income which is twice that of the USA and three times larger than that of Europe.

Human resources are also important: at Mitsubishi, 30 people were responsible for following competitor patents in 1990.

– Training and awareness for information collection:

Training of people for research and processing of information is huge. In 1990, there were 31 universities, colleges and institutes specializing in information sciences. The University of Chiba was created in 1935 and trains over 300 scanners every year. In Osaka, a university was created to train 900 scanners. In addition, employee awareness of information is permanent.

Finally, information sharing between employees is another strong point for the Japanese system. Collected information can be consolidated during regular meetings between the different managers (research, production, studies, commercial, etc.).

– Means of acquiring information:

Japanese corporations have access to much greater pre-processed information than those of the USA and Europe. Besides the patents which represent the most efficient source of information, many other sources are available:

– worldwide databases,

– publications,

– surveys of the opinions of international experts,

– industrial missions,

– exhibitions, symposia, conventions, trade shows, etc.,

– students and interns,

– the acquisition of products and samples,

– industrial negotiations,

– sales networks, joint-ventures, partners, etc.,

– foreign installations,

– foreign research contracts,

– Japanese corporations also use other more aggressive forms of information collection such as harassment, recruiting employees from competitors and industrial espionage.

In the 21st century, Japan is facing its third recession in ten years. During the second half of the 1980s, political policies encouraged the development of a trading bubble (increase in real estate prices, excess debt, over-investment). At the beginning of the 1990s, the interest rate increase triggered the explosion of these "bubbles" and a violent drop in activity. Besides this explanation of the crisis in Japan, we should also note that the Japanese intelligence model served as an example for numerous nations and corporations who have now become very powerful in information management. In order to respond to industrialists' questions concerning the economic success of Japan, in the 1980s Y. Otu, Director of the Strategy Department at MITI, did not hesitate to arrogantly say: "Japan was defeated during the Second World War in part because of the supremacy of American information…Why doesn't American industry develop the same type of excellence today to cope with Japan?" It seems that he was heard, if we look at the evolution of the American economy and intelligence system.

1.4. Conclusion

The need for information as well as information research and processing is not new. Man has always felt the need to get informed, whether to survive in a hostile natural environment, to satisfy his natural curiosity, to win wars or to ensure economic and political power.

However, in an economic world, being organized to manage strategic information has become vital for the survival and future position of the corporation. The company is an open system constantly interacting with an increasingly turbulent environment marked by new technology, globalization and revolution. This instability is creating a strong feeling of uncertainty for managers in their decision making as well as in anticipation and crisis management. A paradox exists between their needs and an overload of information. To reach their performance and competitiveness objectives, they must innovate.

Scanning is implemented to decrease uncertainty, anticipate unexpected events and improve innovation strategies.

The preceding arguments, with the catalyst example of the Japanese success, encouraged an increasing number of corporations to adopt a scanning approach. Environment turbulence, the uncertainty that it generates, a lack of information, an over supply of information and the necessity to innovate are still topical today.

A new threat is also emerging. In his report addressed to the European Union, D. Campbell states that: "large governments regularly use interception for any modern type of high throughput communication, including written messages, calls from cell phones and email over the Internet, in order to ensure commercial advantages for some corporations."

The author also makes reference to Echelon, the global scanning network implemented by the National Security Agency and its partners (UK, Canada, Australia and New Zealand). Created in 1947 to intercept telecommunications from the Eastern Bloc, this network did not detect signals concerning risks of attack and is used today for Economic Intelligence. This is serious enough business to be put on the agenda of the European Union Interior Cabinet meeting on June 29th 2002...

In fact, with the global network scanning threat, shouldn't countries organize and coordinate more? Shouldn't their scanning policies, which are inseparable from corporations, intensify?

For all these reasons, organizing environment scanning remains an absolute necessity for corporations and governments.

Chapter 2

Evolution of the General Concept of Surveillance

Since the 1960s, the general concept of environmental surveillance (which includes watch and intelligence) evolved at the same time as changes in the corporate environment. This chapter analyzes the evolution of surveillance.

Even though surveillance is not a new activity, the outcome of its challenges and its formalization within corporations are new.

The relative newness of these concepts explain the instability of terminology and knowledge – theoretical as well as practical. That is why the semantic question is regularly raised. Most authors emphasize the problem by defining the notions of surveillance – watch and intelligence – because there are so many definitions and terms representing them. It is compounded by translations of expressions between English and French.

Studying books and articles published since 1967 – where we can presume that they correctly reflect the authors' terminology preference – we can account for at least 25 different expressions in English publications and as many in French articles. The profusion of terms for notions of surveillance, watch or intelligence reveals semantic problems and the necessity for an international consensus.

Instead of going through a tedious review of all prior definitions and terms – which would only add to the confusion – we will instead highlight the fundamental points of reference of the evolution of surveillance.

From the analysis of publications and from our observation, we notice three periods in the evolution of the notion of surveillance: an emergence phase, a development phase and a consolidation phase.

This evolution is represented in the following table.

	EMERGENCE PHASE	DEVELOPMENT PHASE	CONSOLIDATION PHASE
ENGLISH EVOLUTION	from 1967 to 1979	from 1980 to 1990	from 1991
FRENCH EVOLUTION	from 1970 to 1990	from 1991 to 2000	from 2001

Table 2.1. *The three evolution phases of the general concept of environmental surveillance of corporations*

The three phases are presented according to a single framework: author definitions, terminologies used and characteristics of each period.

2.1. The emergence phase

2.1.1. *Scanning, F.J. Aguilar (1967)*

Between 1954 and 1961, the foundations of strategic planning models appear in articles from the *Harvard Business School* and the premises of the notion of surveillance are presented. The fundamental concepts of opportunities and threats from the corporate environment are defined and the implementation of surveillance methods is suggested to allow for an anticipatory adaptation of the corporation. However, at the end of the 1960s, the real starting point of the notion of surveillance emerged.

In 1967, F.J. Aguilar was the first to become interested in the process of scanning the corporate environment. His major contribution occurred shortly after the first strategic planning models from Gilmore and Bradenburg, Learned, Christensen, Andrews and Guth and Ansoff.

In his reference book *Scanning the Business Environment*, he uses the metaphor of radar to explain that the corporation must have a scanning system to examine its environment, and presents it as: "The acquisition of information concerning events, trends and interactions in the corporation's environment, for which the knowledge will constitute assistance for the identification and understanding of strategic opportunities and threats for high level management."

In his definition, F.J. Aguilar mentions the three high points of scanning activity: 1) acquisition of environmental information, 2) identification of strategic opportunities and threats, 3) understanding of strategic opportunities and threats. For the author, scanning is clearly helpful and is an external strategic diagnostic tool. We must mention that it explains the concept in its informal and individual dimension, which is meant for high level management.

2.1.2. *Weak signal detection, I. Ansoff (1975)*

The article by I. Ansoff, "Managing strategic surprise by response to weak signals" (1975), is an essential contribution to the evolution of the surveillance concept insofar as an emphasis is put on the importance of detecting almost undetectable information about the environment to avoid strategic surprises.

Unexpected events such as armed conflict and wars (Pearl Harbor, Yom Kippur), the oil crisis of 1973 or crises in the automotive industry enable us to become aware of the consequences of environmental instability and to show the limits of strategic planning. Strategic plans are built from abundant information that is highly visible to all corporations. Ansoff reports that modern planning techniques are not adapted to unexpected events. In an unstable environment, the corporation must be able to detect weak signals heralding these surprises. Corporate evolution can no longer be planned by simple extrapolation of prior data, ignoring the unsteadiness of the environment.

Ansoff recommends greater flexibility, by recommending a gradual response during growth combined with a response to weak signals, as opposed to strategic planning which relies on strong signals. The perception of weak signals must enable the corporation to avoid surprises which would decrease its reaction time and its chances to seize an opportunity or face a threat.

In *Implanting Strategic Management*, published in 1984, he reiterates and clarifies his recommendations by using the expression from Aguilar: "the corporation must have a radar surveillance system to detect weak signals in its environment." He explains that surveillance must be systematic, continuous and, especially, apply to all environmental fields: competitive, technological, economic, social and political.

2.1.3. *Emergence of the notion of intelligence*

British and American intelligence cells (1950)

The notion of intelligence appeared in the post-War period. The day after the Second World War, the corporate panorama changed. It went from being a black box to an open system interacting with its environment. The consumption society was expanding and marketing was becoming more important. The need for information to satisfy customer needs and especially to cope with competitive pressure explained the emergence of marketing intelligence cells in Great Britain and competitive intelligence in the USA in the 1950s.

The intelligence system, Luhn (1958)

In 1958, Luhn noted the definition of intelligence as given in a dictionary: the notion of intelligence can generally be defined as the "capacity to understand interrelations between available facts in order to guide action toward a desired goal".

Intelligence appears as the ability to connect events to give them sense. Several more recent dictionaries and books emphasize this first definition of intelligence (shown above). The quotation also highlights the proactivity of intelligence and its strategic purposiveness in reaching set objectives.

In a mostly technical approach, Luhn, a researcher–computer specialist at IBM, was the first to propose an automatic system for collecting, processing, storage and distribution of information for corporations which he called a business intelligence system.

Organizational intelligence, Wilensky (1967)

The process proposed by Luhn could be found in 1967 in *Organizational Intelligence* as defined by Wilensky: "the collection, processing, interpretation and communication of technical and political information necessary to the decision process."

The author emphasized that this process could help the decision. We should note that he mostly referred to the technical and political environment.

Wilensky then explained in detail the three components of organizational intelligence:

1) Contact intelligence refers to relational networks where members can collect, process and distribute information, as well as carry out influencing actions such as lobbying.

2) Internal intelligence focuses on the surveillance of the corporation itself.

3) Intelligence concerning facts and numbers highlights the value added to information provided to decision makers.

During this period, the surveillance activity for the scientific, technical and technological environment emerged in France under the term *technological intelligence*.

2.1.4. *France: pioneer of technological intelligence (~1970)*

There are at least three reasons explaining the development of technological intelligence in France.

The French Government carried out an innovation policy early in the 1970s. From 1971 to 1981, Thierry Gaudin, General Engineer for Mining Engineering at the Department of Industry, was responsible for the implementation of an innovation strategy. In 1979, the Agence Nationale de la Valorisation de la Recherche (ANVAR, National Agency for Research Appreciation) was reformed. Development assistance, centralized by the government, was replaced by regional innovation assistance. The government encouraged companies, especially small businesses, to develop a technological intelligence approach and offered them two supporting organizations: ARIST – Agences Régionales d'Information Scientifique et Technique (Regional Scientific and Technical Information Agencies) – and DRI – Réseau National de Délégués aux Relations Industrielles (National Network of Delegates for Industrial Relations) – the latter being responsible for coordinating relations between researchers and industrialists.

If the concept of technological watch first emerged in France, it was partly due to the sensitive nature of its industries such as aeronautics and energy. In these extremely competitive fields, in a constant state of alert and with high technological content, France has often proven to be very vigilant. In contrast, manufacturing sectors were rarely mobilized at that time (Martre report).

Finally, scientists, who at that time were numerous in France, had a natural aptitude for research and collection of information. It is an activity that they practiced every day in their job.

French scientific and technical fields were the first to consider the concept of intelligence. Even though the practice of technological watch is old and frequent in French corporations, only in the middle of the 1980s did formal definitions emerge.

In *L'excellence technologique*, J. Morin highlights the vital missions for an activity consisting of: "Scanning corporate technological environment for strategic purposes, detecting threats which, if anticipated in an intelligent manner, can sometimes be transformed into innovation opportunities (...). The surveillance system then plays the role of insurance with a premium that has to be paid. Its objective is to protect from nasty surprises, anticipate threats and opportunities for better management, save time on events and competitors."

This definition included the strategic reach of surveillance as well as all the concepts introduced by Aguilar and Ansoff: surveillance of the corporate environment – the technological environment in this case – detection of threats and opportunities for protection acts against strategic surprises and saves time. The notion of insurance is original. Morin implicitly maintained that any corporation which does not put forth surveillance methods for its environment is not protected and puts itself at risk.

2.1.5. *English and French terminology*

The terms *scanning* or *environmental scanning* have been used in English publications since 1967.

A few French authors like Marteau have subsequently used *scanning* as it is and have translated it to *balayage* or, more frequently, *surveillance*. For lack of a single word that would translate an idea, Lesca said he would use "words or expressions without distinction: to perceive the environment, scan/scanning, monitor/surveillance, be on the lookout, be listening, detect/detection" and translated the American expression Strategic Information Scanning System by *Système d'Information pour le Management Stratégique de l'Entreprise (SIMSE)*. Others use the word *vigilance*. *Surveillance* is mostly used in France; its translation, *Watch*, is rarely used across the Atlantic.

As for the term *Intelligence*, it started being used late in the 1970s in English publications only.

2.1.6. *Characteristics*

During this period, some corporations became conscious of the necessity of scanning their environment and were sensitive to the concept of scanning, surveillance or watch. The first empirical studies on this subject emerged (Kefalas and Schoderbek, Denning, Keegan,

King and Cleland, and Wall). This phase of emergence was characterized by the increasing focus on information research and data collection. In fact, up to the 1980s, these tools, along with information research and collection methods, were the ones studied the most. The main objective was the development of large data files on industries and competitors.

2.2. Phase of development

2.2.1. *Predominance of the concept of Competitive Intelligence*

Michael Porter's contribution (1980)

The beginning of the 1980s marked a real turning point in the evolution of the concept of surveillance in an exaggerated competitive context where competitive analysis became central. Michael Porter, a teacher–researcher at Harvard Business School as well as a consultant in both corporate strategy and industrial economy fields, persuaded corporations of the necessity for an organized and formalized intelligence system.

For the author, analyzing all important competitors, whether they are current or potential, is vital. In order to reinforce its position in a market, a corporation must have a deep understanding of its competitors. Also, in order to respond to questions about these competitors, a leader requires a large basis of information. He explained that information often arrives in bits and pieces. Being able to put this together through a formal process involving documentation to make it logical and to improve our knowledge is vital. An incredible number of sources for intelligence data are inventoried.

Porter proposed a first Competitive Intelligence process model which exceeded the information collection phase since it involved data processing (classification and summary) and communication to the strategy expert. The connection between the Competitive Intelligence and strategy formulation processes was emphasized.

Aguilar and Ansoff suggested surveillance of the corporate environment by detecting weak signals indicating strategic surprises, and Porter insisted on the organization and formalization of this surveillance by specifically focusing on the corporation's competition.

Going from the notion of scanning to the notion of intelligence also involves great proactivity. It is no longer enough to carefully monitor the corporate environment until a signal is detected before reacting. Now we must search for information and transform it into intelligence to give it sense.

Starting in the 1980s, a larger number of corporations implemented and organized their intelligence activities. The infatuation for this concept accelerated with the example of Japan, where the major development was largely explained by its capacity to collect, process and use environmental information. A new function appeared within the corporation. American intelligence professionals created the Society of Competitive Intelligence Professionals (SCIP) in 1986.

The creation of SCIP

SCIP is a professional association for the promotion of intelligence and its practice in corporations. In cooperation with John Wiley & Sons, it launched the *Competitive Intelligence Review*. Awareness and education seminars multiplied and publications were mostly authored by practitioners or consultants primarily proposing organizational methods and techniques for better intelligence formalization.

SCIP gives the following definition: Competitive Intelligence (CI) is the control process of the competitive environment. CI enables managers from companies of all sizes to make informed decisions using marketing, research and development, etc. and to develop long term strategies. Efficient CI is a continuing process involving legal and ethical information collection, non-complacent analyses and controlled distribution of intelligence used by decision makers.

We again find the strong competitive orientation previously given by Porter. The integration in strategy, process continuity and proactivity were emphasized in this definition. Because of the double meaning of intelligence, professionals emphasize the importance of respecting the legal and ethical aspects in the information acquisition phase.

In the early 1980s, the influence of the CI concept began to be felt in France. Notions of Surveillance, Strategic Watch and Economic Intelligence emerged consecutively.

2.2.2. *Emergence of vigilance, surveillance, Strategic Watch and economic intelligence in France*

Vigilance, J.M. Oury (1983)

In his book, *Economie politique de la vigilance*, J-M. Oury was the first to highlight the dangers of a lack of vigilance and the importance of its effectiveness.

Citing examples of vigilance from technicians – making sure planes can fly safely – from production teams – vital to planning operations – previously prosperous City–State merchants from Genoa, Venice, or Amsterdam, CEOs, managers, senior officials, politicians as well as soldiers or hunters, the author shows that nothing works without vigilance.

However, he is surprised that the economic world attaches so little importance to this idea, when the direct or indirect costs of a lack of vigilance can reach billions of dollars.

His concept of vigilance rejects any notion of passivity. It is closer to the notion of intelligence than watch. In fact, for the economist, the efficacy of vigilance is based on the development of a coherent response with underlying expectations and representations. Based on the illustration of the soldier, he shows the effective conditions of vigilance: the watchman must have planned what actions he will take when the enemy appears and have the means to accomplish his actions.

Vigilance then is an activity requiring permanent efforts of observation and investigation. It appears directed towards the representation of an expected event and towards searching for signals announcing it, as well as towards the development of a response taking advantage of this detection. The author identifies three specific orientations of vigilance: the first shows vigilance as an expectation, the second makes it seem passive, and the third one gives it effectiveness.

These notions of attention and vigilance have recently resulted in original and very promising works. Starting with the dangers of the obsession of decreasing delays in innovation, S. Brion developed a model of organizational vigilance and applied it to the process of industrial product design. The application of the concept of vigilance seems essential to continue to be efficient without losing reliability. The author demonstrates that the ability to develop a project for the market quickly is based on a principle of reciprocal and collective vigilance, and proposes devices and tools for its implementation.

Surveillance, R.A. Thiétart (1984) and H. Lesca (1986)

Starting from Wall's studies as well as Cleland and King, and inspired by Porter's book, R.-A. Thiétart dedicated a chapter of his book *La stratégie d'entreprise* to corporate environment surveillance.

One of the key points of efficient strategy formulation for the author is the use of a surveillance system of the competition's environment. Constant research and information analysis of the environment is vital for the corporation to anticipate development opportunities and threats and to react quickly.

He defines the surveillance process as a dynamic process which is constantly repeated and is fed with data from all the different sources that the corporation can use.

Information thus collected must be analyzed in order to provide the necessary elements for quick strategic action adapted to the specific circumstances of the environment. The analysis is part of the surveillance process in the model proposed by R.-A. Thiétart: decision makers make their decision based on available strategic information. As with Porter, he mainly deals with surveillance of the competition.

A research trend took off in France in the middle of the 1980s. H. Lesca, whose research initially involved information management – like Lemoigne or Boss – emphasized the importance of strategic information for the manager. With his team at EAS in Grenoble, he specialized in the concept of scanning introduced by Aguilar.

We define environmental surveillance as the process by which the corporation examines its environment in order to adapt and survive. However, the first definition and technology associated by this French research trend evolved from 1991.

The infatuation of practitioners for watch from 1985/1988

Toward the end of the 1980s, the concept of watch in French corporations was still emerging. The first literature on watch started appearing and was mainly written by practitioners proposing methodologies to handle a strong formalized need for the watch activity in companies. Martinet and Ribault observed five types of watch taken from the five strengths of Porter.

Technological watch combines information research involving scientific and technical knowledge resulting from fundamental research and applied to products (or services), manufacturing processes, material, files, information systems and provisions of services in which the image factor is very strong and is linked with commercial watch.

Commercial watch involves clients, markets and suppliers. Environmental watch covers the rest of the environment: sociological, political and cultural aspects, etc.

Strategic Watch

In order to understand the global nature of watch, i.e. all the different watches defined above, we use the expression Strategic Watch. Strategic Watch represents the corporation's effort of prospectively listening to the environment (by collecting advance information and not by calculating statistical forecasts). It is a generic expression combining several forms of watch such as commercial watch, technological watch, competitor watch, political watch, etc. Its purpose is to capture opportunities and to prevent risk as soon as possible.

With this definition, the role of Strategic Watch in the future and the detection of breakthroughs are emphasized. The author does mention that he sometimes prefers the expression *prospective environment listening* to Strategic Watch.

H. Lesca proposed a cyclic modeling of the Strategic Watch process and refers to its four critical phases. The *zoning phase* consists of defining the part of the environment that will be monitored by the corporation. The *hunt phase* is the series of research tasks for gathering advance information. The *selection phase* sorts collected information according to its strategic value. Finally, there is the *method creation phase* where, from fragmentary information, the puzzle can be reconstructed, or in other words, a series of meaningful representations can be created.

Proactivity and the interlocking of Strategic Watch in the strategic decision does not seem as important as it does with intelligence. In fact, watch differs from intelligence by not being allowed to modify the environment it continuously observes.

It has a detection role, whereas intelligence has a mission to position the corporation in the environment in which it is involved, using a strategy of influence and coercion of the actors of this environment (lobbying, propaganda, press campaign, networking).

The difference established by P. Baumard between watch and intelligence was not always adopted in France at the time, particularly with actions of influence of intelligence. In fact, other authors regret that this dimension was ignored in France. According to them, intelligence must carry out a number of actions: it must include influential actions such as lobbying to have an impact on the corporate environment.

In France, watch was initially preferred to the term intelligence. However, the infatuation for CI in English-speaking countries, and the pressure from supporters of a more aggressive watch, gradually imposed the concept which in France is translated as *Intelligence Économique* (Economic Intelligence) (or sometimes *Intelligence Économique et Concurrentielle* (Economic and Competitive Intelligence)). This expression was also chosen to emphasize the difference between intelligence in terms of information as it is practiced, or government security and information to serve corporate economic interests.

The French development phase then began. SCIP France was created in 1992, but the concept of Economic Intelligence actually took off in 1994 when the report from the State General Planning Commission presided over by H. Martre, *Intelligence Economique et Stratégie des Entreprises* (*Economic Intelligence and the Publication of the Martre Report*) was published.

As a result of France's acknowledged delay in the field of intelligence, and with the urgency of catching up to guarantee its competitiveness, the authorities created a large awareness campaign for the practice of intelligence, with specialized training as well as information resources available to corporations. Seminars and colloquiums on surveillance, watch or intelligence multiplied, and the number of companies developing watch or intelligence activities increased.

This movement began in 1989 during the publication of the report from the State General Planning Commission presided over by A. Riboud. One of the workgroups was called *Veille technologique et politique de propriété industrielle* (*Technological Watch and Industrial Properties Strategy*). It accelerated significantly when the Martre report was published. The definition proposed in this book serves as a reference for many authors:

"Economic intelligence can be defined as the series of coordinated actions of research, processing and distribution of useful information for the use of economic players. These different actions are legally carried out with all guarantees necessary for the protection of a corporation's capital in the best quality, delay and cost conditions (…)"

Useful information is information needed by the different levels of decision making in the corporation or community, provided in a coherent manner, to develop and implement the strategy and tactics necessary for reaching the organization's objectives in order to improve its position in a competitive environment.

The notion of economic intelligence exceeds partial documentation (scientific and technological, competitive, financial and legal, etc.) watch, competitive capital protection and influencing actions (Martre report).

This definition is the result of a detailed collective research study where each term was meticulously chosen. It particularly highlights certain aspects of the Economic Intelligence (EI) activity:

– the coordination of the different phases of the process (research, processing, distribution and use);

– the usefulness of information, which implicitly favors quality over quantity of information;

– the legal framework in which the process must be done to separate economic intelligence from espionage;

– the security and protection of the company against these possible illegal practices;

– the effectiveness of the process (quality, timeframe and cost);

– the overlapping of EI in decision making and strategic tactics;

– the objective of competitiveness for the corporation.

The Martre report had a large influence in the clarification, reputation, acceptance and the acknowledgement of the concept of EI. As a result of this, it enabled often criticized French corporations to catch up.

The difference in terminology between English and French countries appeared early in the 1980s.

2.2.3. *Terminologies*

At this stage, it is useful to explain the French translation of the English term *intelligence* which is written the same way in French: intelligence, in its most popular sense, is the ability to understand.

The second translation associated with the word intelligence is the word information. Intelligence was unfortunately translated as information in the French version of the 1980 book by Michael Porter.

Unfortunately, *information* can have two meanings. The first one is the current term for information: information that we give or receive. The other meaning has a strong military, warlike or even police-like connotation. We speak of the intelligence service and intelligence officers. This would be a government intelligence service (such as the CIA for the US Government or MI5 for Britain). This last explanation is one of the reasons why the concept of intelligence was so difficult for French corporations to accept and implement. In the manufacturing industry it is particularly linked to espionage.

The first reports involving espionage cases date back to the end of the 1950s, when intelligence professionals were starting to bring their expertise to corporations. They integrated more easily with the communities working on this area, publishing articles, becoming involved in university training programs or offering consultations. The context is important because it forms the basis of the reluctance towards the activity of intelligence and of the opposition between two French schools of thought.

The article from J.L. Wall was published in the *Harvard Business Review* in 1974. The author was Assistant Professor at the University of Western Illinois and a reserve officer for Military Intelligence. Mostly using the results of his investigation, R.-A. Thiétart analyzed the concept, without calling it intelligence. The author instead used the term surveillance or strategic surveillance and competition.

To dispel the persistent resistance to the use of the term *intelligence*, supporters of the concept and practice of intelligence were always quick to emphasize that 95% of information needed by the corporation was available from open sources, and that espionage was not a part of intelligence activities.

That is why the term *watch* was preferred to *intelligence* and even *surveillance* which is too often associated with the prison or police environment. For certain authors, however, watch does not completely satisfy their definition, as it is too passive.

In fact, for an IBM Marketing Intelligence manager, watch is a bad translation of intelligence. It indicates that the company is listening to its environment but does nothing as long as it has not detected a signal; it is too passive, whereas intelligence signifies a more proactive attitude.

We should mention that even though most researchers, practitioners or consultants insist on the legality of watch or intelligence activities, there is a divergence with authors who claim that acquisition and use of information is offensive and warlike. This position was confirmed in France in the 1990s by authors who did not hesitate to call it economic war.

2.2.4. *Characteristics*

In the 1980s, an infatuation for the concept of *Competitive Intelligence* emerged. The idea was not only to collect data and develop static analyses but to analyze competition in detail and to make sense out of scattered information, and to transform data into intelligence. The concept of CI gradually evolved into Business Intelligence or SI, involving all sectors of the corporate environment together with the competitive sector.

2.3. Phase of consolidation

2.3.1. *From practice to theory*

During the development phase, each corporation experimented with the implementation and operation of its surveillance system. This learning period made improvements and a better adaptation to the identity of each corporation possible. The field of surveillance first constituted a body of practice before a body of knowledge.

A position of stability seems to have been reached in English definitions. The difference between CI – focused more on competitive surveillance – and SI – more global – is clearer. Modeling around the intelligence system (process, organizational methods, tools, etc.) is more advanced.

According to several observers, the concept of intelligence is accepted today by French corporations who have made up lost ground and are now current in this field, based on the aspirations in the Martre report. It has achieved maturity. In the IHEDN study, Economic and Strategic Intelligence is defined from the qualitative analysis of definitions given by 950 French corporation executives:

"Economic and Strategic Intelligence (ESI) is an organized approach serving the corporate strategic management, to improve its competitiveness by collecting, information processing and distribution of knowledge useful to the control of its environment (threats and opportunities). This decision support process uses specific tools, mobilizes employees and is based on a coordinated internal and external network."

Compared with the Martre report definition, other elements were specifically emphasized:

– the authors insist on the organization and formalization of the activity;

– whereas the boundaries in the Martre report are wide, involving corporations as well as all economic players and communities, Bournois and Romani are clearly positioned at the corporate level;

– corporate competitiveness is placed first in the ESI objectives;

– it no longer involves only useful information, but useful knowledge: the mission of knowledge creation from ESI is put forward;

– finally, vital ESI system factors – particularly tools, employees and networks – are integrated in the definition.

Nevertheless, this last definition has its limits and overlooks important notions that the Martre report identified. First, it does not make the distinction between watch (though much practiced and used in France) and intelligence. Second, it does not describe all watch and intelligence functions, particularly those that could help in distinguishing them. Finally, financial resources, as with notions of efficiency and effectiveness of intelligence, are forgotten. Similarly, the objective of performance is not clearly defined.

For these reasons, the definition of watch and SI would be as follows.

SI is a formalized process of research, collection, information processing and distribution of knowledge useful to strategic management. Besides its information function, the main goals of SI are to anticipate environmental threats and opportunities (anticipatory function), to propose and/or to engage in (proactive function), to help in strategic decision making and to improve competitiveness and performance of the organization. It requires a organizational network structure and human, technical and financial methods.

SI is more proactive, and more integrated into the strategic decision process than Strategic Watch, on which it builds.

2.3.2. *Terminologies*

In the English-speaking world, the terminology is stabilized. We use the terms intelligence, business intelligence and SI to describe global intelligence activity. CI is used to highlight the importance of competitive surveillance in the general surveillance of activity in the environment.

This is not yet quite the case in France. The ESI formula was one of the recently proposed terminologies. However, in practice, corporations frequently use watch or EI.

Surveillance for us is a generic term to describe Watch and/or Strategic Intelligence (WSI) practiced in the corporation. It will therefore be frequently used in this book to describe watch and/or intelligence.

We make the distinction between watch and intelligence, as described in the previous proposed definition, by their degree of integration in the strategic decision and their degree of proactivity. Watch becomes intelligence when it consists of making recommendations to the recipient – this could correspond to a first level of proactivity. Intelligence can also consist of proposing or carrying out actions – this could correspond to a second level of proactivity.

2.3.3. *Characteristics*

After the fervor generated by the practice of surveillance in the phase of emergence, and the experience built during the previous phase of development, executives began to question the real impact of the activity on corporate profits. It was difficult to evaluate the results of surveillance (watch and/or intelligence), thus more operational concepts were preferred such as "benchmarking". This problem is still of interest, especially since important human and financial resources have been allocated to this new corporate function.

On the other hand, we question the integration of surveillance results in the strategic management of the corporation, and the ability of the concept of intelligence to serve strategic decisions.

2.4. Conclusion

From the analysis of publications on these themes, three periods are important in the evolution of the general concept of surveillance; emergence, development and consolidation respectively. This evolution is represented in the following illustration.

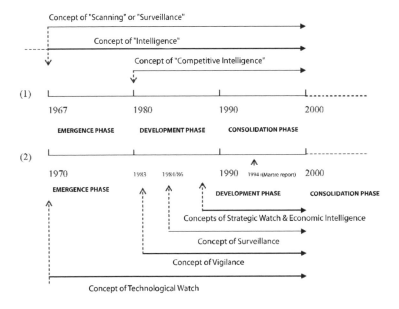

Figure 2.1. *(1) English and (2) French evolution of concepts of Surveillance*

We think there has been a gap between the English and American evolution (1) and the French evolution (2) of the general concept of surveillance, which has tended to disappear. The terminologies used on both sides of the Atlantic followed a progression throughout these three periods.

Across the Atlantic, since 1967, scanning has attracted the interest of an increasing number of companies; it was gradually replaced by CI and more globally by intelligence in the 1980s.

Although France was a pioneer in terms of technological watch, interest in general corporate environment surveillance really appeared in the middle of the 1980s, approximately five years after its appearance in England and America. Early in the 1990s, the concepts of Strategic Watch and EI opposed each other. Despite cultural resistance, EI dominated from the mid-1990s.

What have we learned from the evolution of similar concepts? For the purists, surveillance, watch and intelligence are different concepts. What differentiates them?

To summarize very briefly, we can consider that scanning (or surveillance) is an attitude of careful observation of the corporate environment; it can be compared to a radar, having a function of informing and alerting when an unusual event occurs.

Watch is a more anticipatory function to which a larger and more sophisticated information function is added. Its analysis function can disclose impacts on the organization by predicting events that will occur, but it does not influence the decision making process.

Intelligence goes even further in the processing of information. It exceeds the identification of potential impacts and makes recommendations to the decision maker. It can also propose or even carry out actions. It is more global, more offensive and is more involved in the strategic decision process than watch.

In conclusion, watch is a component of intelligence.

The evolution of the notion of surveillance actually followed the one of strategy. Scanning, which was suitable for a strategy of adaptation, has become an obsolete tool. From their respective functions, watch and especially intelligence are better surveillance activities for strategies of intention.

These different concepts of surveillance actually complete each other. They can be placed on a continuum toward a form of surveillance that becomes increasingly global, proactive and involved in the strategic decision process according to the following three axes diagram:

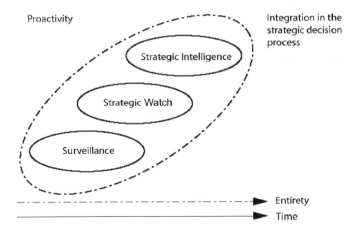

Figure 2.2. *From Surveillance to Strategic Intelligence*

Even though the players involved are conscious of these differences, in practice surveillance, watch and intelligence are very often used as synonyms. We can observe that some will speak of surveillance or watch when they mean intelligence and conversely, while others will use the term intelligence when talking about surveillance or watch, by misuse of language.

Today the concept of intelligence seems to have acquired legitimacy, and takes shape in numerous corporations reinforced by new dimensions. The Internet and new information technology have given it strong impetus. Collection and distribution of information have accelerated. By leading to the production of knowledge, the concept is increasingly linked to knowledge management. Finally, the role of the human and collective dimension is emphasized in the effectiveness of surveillance.

Chapter 3

The Global Measurement Model
of Strategic Intelligence

This chapter proposes a definition of Strategic Intelligence (SI), effectiveness and a model for the evaluation of the effectiveness of SI and its impact on the performance of the corporation. Its final objective is to develop a measuring tool which will give a control panel to control the SI activity.

This chapter begins by highlighting the advantage of measuring the effectiveness of SI and its impact on the performance of the organization. It then proposes a definition of SI effectiveness and a definition of the corporate performance, before examining both concepts in detail.

Finally, it presents the general architecture of a measurement model from the field of management control already applied to information systems and adapted to the specific case of SI systems. Finally, we suggest a measurement for organizational performance.

3.1. Overview of the literature on SI effectiveness evaluation

The theme of effectiveness, and especially the measurement of surveillance effectiveness, is not really addressed in the existing literature. The concept of surveillance effectiveness is itself not defined. However, as we have mentioned, most of the previous studies often implicitly and partially highlight explanatory variables of surveillance effectiveness. Consequently, our global approach requires that we consider all these studies.

The importance of measuring surveillance is recognized by several authors. In 1994, the seventh clause of the Martre report said: "The implementation of an Economic Intelligence system in a corporation must integrate a device to control the effectiveness and efficiency of the system at the very beginning of the project".

The last study on Economic and Strategic Intelligence (ESI) practices of corporations emphasizes the necessity of a control panel to control and manage ESI. In fact, six years after the Martre report, we must admit that only small progress has been made on this point. Some figures in particular are eloquent, and represent the weakness of French corporations: 40.9% of ESI services do not have a system to evaluate the quality of information received compared with expectations; 54% of ESI services do not receive a return on the quality of their services; 90.9% of corporations using ESI do not have a control panel to control this activity; and finally only 8.1% of French-owned corporations have a control system, whereas they are more easily found in American corporations. Unfortunately, no detail is given of indicators of the control panels used, or in the way these 8.1% measure their surveillance. We can only establish that the most advanced companies with ESI practices have more control tools and represent the elite in the field.

The study of surveillance measurement started in the 1990s. In his article published in 1991, H. Lesca proposed a diagnostic tool for Strategic Watch (SW) for small businesses, using in-depth interviews with corporate watch experts. The name of the resulting tool, the *Fennec* program, was based on the name of a little desert fox which survives because of the size of its ears, which are true surveillance radars of its hostile environment. *Fennec* is designed to be used by small businesses or autonomous divisions of larger corporations. It displays results for controlling SW in a control panel based on nine global indicators, measured with the help of a survey given to executives. The first three indicators are meant to establish the basis of the commercial, competitive and technological watches practiced by the company. The responder must indicate their level of quality: priority effort, must progress or satisfactory. The author presents the next six elements called progress paths: style of direction, SW formalization, information sources, transmission of information, strategic use, and motivation of personnel.

Concerning the state of SW affairs section, only three types of watch were analyzed; on the other hand, the author does not provide classification criteria in the three levels proposed, and relies totally on responder subjectivity. As for the progress path section, the approach is also partial. We find no financial indicator (such as the SW cost for example), or indicators for results or SW impact. In addition, the researcher settles for naming the six determining elements of SW quality with no explanation in this article. Only two of them are the subject of a brief explanation: the style of direction and transmission of information. Finally, Fennec was developed only from the point of view of professionals, without considering the opinion, especially the expectations, of executives using SW.

The first book specifically targeting the measurement of intelligence effectiveness was published in 1996. In his booklet titled *Measuring the Effectiveness of Competitive Intelligence*, published by SCIP USA, J.P. Herring presents an exploratory study carried out by face-to-face interviews with 18 senior managers from eight American corporations. His study revealed that, in the corporations studied, the evaluation of intelligence was not done in a formal or systematic manner. Three main results were obtained. The author first noticed a gap between expectations and beliefs of developers and users of intelligence. The former are focused on the development process of intelligence (information collection, database design, distribution of relevant analyses, etc.), whereas the latter are almost exclusively interested in the contribution of the intelligence activity to the performance and success of their organization, and demand a tangible impact on their business. The second result suggested targeting intelligence in key strategic domains for measurable effects. According to the consultant, these sectors are often the strategic plans and decisions, product development, sales and marketing and management priorities. Finally, he recommends aligning fundamental intelligence operations (collections, analyses, etc.) and designing intelligence products corresponding to management expectations. From the analysis of different fields, four effectiveness measurements were proposed: time savings, cost savings, cost reduction and increased profits. His study led to the proposal of a guide in the form of a diagram or checklist, to measure and communicate the value of intelligence to management and to other users in the organization.

One of the strong points in J.P. Herring's methodology is his emphasis that it is as important, if not more so, to measure the effect of surveillance effectiveness on corporate performance as it is to measure the surveillance effectiveness itself. He also insists on the necessity of involving executive users as well as intelligence developers in the process of evaluation. The author directs us on interesting paths to build a tool for measuring intelligence and its impact (knowledge management, information systems, new performance measures, etc.). However, the proposed guide contains more recommendations than concrete measures of effectiveness and examples of the impact of intelligence. On the other hand, it can seem abstract for intelligence professionals who would like to implement it, but who are waiting for more pragmatic methods.

The question of the evaluation of surveillance effectiveness is discussed in more general research studies.

For Jakobiak, along with other authors, wanting to quantitatively evaluate intelligence is somewhat like a bet. The author nevertheless proposes an operation control and an estimation of intelligence effectiveness from operating indicators (input, flow, output, use of information) and results (number of research programs, patents registered, etc.). Still, the evaluation is partial; it does not take into consideration the opinions of users and mainly focuses on the operation and results of a technological type of intelligence.

Some studies use satisfaction measurements or propose general notation scales. Ballaz for example noticed that 56% of Purchasing Directors were satisfied with the organization of SW in their companies. Referring to the second annual study conducted by the *Futures* Group, Harkleroad learned that decision makers interviewed gave a grade of 6 out of 10 to intelligence effectiveness at their companies. Finally, according to Bournois and Romani, ESI services have a vague idea of the quality of their services in relation to client expectations. On a scale of one to five (five being the best grade), the majority gave themselves a three (49.5%), but only 22% of corporations practicing ESI gave themselves a higher than average grade.

Evaluating the effectiveness of surveillance from satisfaction and/or notation scales is necessary but insufficient. These measures only represent a portion of surveillance evaluation and are very subjective, especially when the classification criteria are not really defined. Other measures should be considered: for example, the evaluation of methods used, objectives set and results obtained.

In fact, studies of results (and benefits) of surveillance which directly involve its effectiveness are rare. When the subject is addressed, it is mainly in terms of success stories, often recalled in several publications.

3.2. Intelligence and performance

The fundamental and recurrent concern of strategy is to identify variables, explaining the performance of corporations and sources of durable competitive advantages. A permanent question is raised in strategy: why, at a given moment, are there differences in performance between companies (Métais)?

For many specialists, the capacity of a company to scan its environment can largely explain its competitiveness and performance. For Peters and Waterman, the most competitive corporations are the ones most able to listen to their environment in general, but first and foremost to their clients. Similarly, according to Diffenbach, environmental analysis is especially useful to increase corporate effectiveness. For some authors, reaching a better performance is the central objective of surveillance.

Paradoxically, the problem of the intelligence–performance connection – and the impact of intelligence on performance – is rarely the main object of the study.

In the Dollinger study, carried out among 82 small company executives, the intensity of watch activities – measured by the ratio of the number of hours the executive spent with potential informers to the number of hours worked per week – explains the significant variation of performance.

Daft, Sormunen and Parks establish that the surveillance practiced by the sample firms with the best performance is more frequent, uses a larger variety of sources and covers a larger number of environmental fields, especially when strategic uncertainty of the environment is high.

In his empirical exploratory study among 40 small businesses in the Rhône-Alpes region, Vergnaud-Schaeffer demonstrates that there is an influence of the behavior of companies in terms of watch on their performance.

The Subramanian, Fernandes and Harper study is an extension of the Daft study. The authors conduct their study among 101 firms in the *Fortune* list and emphasize a relation between the existence of advanced watch systems (reactive and proactive) and company performance. In 1994, a Subramanian, Kumar and Yauger study carried out in the hospital sector confirmed this result.

Starting from the observation that not enough research attempts to find the relation between watch and performance of the corporation, Audet set the objective of identifying SW characteristics liable to be associated with business performance in the high tech field.

From his analysis of previous research studies on this problem, the author recalls the three SW dimensions which are most associated with performance: the intensity of SW, the integration of information into the strategic process and the appropriateness between SW intensity and the uncertainty perceived by the environment. His research is based on the study of four high tech companies and proposes new dimensions: the strong propensity for innovation from the managing team, the strategic management of their information networks and an SW motivated by the search for opportunities and carried out over a long period of time.

In this last piece of research, the preliminary conceptual context of the author does not take into consideration all results from the previous studies, notably from Subramanian. On the other hand, even though the dimensions retained seem to be linked to performance, no study obtained results which can be sufficiently generalized to confirm these hypotheses with certainty. Finally, the new dimensions proposed were suggested by prior studies. We can thus presume the existence of a connection between several characteristics of surveillance and corporate performance.

As in the case of the measure of surveillance effectiveness, the surveillance–performance link is discussed in some studies where it is not the main object of the study.

In 1982, Stubbart highlighted the existence of a direct link between performance and surveillance. However, the study showed that the association can be negative: in many cases, performance problems lead to a change toward irregular surveillance. Three reasons can explain this probable evolution. First, substandard performance often leads to cost reductions, and since surveillance activities have not proven their profitability, they become a vulnerable target. Second, a company's bad results often precede a change in management and the chance that the new management has similar points of view on the usefulness and organization of surveillance is slim. Finally, a sudden decrease in performance can be caused by unexpected but important events. Managers are then tempted to interrupt ongoing surveillance in order to pool all surveillance resources for solving the problem. The combination of these three factors can have an ironic effect: it is when environmental surveillance could be at its most useful that it may not be in practice.

Another surprising effect was mentioned later by Kaish and Gilad. The authors noticed a decrease in surveillance activity when companies reached sufficient experience and profitability. According to them, executives would focus on internal management and would abandon the search for new opportunities as soon as they reached a satisfactory level of performance.

The results for both these studies raise the question of the nature and causality of the relation between surveillance and performance.

All prior studies on this subject specify that causality is not discussed. The most recent one is from Bournois and Romani.

The study was carried out among 1,200 large French corporations and emphasized the surveillance–performance link. The authors proposed a descriptive model for the surveillance practices of these firms. In this context, they asked themselves if corporations that practiced EI had different financial results than those who did not, or who only had the intention of practicing it.

A simple statistical analysis by the Chi square test has shown that the variables EI and financial results (losses or benefits in 1998) were not independent.

According to the authors, this first statistical result emphasizes that practicing or not practicing EI is directly or indirectly linked to economic performance. However, they note that some will prefer to reverse the proposition and suggest that having benefits offers the opportunity of investing in EI. Their explanation: statistics do not solve the causality question.

They relate the practice of ESI to financial performance, when the relation between the effectiveness of EI and the corporation's performance should be studied instead.

In fact, a company can practice surveillance without any impact on performance, if the surveillance system is ineffective. The higher the level of effectiveness of the surveillance practiced, the better the performance should be.

To summarize, a relation should not be made between the practice of intelligence and the performance of the corporation, but between the performance of intelligence and the performance of the corporation. Before studying this relation, it is necessary to create a prior step of definition and measurement of SI effectiveness. Our studies focus on this problem.

It is, however, vital to consider another essential link between surveillance and performance: decision. Surveillance can be of very high quality and provide the right information at the right moment, without increasing performance, if the decision was not the right one, if it was not carried out, or if it was carried out only partially, or late, etc.

It is possible that the decision maker may still make the wrong decision even with very good information, because a multitude of variables can influence the quality of the decision (power battles, decision maker's own rationality, etc.).

On the other hand, as we know, performance is defined by a large number of parameters; in this context, models of excellence illustrate this idea thoroughly. It is dependent on the quality of the decision, which in turn depends on many parameters including quality of the surveillance, etc. We enter into a complex cause and effect chain (explanatory factors => effective surveillance => strategic decision, then tactics and operations => performance).

Measuring the impact of surveillance on performance seems impossible because of the large number of interdependent variables. How can we specifically isolate the role of surveillance? Our first objective is to propose a model for measuring the effectiveness of surveillance, but we will attempt to propose a solution for this specific problem – the effect of surveillance on performance – while taking into consideration the previous warning.

In all the studies, a link is established between performance and certain characteristics of surveillance: consistency, intensity, frequency, progress, the variety of sources used, its extent, its appropriateness with perceived uncertainty and its integration into the process of strategic decision, etc.

These characteristics can represent variables of surveillance effectiveness insofar as they contribute to the goal of better performance. The intelligence–performance connection is often studied from a limited number of effectiveness variables presumed to be linked to performance. However, these are hypotheses or propositions from research with results which cannot be generalized, notably because of the size of the sample.

3.3. Definition of corporate performance and surveillance effectiveness

3.3.1. *The general notion of performance*

In his analysis of the general concept of performance, A. Ancelin-Bourguignon starts with a triple observation:

– a frequent lack of definition,

– a large variability in existing definitions,

– a problem with translating the word *performance* from English.

In the 13th century in old French, "parformer" meant accomplishing, executing. In the 16th century, in mid-French, "performance" was the corresponding noun.

In the middle of the 19th century, performance meant results, and possible success, of a racehorse on a racetrack. At the end of the 19th century, it applied to an athlete or a sport; we spoke of results and sports achievements. At the beginning of the 20th century, we spoke of the performance of a machine by measurements representing its possibilities, its efficiency or its exceptional reliability. The word performance then represents success and achievement. It is the result of an action or operation. It is always positive (a substandard performance represents failure or a mediocre result).

During the last few years, the meaning of the word has been somewhat extended, since we now apply it to results of organizations and governments.

3.3.2. *The general notion of effectiveness*

The word effectiveness has two meanings:

– the first characterizes what is efficient, i.e. which produces the effect expected. In the first sense, effectiveness is similar to performance by representing the satisfaction of expected effects – or results,

– in the second sense, effectiveness represents the ability to produce maximum results with minimum effort – or cost.

The notions of productivity and optimization are introduced here, effectiveness also represents efficiency.

The term *efficiency*, from English literature, is not listed in any common French dictionary. However, in management literature, several authors distinguish between efficiency and effectiveness. The measure of effectiveness consists of comparing results obtained with objectives set, whereas the measure of efficiency compares results with resources engaged.

3.3.3. *Performance and effectiveness*

We notice a frequent absence of definitions of performance, even in books dedicated to this subject. However, there are some formal but variable definitions.

The definition of performance and its measure can be quite varied. In its narrowest sense, performance and effectiveness are synonyms. They represent the achievement of objectives; measuring them consists of comparing the results obtained with those initially set. In its broadest sense, performance becomes the achievement of objectives with optimization of methods, in the best conditions of satisfaction – three components of measurement, efficiency, effectiveness and satisfaction are combined. According to the analysis and previous definitions, the two notions of effectiveness and performance are equivalent, and can therefore be substituted.

3.4. The definition of the concept of measurement

The objective of this section is to define the concept of measurement by demonstrating that evaluation and assessment are synonyms. Control generally follows measurement. That is why we also explain this concept. We will be better able to understand the measurement of surveillance effectiveness and its impact on the performance of the corporation.

3.4.1. *Measurement*

Measurement is the action of determining the value (of certain dimensions) in comparison with a constant size.

Its synonym is evaluation (dictionary definition). According to the dictionary, measuring has three meanings:

– evaluating (a length, a surface, a volume, etc.) by comparison with the same type of standard;

– determining the value of a measurable size;

– judging by comparison. Proposed synonyms are then evaluate and estimate.

The first meaning is directly related to measurement, supposedly the most objective possible, and the two other meanings refer to the notions of value and judgment resulting in more subjectivity.

3.4.2. *Evaluation*

Evaluation is related to measurement as well as to judgment and value.

The notion of value can be defined as the measurement of a variable quantity or size, which sends us back to the concepts of measurement and evaluation. It can also refer to price (exchange value or usage value). Finally, it can refer to the subjectivity of people who judge the value of an object. The analysis of the notion of value, at the basis of the evaluation, explains the objective and subjective parts present in any evaluation.

3.4.3. *Assessment*

Assessment is a synonym of evaluation. It also includes notions of measurement, estimation and judgment.

In conclusion, we can consider that measurement, evaluation and assessment are similar terms and that they all contain the notions of value estimation (measurement) and value judgment, which can also be interpreted as approximation and subjectivity.

Control is a broader concept than measurement, evaluation or assessment. It means verification (we verify that things happen the way we want them to, i.e. according to set objectives) and control simultaneously. It implies the use of measuring tools to evaluate the results obtained and the methods by which they were obtained.

3.5. A measurement model for surveillance effectiveness

3.5.1. *The importance of evaluating intelligence effectiveness*

Obtaining a way of determining the contribution of surveillance systems to corporate success remains a challenge for surveillance specialists. This opinion is shared by most analysts. In the analysis of previous research, we demonstrated that the establishment of a measurement of surveillance effectiveness was an essential precondition for the study of the connection between surveillance and performance. However, the measurement of surveillance effectiveness is important for other reasons:

– for the future position of the specialized entity or surveillance system;

– for its survival, continuity and to justify its role;

– to justify its budget and its requests for additional resources from management;

– to evaluate its economic interest and its feasibility;

– to help its progress, by supporting organizational training;

– to encourage its effective use and to motivate specialists and users;

– for its effective and efficient management (cost evolution control);

– to verify that objectives are reached and to correct malfunctions;

– to control the quality of information produced, etc.

Developing a measurement of surveillance effectiveness is therefore highly justified.

3.5.2. *An evaluation model for information systems adapted to surveillance systems*

Control and performance measurement activity is part of a general logic of management systems, combining three groups of actions:

– the choice of objectives;

– organization, i.e. the implementation and layout of resources meant to help reach these objectives;

– coordination and control, i.e. the implementation of techniques for the evaluation of results, and the methods by which they were obtained. Measurement is implied here and is inseparable from control (Tabatoni, Jarniou and Reix).

The surveillance management field can no longer ignore this model. As with information systems (IS) in general, surveillance systems are characterized by a low level of control. This can be explained by their relative newness, by the difficulty in assessing results, by resistance from professionals not wanting to be evaluated, etc.

As we have seen with management expectations however, improving IS management control (surveillance systems in our case) is now a clear objective for many companies.

The fact that surveillance systems (watch or intelligence) belong to corporate information systems is established. By analogy, we are attempting to adapt the control and measurement of information systems to the control and measurement of surveillance systems. Four elements should be considered:

– the different measuring types or categories;

– the different objects being measured;

– the choice of measurement methods to be implemented;

– problems linked to key measurement concepts.

Different measuring techniques

Based on the dominant perspective, measurement of the surveillance system can be divided into three types according to the user involved:

– *Technical:* focused on the tool whose operation is being monitored.

This approach requires the consideration of the methods used (and the quality of these methods) to carry out the surveillance activity (organizational, process oriented, human, technical and financial). The measurement can involve the evolution of the response time of the surveillance entity, information flows of surveillance networks, failure rates, or problems encountered with response to a specific information request, etc.

This component is particularly interesting for managers responsible for surveillance.

– *Economic:* expressed in terms:

– of cost (generally linked to the use of tools: computers, search engines, etc.);

– of efficiency: comparing results with methods involved (only financial methods are used here including the costs previously mentioned);

– effectiveness: evaluating results in relation to objectives set (a central measure in our research).

– *Organizational*: evaluated in terms of user satisfaction or in terms of corporate performance (or impact on performance).

The last two measurement methods (economic and organizational) are the most interesting to managers. They are also very relevant for our research on measurement of surveillance effectiveness and its impact on corporate performance.

We have here all the notions identified during the definition and measurement of performance (or effectiveness). Notably, we have the three traditional measurements of effectiveness; efficiency, user satisfaction and a measurement of quality (quality of methods implemented, of the product used – information – and services offered).

Different objects being measured and the research model

Based on the perspectives from the previous measures, we can evaluate different variables.

Resources used by surveillance systems: in our case, we use methods in a broad sense as something used to arrive at a result. As we have already discussed, in the technical perspective of measurement, these resources will be financial as well as organizational, technical, human or process oriented (linked to the surveillance process).

The product (information) and services offered: this means the quality of information and the functions provided by surveillance systems: informative, anticipative and analytical functions, etc. It is vital at this level to consider what the different users will use. We have chosen to focus on executive users, or those responsible for strategy, who use the product of surveillance to make important strategic decisions, those decisions which commit the future of the company.

Usage processes: what is used? In what conditions?

The results of the system itself and its impact: has the use of the surveillance system given measurably better results – lower costs, increased sales, more innovations, greater financial gain, etc? We should note however that results obtained come from decisions made as well as uncontrollable external factors.

When all is said and done, these four elements characterize global surveillance effectiveness and its impact on corporate performance within the following simplified model.

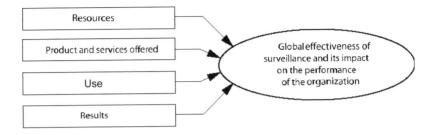

Figure 3.1. *Simplified research model*

The following model presents the different variables, and perspectives of the control and measurement of surveillance systems studied in our research.

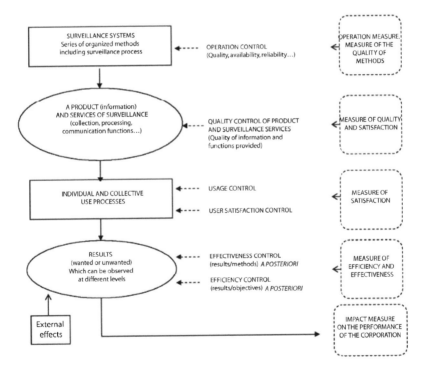

Figure 3.2. *Measurement model of global effectiveness of surveillance and its impact on the performance of an organization*

From the model presented, we will use two complementary methods. The first one involves (the) executive user(s). It is based on results, use, products and services offered, and it corresponds to measurements of efficiency, effectiveness, quality and satisfaction.

The second approach focuses on the people responsible for surveillance. It involves the approaches, broadly speaking, implemented to carry out the activity, and corresponds to measurements of operations and of quality.

Both these approaches will take place following the development of two questionnaires, one intended for executive users and the other one for those responsible for surveillance. The first questionnaire is more important for the evaluation of surveillance effectiveness as defined – reaching the objectives – but the two evaluation techniques will complete each other to evaluate the global surveillance effectiveness and its impact on corporate performance.

Prior choices and problems linked to key measurement concepts

Three questions are raised during the design and implementation of an evaluation system and consequently in the context of this research.

An initial reflection on desired outcomes and on the extent of the measurement must be done. In the context of our research, the objective is to develop a tool to measure the effectiveness of the surveillance system and its impact on performance, intended both for executive users and surveillance professionals. It must lead to a control panel for controlling surveillance. This expected and recommended tool should rely on a limited number of effectiveness indicators for surveillance and corporate performance. The traditional implicit objective of the evaluation is to favor organizational knowledge. In the context of the extent of the measurement, we want to evaluate the global effectiveness of the surveillance system.

We must then use a measuring tool. The audit is one of the possible choices mentioned in the literature. Its advantages correspond to our subsequent case study methodology. The collection phase precedes the analysis and diagnostic phases, leading to a conclusion in the form of recommendations. The advantage is to launch curative and/or preventive actions based on a rigorous methodology (Reix, 1998: 369). In our research we will not only make a diagnosis; the objective will chiefly be to complete the initial conceptual model and to develop the corresponding measuring tool. Our wish is to provide a tool for controlling an efficient surveillance activity for surveillance users and managers.

Finally, we should keep in mind that choices involving the evaluation of surveillance systems are contingent (they must be adapted to the context) and progressive (Reix, 1998). In fact, the literature has an abundance of examples of companies who failed by trying to apply predefined models. On the other hand, surveillance is a complex activity involving numerous players – an organization, techniques, technologies, etc. It requires a long learning curve to improve.

Problems linked to key measurement concepts

Measurements of efficiency, effectiveness, satisfaction and quality often raise problems for researchers, and deserve some explanations.

The measurement of effectiveness is difficult for at least two reasons:

– the objectives assigned to surveillance must be explained in detail. There is a problem of definition that we have widely covered in Chapter 2. There will need to be detailed information on functions and objectives of the two forms of surveillance, which are watch and intelligence;

– the contribution of the surveillance system to the production of observed results must be clearly highlighted. There is a problem of imputation. Aligning the objectives of surveillance to corporate objectives – recommendations made during the proposal to measure performance – limits this problem.

The measurement of efficiency consists of comparing results from the approachs used, and is usually done from cost and productivity analyses. Applied to technical factors it has few problems, but applied to job factor measurement, to intellectual tasks, problems arise.

User satisfaction is a frequently used indicator in the world of information systems. Opinions are taken by scale questions from five or seven points on the Likert Scale. We obtain partial or global satisfaction indices (by weighted sum), helping to follow the evolution of satisfaction over different predetermined dimensions. The most complete questionnaires involve the quality of information provided (precision, reliability, timeframe, etc.). When use of the system is optional, simple satisfaction indices are the measure of usage rate (the number of users of the system over the resource involved) and the intensity of usage (the number and duration of uses).

There is low correlation between efficiency and effectiveness measures and satisfaction measures. That is why it is preferable to use these three measures in a complementary way.

The concept of satisfaction is automatically linked to the concept of quality. A last section enables us to highlight the importance given to the quality methodology in our research.

3.6. The importance of total quality management (TQM)

3.6.1. *The origins of TQM*

In a certain measurement, the evolution of surveillance is similar to that of quality (the example of Japan, the role of private associations, of education and training, promises about performance, the necessity of a dedicated responsible person connected at high level, the implication of top management, etc.).

The quality of a product is a powerful sales argument. In contemporary history, important events improved it: the normalization by Gribeauval, serial production by Taylor, statistical control by Shewhart. The most memorable remains the new norm that the Japanese imposed blazingly on American, then worldwide markets.

Japanese executives were able to take advantage of the management theory imported in the 1950s by the Americans Deming and Juran. This later spread under the acronyms TQC (Total Quality Control) and TQM (Total Quality Management).

The strength of this approach is the significant improvement of the corporation's effectiveness, while at the same time improving teamwork and the decision making process. That is how corporations focused their policy on the search for continuous improvement. At the heart of this policy is client needs satisfaction, around which all functions of the company are concentrated.

The American association for quality, launched in 1947, and its French counterpart, created 10 years later, play an important role in the evolution of quality management.

3.6.2. *Principles and definitions of quality*

Quality management is based on three general principles:

1) The company is a system, i.e. a series of interdependent elements focused on a common goal, with a stable and well-defined policy of cooperation with its personnel, and a multi-line organization.

2) The theory of variations, consisting of studying the gaps in any process, compared to a standard.

3) The decision errors compared to forecasts, which are not seen negatively but as an accumulation of experiences and thus knowledge. This last principle and, more globally, the spirit of quality methodology are synthesized in the PDUA (Prepare–Develop–Understand–Act) cycle proposed by Deming.

In an approach based on use, quality is the ability of a product or service to satisfy the needs of users, or the ability of a series of characteristics to satisfy requirements.

The only judge in this case is the user. The problem, particularly in the field of surveillance, is to respond to expressed needs of users as well as their implicit requirements. On the other hand, the ability of a product or service to satisfy the needs of these clients is the result of a complex surveillance process. As a result of this, the quality of the product (or service) depends on the quality of the process that is at its root.

Consequently, quality management is a series of methods and practices intended to mobilize all the players in the corporation for the lasting satisfaction of client needs and expectations at a better cost (Detrie).

3.6.3. *The measurement of quality*

"Measuring quality means obtaining numbers and quality indicators expressing the degree of compliance of products and services with client requirements" (see Gogue). The measurement of quality is difficult to determine, as the objectives of surveillance, or even of the corporation, cannot always be quantified. This problem is one of the reasons why the AFNOR norm concerning watch and intelligence activity written in 1998 was never adopted. However, having one measure of imperfection is better than none.

The new TQM 2001 standard includes nine themes analyzing the management aspects of the corporation, with the help of a quality self-diagnostic of 30 questions in all nine themes. 700 points are attributed to methods and 300 points to results:

1	Executive commitment	120 points
2	Personnel management	100 points
3	Quality strategy and objectives	80 points
4	Resource management	70 points
5	Process	330 points
6	Personnel satisfaction	70 points
7	Client satisfaction	110 points
8	Integration with collectivity	30 points
9	Operational results	90 points
Total		1,000 points

This logic will be widely used in research, which will consist of developing a measuring tool in the form of a questionnaire, and given for example as here, in the context of a quality self-diagnostic of surveillance. The methodology is also interesting in the case of benchmarking operations. Grades are given on traditional semantic scales and transcribed in an evaluation grid.

We defined the notion of effectiveness in the strict sense, such as reaching objectives. On the other hand, we proposed a measurement model of surveillance effectiveness based on measures of effectiveness, efficiency and satisfaction in a clear spirit of quality management. It is now a question of explaining our approach concerning the measure of corporate performance.

3.7. The measurement of corporate performance

This book also proposes the measurement of the impact of surveillance activity on corporate performance. This section presents the different concepts of performance and the most recent performance measurement systems.

3.7.1. *The different approaches to corporate performance*

There are four schools of thought relating to performance or organizational effectiveness: economic, psychosocial, ecological and systematic.

Economic approach: the efficiency

In the economic conception of the corporation, performance is measured by reaching formal objectives, which are presumed to be known and shared by members. For executives, the main dimensions are production, productivity, profit and efficiency. This school of thought uses benchmarking to compare current performance to past performance, expected performance and performance from the competition.

The economic efficiency is the ratio between production quality or quantity and resources used for this production. Two dimensions account for economic efficiency: the economy of resources and productivity.

The economy of resources is the degree of decrease of resources used in the context of the system's correct operation. Four indicators measure this dimension: percentages of reduction of expenses, errors, scrap and waste (including raw material and finished products, as well as energy, time and equipment).

Productivity is the ratio between the quantity of finished products and resources used for their production within a timeframe.

Psychosocial approach: the value of human resources

In the psychosocial approach, corporate performance is evaluated by the value of human resources, represented by four components: mobilization of employees, job atmosphere, employee productivity and employee skills.

Employee mobilization means the interest and motivation of employees for their work and company. It is expressed in their effort to reach the goals set. The corresponding indicators are the rate of turnover (resignations), absenteeism rate, initiative shown, participation in emergency situations, punctuality and diligence. It is often measured by questions of motivation at work, commitment toward the company and involvement with the job.

Job atmosphere enables us to find out if employees feel that they are treated well in and by the company. It is expressed by the degree to which work experience and working for the company are evaluated positively by the employees. Behavioral or psychological indicators are the absenteeism rate, illness and accident rate, rate of grievances, turnover rate, number of lost days for work stoppage, reasons for resignations and number of deviant acts (sabotage, robbery, etc.). The best measures of atmosphere are achieved by standardized questionnaires. These make it possible to evaluate authorized work autonomy and consideration.

Employee productivity is represented by the performance of the employee or the economic value of services rendered by employees.

Corresponding indicators are the quantity of outputs (products, activities, services) over a given period, the economic value of outputs, quality of outputs (number of repeats, losses, returns) and output production cost. If these indicators are not available, management opinion may be sought. Assessments by intuitive data, objectives and behavior are requested. Regardless of the approach, the opinion will be based on production quantity, value and quality as well as on the quality of actions deemed essential in the production process.

Employee skill is expressed by the degree to which employees have perfected their existing skills or acquired new skills. Indicators of this vital dimension of social effectiveness are the percentage of people who have received new or broader responsibilities and the internal mobility of employees.

Systematic approach: continuity

This concept mainly refers to a general model of systems, and contrasts with the approach by a particular objective. Continuity is expressed by the degree in which the stability and growth of the company are ensured. It is made up of quality of product, client satisfaction, financial performance and business competitiveness.

Quality of product is a vital criterion because it determines the choice of consumers in an increasingly competitive environment. Consequently, it helps in the stability and growth of the company, its capacity to adapt to new constraints in the environment and to retain a good operation. It expresses compliance of products and services to quality tests and to client demands. Corresponding indicators are the number of returns, the number of complaints and improvements in product quality.

The quality of customer service is the reflection of the way in which the company has been able to respond to client needs. Indicators are lead time, frequency of delays in delivery, the range of services of products offered compared to client requirements, and the degree of customer loyalty (number of clients from one period divided by number of clients from the previous period). Customer service quality is mainly evaluated from data provided by the consumers of a product or users of a service.

Financial performance is measured by general profitability (income after taxes divided by total assets). The evolution of this ratio over three to five years and the comparison with the industry standard enables us to evaluate performance. The same methodology can be used with sales, profit margin and production costs, etc.

Competitiveness is represented by the protection and development of markets served by the corporation, as well as the maintenance and improvement of the quality of goods or services offered in these markets. It is evaluated by comparison with results from competitors. The corresponding indicators are production costs, level of revenue by industry, services export level and market share.

Ecological approach: corporate responsibility

This concept is based on the premise that all organizations take their resources from the environment and return the products of the transformation to this environment. These exchanges can generally be profitable for this environment. The challenges for the ecological approach are revitalization, protection and appreciation of the physical, economic, social and cultural environment in which the corporation evolves. Respect for regulation, social responsibility and environmental responsibility are the three key components of this ecological dimension.

Respect for regulation is the degree to which the company observes the laws and regulations controlling its activities. The amount of penalties paid for an offence is the indicator used.

Social responsibility is evaluated by tools proposed by different authors. The Council on Economic Priorities, for example, evaluates corporate performance over a dozen criteria such as the amount given to charity, the number of minority members in executive positions, the degree of implication in the production of offensive weapons, the degree of implication in the nuclear industry, etc.

Environmental responsibility can be illustrated by the 10 basic principles proposed by the Coalition of Environmentally Responsible Economics. Named Valdez Principles in memory of the Alaskan catastrophe, they are, for example, protection of the biosphere, sustainable use of natural resources, reduction and disposal of waste, intelligent use of energy, etc.

The presentation of these four approaches to corporate performance shows that the evaluation of performance is in reality a vital selection process. In fact, selecting the approach and appropriate indicators makes it possible to choose the strategy to adopt by setting the desirability standard for actions and products. On the other hand, it offers the possibility of managing performance by indicating the necessary adjustments for its improvement.

Morin, Savoie and Brunet highlight two important elements in the context of this research. On the one hand, performance is defined in different ways according to value, training, status and experience of evaluators and their notion of how to use it.

On the other hand, the evaluation of performance through appropriate indicators is a fundamental exercise in the success of corporations. That is why it is useful to present the most recent and appropriate systems of performance measurement for our research (notably the prospective control panel (PCP) of Kaplan and Norton).

3.7.2. *Contemporary performance measurement systems*

There is no consensus on definition or on the way to evaluate corporate performance. However, it is a general and central theme in management sciences.

In reality, there is more than one performance measurement system, and the field is far from stabilizing. In fact, new methods and new indicators appear on a regular basis. Consequently, the operationalization of the notion of performance in the context of empirical research is problematic for researchers, insofar as there are several performance criteria.

Before presenting contemporary examples of performance measurement, particularly the PCP of Kaplan and Norton, we must emphasize the importance of useful information to executives for corporate control.

The information that an executive really needs to control his corporation

For many specialists, performance measurement raises the question of information that the executive needs to control his company. This information is crucial because that is where strategic and tactical decisions and plans are made for the use of managers as well as shareholders. In this capacity, the scope of the relationship between surveillance – mainly responsible for providing high added value information – and performance is very important.

Executives are concerned with managing for the future, and need to have an information system integrated into the strategy rather than isolated tools, which have mostly been used to understand the past. P. Drucker observes four main groups of information which help executives establish a diagnostic to enable them to form relevant opinions:

– *vital information* groups cash flow and cash projections, stocks/sales ratio, accounts receivable, etc.;

– *information on productivity* emphasizes the increasing interest in EVA (Economic Value Added). EVA expresses the idea that as soon as a company does not earn higher profit than its capital cost, it does not create wealth for shareholders. The EVA measures the productivity of all factors in production. Benchmarking compares the company's performance to the performance of the same industry or of another industry. It is also part of this category and completes EVA;

– *information on skills* is a category based on the founding article by Hamel and Prahalad. That is where innovation is presented by P. Drucker as a fundamental skill that all companies should have. According to the author, companies would find the implementation of systematic methods to assess their innovation performance very useful;

– *information on the allocation of scarce resources* (capital and employees). The systematic process of capital allocation generally uses four measures: the profitability period, investment performance, cash flow and current net value. The author emphasizes the importance of the retrospective measure at this point: "nothing is more liable to improve the performance of a company than the evaluation of the results of capital allocation in relation to promises and expectations which led to their authorization" (P. Drucker). He regrets that there is not an allocation process for human resources combined with expectations, and a systematic evaluation of results of permanent staff.

Recognizing the multitude of sources of information, the author insists on the necessity for companies of all sizes to have the assistance of data processing specialists. This recommendation is all the more relevant as performance measurement systems often demand an overabundance of information.

The Activity-Based Costing (ABC) method and the PCP are examples of the most recent performance measurement systems.

The logic attached to PCP is appropriate for our research in more ways than one. That is why we specifically develop this method, which will serve as a basis for the creation of corporate performance measurement in connection with the surveillance activity of the organization.

Examples of performance measurement systems

Many companies abandoned traditional control systems by cost to adopt ABC.

THE ABC METHOD

The ABC method was made possible with the help of computers and new technologies. It calculates the cost for the complete process of a product or service. It groups in a single analysis what used to be several separate steps: analysis of the value, processes, quality management and cost control, including the value chain.

Some companies integrate ABC in management systems and use activity-based management as a powerful tool to rethink and continuously improve the corporation.

ABC requires a large information collection effort because it is more complex than analytical accounting. In fact, traditional systems consist of breaking up a certain number of costs into several heterogeneous categories. In the ABC approach, each category is broken up into activity measures which require much relevant information research. In addition, the ABC system is based on a much larger number of statistical measures to detect indirect costs (products, processes, marketing channels, clients, markets, etc.).

The start of the ABC method is often combined with a problem of selecting relevant information. Companies are often drowning in an overabundance of information. Ness and Cucuzza give the example of Chrysler, which has collected three times more data that it needed, and mobilized twice the resources necessary. This problem is avoided in the PCP method.

THE PCP OR PERFORMANCE CONTROL SYSTEM

In their founding article, Kaplan and Norton propose a PCP based on financial and operational measures according to four major axes:

– customer satisfaction;

– internal processes;

– innovation;

– learning.

Concerning the customer axis, the authors emphasize the necessity of first defining objectives in terms of time, quality, performance and service. The production timeframe is the time that the company takes to respond to a demand. For an existing product, the timeframe is from order to delivery of the product. For a new product, it represents the availability timeframe (from product definition to the first deliveries).

Quality represents the level of flaws perceived by the customer and the punctuality of the company. The performance–service combination indicates the value creation for the client. Implementing PCP comes down to a prior definition of objectives in terms of timeframe, quality, performance and service in numbers.

The second axis evaluates internal processes with the most impact on customer satisfaction. For example, they involve lifecycle, quality, employee knowhow, productivity, etc. The company must also identify and evaluate its key skills and critical technologies to perpetuate its predominance. It must know its strong points and define its corresponding measurement modes.

Innovation and learning axes represent the idea that the value of a company is directly connected to its ability to innovate, improve and continually learn. That is why innovation is a vital measure of corporate performance. The percentage of sales for new products can be a good indicator of its innovation ability.

In addition, the authors indicate that investors are no longer insensitive to certain measurements concerning new products. The ability and speed of developing and launching new products are other indicators of the innovation axis. Learning can be measured with new products, as the objective may be to stabilize the production of innovative parts for example. Many companies create continuous improvement objectives in customer satisfaction and in internal processes.

Concerning the financial axis, Kaplan and Norton agree with many researchers that these traditional indicators are not good navigation tools because they are too focused on the past. Nevertheless, they retain this financial category for profitability, growth and value for the shareholder. They provide the example of cash flow, sales, equity performance, etc., to which they add indicators geared toward the future: future cash flows and their updates.

Financial measurements represent actions already taken. Operational measurements are indicators of upcoming performance.

The authors compare their PCP to lights and dials in a cockpit. In order to navigate, the pilot needs several pieces of information (fuel, wind velocity, altitude, etc.) informing him of the current environment and what can be expected. Piloting from a single piece of information would lead to catastrophe. Similarly, in the turbulent corporate world, management must have a lot of information to control the performance of the company. The chart answers four fundamental questions:

1) How do our customers view us (client axis)?

2) Where are we the best (internal process axis)?

3) Are we continuing to improve and generate value (innovation and learning axis)?

4) How do shareholders view us?

Norton and Kaplan warn that the PCP is only a tool for translating strategy into specific and measurable objectives. If operational performance seems better with PCP, but it does not lead to better financial performance, the strategy should be rethought.

The PCP is not only a simple evaluation tool; it is also a management tool capable of triggering net changes at vital product, process, client and market levels. It translates corporate objectives into a coherent performance measurement set.

Customization is performed according to corporate mission, strategy, technology and culture. In order to help managers, the authors suggest a method based on a series of interviews and group meetings, mainly at management level.

The advantage of the PMC is that it can be customized: the authors do not propose a single framework that can be applied to all companies. Each corporation must go through its own analysis and decide on its own criteria and performance indicators. In addition, the PCP limits the amount of information collected by ensuring that the manager will only keep the most critical information, thus avoiding information overload. The PMC provides a clear view of the strategy. It is therefore highly confidential.

Our approach is largely influenced by the methodology of these authors, especially since the indicators they propose are very relevant in the context of the surveillance activity (impact on innovation in particular).

By reading the different publications on performance measurement, we notice a clear evolution of the use of traditional methods based on quantitative and especially financial indicators, toward approaches favoring various indicators, including financial indicators, and more quality focused. G. Eckes confirms that financial data can no longer constitute the basis of performance measurement. It must be treated in the same way as any type of data, such as quality, customer satisfaction, innovation and market share, which better reflects economic conditions and the growth perspectives of a company.

The proposed measuring system: a system aligning surveillance objectives and the organization's objectives

Despite this trend, studies concentrating on the surveillance–performance link used traditional, and almost always financial, performance.

In all studies, researchers have a very narrow view of performance. As indicated by Audet, human dimensions of performance are ignored, as are employee satisfaction and executive satisfaction and objectives.

It is especially unfortunate to notice that no method retains criteria or performance indicators with a widely recognized link to surveillance activity, such as innovation.

In his book on surveillance effectiveness measurement, Herring (1999) joins Kaplan and Norton by saying that there is no series of measures that can be applied to all companies. Each corporation must select performance measures related to its objectives, its vision and strategy at the highest level. Research, including Herring (1999), shows that management expects an impact from surveillance by an increase in market share, development of new products, strategic plans, etc.

Herring encourages specialists to attend conferences about new performance measures for companies. He mentions in particular the contributions of the Conference Board and notes the tendency of management to integrate intangible performance measures into traditional financial measures.

The table below summarizes the indicators proposed in the report from the Conference Board in 1995.

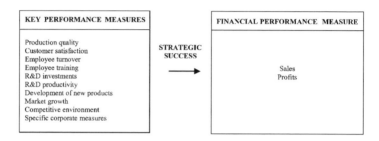

Table 3.1. *New performance measures*

We can use the PCP logic and propose the use of various indicators, reflecting the multiple dimensions of performance, including traditional financial indicators. It is also vital to use indicators liable to be closely linked to the results of the surveillance activity (innovation, sales increase, market share increase, etc.).

In fact, in order to measure a tangible impact from surveillance activity on performance, it is necessary to align surveillance objectives and the objectives of the corporation that it is supposed to serve. For example, if an organization chooses to follow a strategy of innovation, its surveillance system must serve this objective and contribute to an increase in innovations, in the success of new product launches, etc. If the strategy of a corporation is to reinforce its commercial position, its commercial and competitive surveillance system must also serve this objective. The indicators retained would then be increased sales and new clients, etc.

The following table proposes a few performance indicators, based on the four axes of the PCP proposed by Kaplan and Norton.

AXES	PERFORMANCE INDICATORS
FINANCIAL AXIS	Sales ROA Financial results (loss or profit)/Operating results/net Profitability Export rate Cash flow Return on capital Proposed dividend Sales growth, market share growth CRAOI EVA EBITDA …
CLIENT PERFORMANCE	Customer satisfaction index Classification by customers New clients/new markets Respect of delivery due dates …
INNOVATION AND LEARNING AXIS	Number of designed/developed/launched products Success rate of new product launch Percentage of new products in revenue Delay of new product marketing Quality of products Manufacturing lifecycle Improvement rate …
PROCESS AXIS	Manufacturing methods, comparison with competition Lifecycle Unit cost Productivity …

Table 3.2. *Examples of performance indicators*

3.8. Conclusion

From the analysis of general notions of performance and effectiveness, we have considered that, in the strictest sense, performance and effectiveness are synonymous and both represent the achievement of objectives set. As a result of this:

– an organization with a high level of performance (or efficiency) is the one which reaches its goals;

– an effective intelligence (or with a high level of performance) is the one which reaches its goals.

This last definition deliberately puts an important emphasis on an effectiveness measure which consists of comparing results obtained to objectives initially set. However, the effectiveness measurement of surveillance will be more widely studied by also taking into consideration the efficiency measure (the results/methods committed ratio), the measure of user satisfaction and the measure of quality (of methods used, products and services offered). The approach comes from the field of management control and is already applied to information systems, and is adapted here to the specific case of surveillance systems.

Concerning the measure of performance, we propose the use of various criteria (including financial), especially those linked to the activity of surveillance. The evolution of innovation, market share and sales are examples.

From the model proposed, we have observed two different but complementary approaches which will eventually be turned into two measuring tools, in the form of questionnaires. The first one involves the surveillance manager. It concerns the methods implemented to ensure the surveillance activity.

The second approach is addressed to the executive user. It involves the measure of effectiveness in particular (results/objectives) and requires the precise definition of objectives assigned to both forms of surveillance (watch and intelligence).

Chapter 4

Objectives, Products, Use and Context
of Strategic Intelligence

Wondering why and how companies organize surveillance of their environment mostly comes down to identifying the objectives assigned to Strategic Intelligence (why?) and the methods implemented to achieve them (how?).

The core of the general system consists of strictly measuring the effectiveness, i.e. comparing, after the fact, results obtained by the SI system with its initial objectives. The first step is to give information on the objective variable of the measurement model. Then, two other model variables, product and services, will be analyzed, as well as the processes for the surveillance operation. Developing a measurement tool mainly intended for executive users or strategy specialists is based on the analysis of these three elements. The context of SI is also part of the model.

In this model, the SI measure consists of evaluating the resources implemented in SI activity. At this level, a model was developed to explore, describe and measure the five types of surveillance resources: organizational, process oriented, human, technical and financial. It was used as an analysis grid in the empirical part of our research and will enable us to form a measuring tool, mainly for SI managers.

Both measuring tools are complementary. They will serve as a base for the development of a management chart for controlling the surveillance activity.

The objectives assigned to SI come directly from its functions. At this level, the differences between both forms of surveillance – watch and intelligence – are important.

4.1. Functions of surveillance

The major criticism that we can make of the numerous definitions of surveillance is that there is not a significant difference between watch and intelligence. The confusion generated is found in corporate practice, where sometimes companies have a hard time determining if they practice watch or intelligence or nothing at all.

In reality, the disparity between the two forms of surveillance is found at two levels. The first level involves the attitude toward uncertainty and future possibilities. Whereas watch is passive (it experiences change) or at least reactive (it waits for change) or pre-active (it prepares for expected change), intelligence is proactive (it acts, or recommends action, to provoke change). As a result of this, the disparity also exists in the functions of each form of surveillance.

4.1.1. *The main functions of Strategic Watch*

Advance function

The first watch function, its *raison d'être*, is to anticipate threats and opportunities occurring in the environment of companies. Watch must anticipate the evolution of markets, competition and legislation, etc.

Threat and opportunity sources are many and varied. Threats can come from competitors, for example, or from a new upcoming rule or the obsolescence of the corporate scientific and technical capital – a well known threat, especially for technological watch managers. The opportunities can be detecting an acquisition or potential alliances, the development of a new product, reaching a new foreign market, etc.

Information function

The other purpose of watch is to provide information. The information that watch searches for, and collects by different methods and techniques, must be relevant, i.e. have value, and must correspond to user needs. The objective is to satisfy the requirements of users, giving information of value. It can be by putting together an information file on a country or competitor from studies, monographs, etc. The information function is basic for the watch activity.

The information provided by the watch service can however be raw or processed. In this last case, it comes from a procedure of analysis, summary and formatting.

Analytical and synthetic function

Another mission of watch is to analyze information collected, i.e. to break it down and highlight vital elements.

The summary is inseparable from the analysis: it helps in relating and correlating pieces of information that are fragmented, scattered and heterogenous in order to reconstruct a meaningful puzzle. In other words, the summary assembles knowledge elements into a coherent set intended for facilitating decision making.

Analysis and summary are essential functions, particularly when there is information overflow (another purpose of surveillance). They are often preceded or accompanied by a sort and selection operation.

The formatting function

The mission of watch is also to format the analyzed and summarized information. The quality of this formatting can play an important role in understanding displayed knowledge.

The coordination and communication function

Watch must communicate to the right recipients the information that it has collected, analyzed and summarized. Its function is also to coordinate its watch networks to favor the information flows passing through.

The identification of information needs function

The literature sometimes implies that the identification of information needs is one of the functions of watch. It must respond to requirements formulated by users as well as to guess and satisfy implicit expectations.

4.1.2. *The main functions of strategic intelligence*

Watch is part of intelligence. In addition to the functions identified above, intelligence is protective, for certain authors, coordinating and proactive.

The protective function of watch and intelligence

This is a bridge function between watch and intelligence, translating two different protection paths. It is also closely linked to the function of threat anticipation of watch, where it is complementary. In fact, detection or anticipation of threats is logically accompanied by protection operations.

For the Martre or J.-L. Levet and R. Paturel report, it is part of a larger function of scientific and technical capital control of knowhow. This consists of the protection, control and enhancement of corporate knowledge and knowhow. Presented in this way, it mostly involves the technological component of watch and intelligence.

The role of watch for example can be to avoid obsolescence of its knowhow by tracking international technological developments, to enable the registration of patents, etc.

The role of intelligence will be more aggressive. To ensure maximum security for the corporation, it will consist of implementing counter intelligence actions in the case of crises, misinformation, acts of abuse for example. We must nevertheless mention that in most corporations, this last security function is attributed to a specific department instead of only to intelligence.

The coordinating function

The coordinating function is involved with strategies and operations of different company functions. However, this function is not discussed much in literature.

For J.-L. Levet and R. Paturel, economic intelligence plays a role of coordination of strategies by favoring collective reflections. According to D. Rouach, efficient intelligence leads to operation coordination and synergy between functions.

The proactive function

Intelligence has the task of providing actionable information, or in other words, information provided by intelligence activities must be transformed into actions.

The first part of the intelligence proactivity function (proactive function 1) materializes during the distribution of the results of intelligence to users. Knowledge is transmitted in a generally implicit way, in the form of prescription or recommendations of actions. This differentiating element indicates a stronger implication of intelligence in the strategic decision process.

The second part of the mission corresponds to the action itself – for example, implementing actions of influence (proactive function 2). There are very few companies who go this far in intelligence.

Influence or lobbying is an instrument of corporate strategy when faced with globalization of markets, and is mainly used to destabilize competitors. Such activity, especially its methods, is not well known and not much used in France. It often translates into commercial ambition, for example, difficult access to a market. It consists of acting on the environment by broadcasting real and relevant information to a targeted audience. It takes the form, for example, of an agreement protocol with an ecology group in the environmental industry, or of financing the same group to learn its strategy. It can also take the form of putting pressure on authorities regarding a regulation.

We have witnessed a progressive extension of surveillance functions from basic functions (informative and anticipatory) to advanced functions (analytical, synthetic, formatting, coordination and communication, identification of needs, proactivity, etc.).

The table below summarizes the different functions of watch and intelligence.

		FUNCTIONS
INTELLIGENCE		PROACTIVE (1&2)
		COORDINATOR
		PROTECTIVE ("SAFE")
	WATCH	PROTECTIVE
		OF IDENTIFICAITON OF INFORMATION NEEDS
		OF COORDINATION AND COMMUNICATION
		ANALYTICAL, SYNTHETIC, FORMATTING
		INFORMATIVE
		ADVANCE

Table 4.1. *Functions of Watch and Strategic Intelligence*

Largely discussed in the literature, the objectives of watch and intelligence are the result of their respective functions.

4.2. Objectives of intelligence

At this point, it seems necessary to explain the difference between function and objective.

Function is what a person must accomplish in his work. It can be an activity, mission, role, service, task or a job. It can also be a specific action; it then has a role, a specific use.

An objective is a goal to be achieved, a point toward which a strategic or tactical operation is directed, or a specific goal that the action is proposing. Watch and intelligence must anticipate threats and opportunities, satisfy information needs of the user, help in the decision process, etc.

"Objectives correspond to results that the company wants to reach at a given date" (see Desreumaux). This definition, when applied to surveillance activity, explaining its objectives, comes down to explaining expected results.

In other words, the Strategic Watch and Intelligence (SWI) function would be the action (anticipating, informing, analyzing, etc.) and the SWI objective would be the expected result of this action (anticipated threats and opportunities, satisfaction of information needs, decision support, etc.).

According to the literature, the first objective of surveillance is to provide decision support. It is directly linked to the anticipation and information functions of surveillance, especially for decreasing environmental uncertainty.

Cascading objectives result from this vital objective: provision of support for strategic decision making improves decision, which improves strategies, which improves performance, etc.

Several other objectives are also part of surveillance. Despite this multiform set, we can nevertheless observe six large categories of objectives generally linked to the functions already listed. The first category is linked to the anticipatory function of watch. The second category corresponds in a broad sense to the information function of watch (raw information collected, and information that is processed and communicated). The third category is connected to the protective function of watch and intelligence. The fourth category corresponds to the security function of intelligence. The fifth category corresponds to the coordinating function of intelligence. The sixth category mainly involves the proactive function of intelligence.

A seventh function needs to go on a particular level. It is linked to the previous functions and it involves the major objective of competitive and performance impact on the corporation.

4.2.1. *The objectives of Strategic Watch*

Objectives linked to anticipating function

The objectives linked to the anticipatory function of surveillance are:

– better anticipation of threats (intentions of competitors, changes in legislation, political risks, new standards, etc.);

– better anticipation of opportunities (new requirements, new products, new markets, diversification, sales/license purchase, joint venture agreement, etc.).

The objective of anticipation should lead to better reactivity, better crisis management (the company would be better prepared for expected changes), better adaptation capacity, etc.

Objectives linked to the information function in the broad sense (from research to communication of information)

The main function of watch is to provide raw as well as processed (analyzed, summarized and formatted, etc.) information, with the main objective of satisfying user requirements for valuable information.

With this central objective, it should allow a better understanding of the corporate environment, a better understanding of plans and intentions of competitors, decreased uncertainty in decision making (by limiting risks of error), better communication, etc.

4.2.2. *Objectives of strategic intelligence*

Objectives linked to the protective function of SWI

The objectives linked to the protective function would be a better protection against obsolescence of knowhow and technologies (we get closer to the anticipatory function of surveillance in this case) and better protection against misinformation, acts of abuse, etc. (ensuring the security of the corporation).

Objectives linked to the coordinating function

Surveillance would enable better coordination of decisions and operations, as well as better synergy in operations.

Objectives linked to the proactive function

By making recommendations and instructions, surveillance would encourage better environmental control (because the company will act on the environment instead of experiencing its changes) and the implementation of actions (including actions of influence).

Consequently, the series of functions of watch and intelligence activity serves a common objective maintained by most authors and confirmed in all empirical studies about decision support.

It would then enable better strategic choices, more appropriate strategic decisions and better strategies (better success rate of innovation, alliance, fusion or acquisition strategies, etc.).

In order to explain this ambitious objective, take the example of innovation strategies. The amplifying effect of surveillance on the innovation process of the company is widely recognized.

For Rouach and Santi, technological watch is the real booster for innovation. By scanning the market evolution, the marketing watch also makes it possible to design products which are better adapted to consumer expectations of better quality, etc.

4.2.3. *Objectives of competitiveness and organizational performance of SWI*

For the group behind the Martre report, surveillance has become one of the major triggers of the global performance of corporations and nations. Shared by the vast majority of authors, this idea states that the final and main objective of surveillance is the improvement of competitiveness and corporate performance. In reality, it involves objectives of impacts more than objectives in their own right.

Surveillance would improve the competitive position (evolution of market share), decrease costs (R&D, production, etc.), make savings in the budget, (avoiding waste of resources), make savings (or gain) in time, improve innovation, improve quality of products, improve sales, etc.

Prior studies rarely addressed the very confidential theme of surveillance results, and promises suggested by authors have not always been verified empirically.

In addition, the literature highlights the problem of evaluating the effectiveness of surveillance through the results obtained.

First for Lainé, given that the main objective of surveillance is to provide assistance to decision making, its effectiveness can only be measured indirectly, through the quality of decisions taken.

Secondly, the effectiveness of surveillance is often evaluated in a negative way: the system could not detect a threat or it could not avoid a bad decision...

Finally, it is difficult to evaluate the profitability of surveillance since the costs of the activity (important and impossible to estimate in a reliable manner) are at least as difficult to estimate as the gains.

In his research on organizational practices in terms of surveillance with 19 anonymous companies, C. Jamboué established the problems encountered by companies in estimating the results of surveillance. When the results were identified by the people interviewed (surveillance managers in the case of this study), they were always expressed in a qualitative way.

As a result of problems encountered, seven companies out of the 19 studied did not evaluate the efficiency of their surveillance. Some managers talked about the problem of quantifying the value of information, the lack of return for the client user on the usefulness of information transmitted and the impossibility of determining the role of additional information provided by the surveillance system in a decision role based on a multitude of other information.

One of the 12 companies able to attribute concrete results to the activity of surveillance also emphasized the problem with linking a result to the surveillance activity.

Another estimated that it was difficult to get quantitative results when the primary mission of surveillance was to bring better quality to decision making.

The problems raised by the evaluation of value, usefulness and weight of information provided by the surveillance system in decision making explained the problems encountered by these companies in evaluating the effectiveness of surveillance.

Concerning the identified qualitative failings, the author distinguished between those involving activities of the company and those linked to the operation of these activities.

The following table summarizes the results obtained.

RESULTS FOR CORPORATE ACTIVITIES	RESULTS OF SURVEILLANCE FOR CORPORATE OPERATIONS
Research program direction • Starting new programs: launch of a research program on the quality of life linked to the treatment of a class of pathologies (1) • Reorientation: targeting of new energy applications (1) and modification of current research (2) or • Withdrawal of current research: identification of results from American research projects on a current research program (1)	**New methods of work organization** • The use of Minitel for credit applications with the bank's partners enabled productivity gains and a two year lead over competitors (1) • Adoption of new computer tools and new work methods (1) • Modification in the internal research organization (1) • Team spirit reinforcement, making teamwork easier and encouragement in information services (1)
Adoption of new technical solutions • Application of technical solutions used in other activity sectors (1) • Adoption of a new fuel following the surveillance of competitors who are using it in increasing numbers (1)	**Industrial property actions** • New research and development lines toward innovation leading to the creation of products or processes which can be patented, opposing competitive patents (1) • Patenting anticipation (1) • Closing of a competitive unit in Japan infringing a patent (1)
Modification of the corporate activity portfolio (development of new products or modification of existing products) • Launch of a new insurance contract (1) • Galenic modifications of medication and development in urology of a drug traditionally used in cardiology (1) • Development of new training shoes and launch of a product made with recycled cotton before the environmental trend (1)	**Development of foreign relations** • Partnerships created with firms and research teams (1) • Modification in foreign partnership choices after reorientation of research programs (1)

Table 4.2. *Surveillance results from 12 corporations (see Jamboué, 1995)*

The author of the study noted that all parties expressed themselves in terms of examples, but they were unable to provide exhaustive or quantitative indications about the results obtained. In addition, it is interesting to note that most of the examples involved the organization of work. The studies demonstrating the existence of a link between the practice of surveillance and the performance of the organization were based on potential gain in downstream performance, either by ROA or sales growth, for example. In the study, surveillance was liable to improve the internal operation of the company upstream, and thus create additional potential.

It is unfortunate that the study was only based on testimonials of surveillance managers, without considering the opinion of users of the products of surveillance, in particular its contribution in the context of their decision process.

In his study of the Elf Atochem case, the Martre report notes results linked to the activity of corporate surveillance: new research projects, new development projects, cooperation agreements, transfers of technology, (sales – purchases of licenses), sales – purchases of units of production, breaks in activity.

During his studies into salespeople's attitudes towards marketing and commercial watch, Le Bon emphasized three concrete examples clearly attributed to surveillance. The first example discussed the decision of the Frial oil launch by Astra Calve, which was taken after a salesperson informed the commercial management of the launch of Cristy by Lesieur. At Xerox, salespersons were the first to perceive increasing client interest for postscript production printers. At Sodexo, a salesperson made development management take notice of the arrival of Panzani, which affected the catering market for colleges and high schools with the sale of vending machines with prepared foods.

The following table gives an exhaustive list of objectives assigned to surveillance in the literature.

		FUNCTIONS	**OBJECTIVES (EXPECTED RESULTS)**
INTELLIGENCE		6. PROACTIVE 2. Implementing actions 1. Produce recommendations to SWI	**Decision support** Recommendations to users Implemented actions (of influence for example) Fallout examples: Better control on environment
		5. COORDINATING	Decision support Better coordination in decisions and operations Better operational synergy
		4. PROTECTIVE Securing the corporation	Better protection against misinformation, acts of abuse...
	WATCH	3. PROTECTIVE Protect against threats	Better protection against obsolescence of know-how, techniques and technological
		2. INFORMATIVE (in a broad sense) • Inform •Analyze • Synthesize •Format • Identify information needs • Coordinate & Communicate	**Satisfaction of value information needs for users** Fallout examples: Better knowledge of global environment, markets, competitors, technologies, rules and regulations ... Better understanding of competitors' plans and intentions Better communication **Decision support** Fallout examples: Better strategic choices More appropriate strategic strategies Better strategy (innovation, alliances, fusion etc.)
		1. ANTICIPATING • Anticipate environmental threats and opportunities	**Anticipation of threats & opportunities** Fallout examples: Better reactivity Better crises management Better capacity of adaptation

Watch and Intelligence	IMPACT OBJECTIVES ON COMPETITIVITY AND PERFORMANCE	Better competitive position Economy of costs Budgetary economy (avoid wasting resources) Economy (gain) in time Better innovation Better product quality Better sales

Table 4.3. *Objectives assigned to SWI*

The measure of surveillance effectiveness and its impact on performance consists of, among others, comparing the objectives of surveillance with the results obtained. It is a measure after the fact. With this measure, executives can understand the degree of objective achievement of their surveillance system and the impact on performance. In order for this measure to be possible, objectives of surveillance must be precisely set and aligned with the corporate performance objectives, as previously suggested.

Throughout previous empirical studies, we notice that some of the results corresponding to listed objectives do not lend themselves to the measure. Because of this, their operationalization will inevitably return to qualitative and subjective measures.

4.3. SWI product and services

The product of surveillance is information or, to be more precise, knowledge, which the process of surveillance broadcasts to user recipients. Raw information collected is transformed and evaluated (analyzed, summarized, formatted) during the process of surveillance, mainly to serve the strategic decision.

At this level, the question of information value is central: an efficient surveillance system is first and foremost a system which distributes valuable information. Information is distributed with the help of different types of productions and supports which are specific to the activity of surveillance and the organization.

In the context of our measurement model, the executive user or strategy manager must judge the quality of the information and functions (i.e. services) provided by the surveillance system used.

4.3.1. *The value of information provided by the surveillance process*

The value of information depends on eight fundamental dimensions (see Zmud (1978)):

1) relevance of the information (i.e. useful, expected, important);

2) precision of the information (i.e. credible);

3) the fact that the information is factual (i.e. true);

4) quantity of information (i.e. complete, sufficient);

5) reliability and timeliness of information (i.e. valid, current);

6) organization of the information (i.e. orderly);

7) legibility of information (i.e. clean, useful, simple);

8) the fact that the information is reasonable.

The author aggregates these into four categories:

– quality of information (dimension 1);

– components of relevance (dimensions 2, 3, 4, 5);

– quality of the format (dimensions 6, 7);

– quality of the meaning (dimension 8).

The categorization proposed by Zmud lays down vague barriers between the different components of the value of information which in reality overlap and complete each other. Are the quality of information, the quality of its format and the quality of its meaning not part of the relevance of information?

In addition, the author does not take into consideration the user and context of use, or the subjectivity of evaluation information criteria.

We explained the interpretation processes of individuals using representations from the real world. The problem of the relevance of representation, i.e. the value that the information presents for its user, is raised when information is acquired.

In fact, the notion of relevance is directly linked to the use of the information: what is relevant is what is suitable, what is appropriate to an action. To be relevant, a representation must therefore respond to the needs of its user.

Applied to the context of decision, relevant information is information which would enable us to make the right decision and to facilitate the appropriate development of the decision process in all its phases (intelligence of the problem, modeling, choice and evaluation).

R. Reix details the main determining factors of relevance of representations, and most of them are found in the list proposed by Zmud: completeness, absence of noise, precision, respect for time constraints, reliability, form of the representation and accessibility of information. According to the author, the discussion of the notion of relevance of representations is in fact an interrogation of the value that the information represents for its user.

Completeness

Any decision maker would want to have complete information. Problems would be identified better, modeling would be more precise and all alternatives would be considered.

In practice, however, this criterion is rarely respected. In addition, the function of information does not retain all the important elements. Completeness is therefore relative to a given user and decision model.

Absence of noise

The ideal is also to have only information that is useful for the decision involved. Absence of noise, in a way, represents the degree of usefulness of the information provided. The function of information can retain unimportant, useless information.

Precision or the degree of fineness

This represents the level of detail of the representation. However, people have limited capacity for data processing and there is a volume of information threshold where relevance decreases.

Respect for time constraints

THE LIMIT IMPOSED BY DECISION MAKING

The process of using information is a dynamic process under strong time constraints. In order to be used, information must be available in a timeframe limited by the decision making time. Beyond this boundary, additional information, regardless of its value, no longer has any interest, since the decision has already been made.

TOPICALITY

Surveillance systems for the environment often describe progressive processes (evolution of competitive positions for example). As a result of this, the relevance of information decreases with time and hence with the age of information. The delay in receiving information must be reduced and the frequency of observation must be increased.

Reliability

This corresponds to accuracy of information. Information reliability depends on its source and on the judgment of the compiler of the information on the transmitter. Inaccurate information can lead to a bad decision and often irreparable consequences for the company.

Form

Numerical and alphabetical data, drawings, images, etc. are all forms of representations. The wealth of a representation depends on its aptitude in translating all aspects of reality. Information formatting is important for the relevance and speed of decisions made. For example, information summarized in the form of a graph is more quickly perceived in its entirety than that presented as a table.

It is impossible to define the best form of representation, since this very subjective criterion depends on the user's cognitive style.

Accessibility

Where can we find useful information? How much time is needed before finding it? What operations should be done to obtain information? These are questions defining information accessibility. All prior studies demonstrated that accessibility was a quality of information determined by a given use.

In conclusion, the value of information increases with its topicality, abundance, accuracy and reliability. It also increases with its degree of accuracy up to a given threshold, from which it greatly decreases. Finally, it is linked to its form by a subjective and contingent relation linked to the user and context. Similarly, with information sources, the value of information varies with time. In general, it decreases with it.

The following diagram represents the major determining factors of relevance.

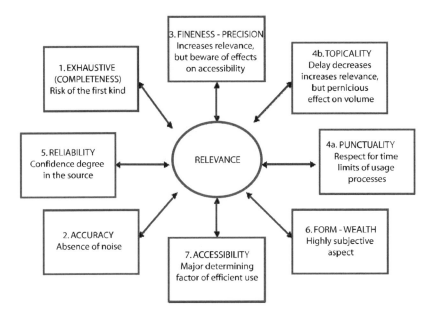

Figure 4.1. *Major determining factors of information relevance (see Reix, 1998)*

Martinet and Marti exceed the traditional analysis of the value of information to adopt a wider angle within the global context of the intelligence activity.

According to them, the value of information depends on the quality of information needs analysis, relevance and quality of sources, quality of the analysis, distribution, feedback and respect for security.

The equation below illustrates their point of view.

$$\text{Value of information} = \begin{pmatrix} \text{Accurate} \\ \text{needs} \\ \text{analysis} \end{pmatrix} \times \begin{pmatrix} \text{Relevance} \\ \text{and quality} \\ \text{of sources} \end{pmatrix} \times \begin{pmatrix} \text{Quality} \\ \text{of the} \\ \text{analysis} \end{pmatrix} \times \begin{pmatrix} \text{Distribution} \\ \text{and} \\ \text{feedback} \end{pmatrix} \times \begin{pmatrix} \text{Security} \end{pmatrix}$$

Figure 4.2. *Value of information (Martinet and Marti, 1995)*

In reality, this equation does not determine the value of information. According to us, it emphasizes the effectiveness of surveillance, which is represented by the product of surveillance effectiveness factors. We find certain phases of the SWI process previously analyzed. Again, it is a partial view, putting aside other fundamental effectiveness factors of surveillance.

4.3.2. *Production of surveillance services*

Products from watch or intelligence services materialize during the formatting operation. This is often documentation of highly variable type and length, according to the status of the transmitter, the recipient and the objective sought. Denominations also vary from one company to another. Their content reflects the functions of surveillance services (prospective, informative, analytical functions, etc.).

The warning note

When valuable information is detected by a corresponding watchman or by watch and intelligence management, it may sometimes be very urgent to transmit it as is to the recipient involved. The alert note is very simply formalized and saves time. This solution can be assessed by a sales watchman for example. He has very little time to process information that he receives.

Ad hoc report

This is a document written by employees during business trips or at conventions, shows and other events. Their mission is to take note of all unusual information which seems interesting for their company.

Competitive monographic publications

The in-depth study of competitors is mandatory for any corporation wanting to acquire or retain a favorable competitive position. Corresponding documents are often voluminous. Summarizing becomes interesting in this case.

SWI synthesis

These documents are mainly intended for the General Manager or Strategy Manager; they combine vital results from the different watches in the company, or report on specific strategic axes of SWI.

Newsletters

Watch and intelligence services often produce periodic newsletters with the objective of informing company employees of important events occurring in the corporate environment. These letters can also be used to support the network of watchmen, along with other sources of information, such as blogs, group emails, websites, etc.

Press reviews

Documentation centers broadcast these publications, but they can also be produced by the surveillance service or be outsourced.

For the products and services provided by SWI, the methodology consists of evaluating the degree of user satisfaction on the quality of information provided by the surveillance system (completeness, degree of information use, precision, respect for delays, topicality, reliability, form and accessibility).

The approach (above) is also about knowing the degree of customer satisfaction on services offered by surveillance (service of anticipation, raw information availability, analysis, summary, formatting, etc.).

4.4. SI uses

The ultimate step of the surveillance system is implementation, since this applies the product of surveillance (information) to the making of strategic decisions (in particular but not solely). In fact, the literature lists several types of uses for products of surveillance, but for all the authors, the main objective is strategic decision support.

The implementation phase is the part of the surveillance process that we have studied in our model's process methods. Three questions are raised concerning the effectiveness factors at this level:

– the use of the product of surveillance, notably its integration into the decision process;

– the surveillance–strategy connection;

– the existence of recommendations for the user.

In fact, the integration of surveillance results into the strategic decision process is often mentioned in the literature as the main factor of effectiveness.

The link between surveillance and strategy facilitates the integration of surveillance results into the strategic decision process. The frequency of contacts between the surveillance manager and the user is an indicator of this link.

The difference between watch and surveillance is more prevalent in this product use phase: whereas watch provides information for decision making, intelligence goes further by making action recommendations to the decision maker. As a result of this, it is automatically more integrated into the process of strategic decision making than Strategic Watch.

Even though the authors highlight that integrating surveillance results with the process of strategic decision is a key factor of corporate success, in practice it is rarely observed. Its measurement is difficult, and in all previous studies, it is based on the perception of respondents. To avoid this problem, Ghoshal and Westney are demanding concrete results to prove this use.

In fact, for many authors, the degree of integration must be important. Surveillance must be involved in each phase of the strategic planning process. Jain notices, however, that results of surveillance practiced by American insurance companies studied are not used, because there is no formalization of the planning process. He deduces that a formalized strategic planning process is mandatory in order for the surveillance activity to be efficient.

Despite recommendations from authors, studies show the problems encountered by professionals in the study, in ensuring that their results can be used in decision support, or for feeding the strategic planning process.

In Fahey's study, only one company in 12 integrates information from surveillance into its strategic planning process. There is interaction between surveillance and planning personnel in only two companies. Most of the companies studied in the Diffenbach report integrate the products of surveillance into strategic planning. This integration is stronger at group level (69% of respondents) than at division level (56%).

Klein and Linneman noticed that there was no integration in the companies they studied. Ghoshal and Whestney did not settle for responses; they required concrete examples of the use of information from surveillance. In 44 out of 63 cases, information from surveillance was used, both in the strategic decision process (17 cases) and in strategic planning (27 cases).

The Surveillance Manager plays an important role in terms of surveillance integration into the strategic decision process. His actual influence was studied in the IHEDN study. The authors wondered if he had the authority to influence the strategic decision process or if he was limited to implementing actions decided by management.

Results of the study show that the SWI manager is perceived more as a strategic proposition force contributing to the formulation of corporate strategy (62.2%) than as a lever of implementation of a policy created by executives for the company's overall operations (37.8%). On the other hand, meetings with executives revealed that RIES always succeeds in making executive committee members more aware, resulting in a more efficient decision process because of their interventions.

According to the results of the study, the RIES strategic proposition strength is supported by:

– the nature of competition: European competition represents 72.7%;

– the corporate structure: RIES action effectiveness is perceived as maximum when the organization is divided by geographical zones (91.7%);

– the prevalence of prior attacks: the more prior attacks the company experiences, the more efficient the RIES action is perceived to be and the more its recommendations are integrated into strategic decision support.

In contrast, when competition is global, the corporate structure is divided by product and there have been no major identified attacks, RIES is not perceived as a strategic proposition strength. Instead, it responds to the recommendations of the Executive Committee.

As for research model use, we have to evaluate the use of surveillance product (information) and, notably, its integration in the strategic decision process and user satisfaction for the general surveillance system.

As indicated in the section dedicated to measuring satisfaction, simple satisfaction indices (for optional system use) are the rate of use measurement (the number of system users by the involved resource) and the intensity of usage (number and duration of uses).

4.5. Context of surveillance

4.5.1. *The influence of corporate environment*

Some characteristics of the environment seem to play an important role on the type of surveillance practiced: instability, complexity, competitive intensity, competitive aggressiveness, the nature of the business sector, and government policy concerning SI.

Perceived instability and complexity

In all studies involving this theme, there is correlation between the degree of instability or degree of uncertainty perceived and the practice of surveillance.

In their study of surveillance at the level of individuals within a company, Kefalas and Shoderbek measure the degree of environmental turbulence with the help of goal indicators (sales change rate, new product introduction rate, etc.) and the perceived subjective uncertainty indicator. They notice that managers spend more time on surveillance when the environment is qualified as dynamic. Nevertheless, the difference is low (1.9 hours for the dynamic environment of the agricultural mechanical industry and 1.7 hours for the stable environment of the food packaging industry).

Klein and Linneman and Daft *et al.* noted a correlation at the corporate level: Klein and Linneman measure environmental instability by the uncertainty perceived, and Daft *et al.* measure environmental instability by environmental complexity, perceived change rate and the importance given to the environmental field involved.

The nature of competition

The practice of ESI is more important for companies evolving in an environment where competition is strong and/or global.

To qualify the degree of competitive aggression, we can use the number of attacks as indicators. These show that companies who detected or experienced prior attacks practice ESI more, and in a more innovative and dynamic way.

The nature of the business sector

Contrary to preconceived ideas, the superiority of high tech corporations in terms of surveillance has not been verified in studies. According to results from Bournois and Romani, three sectors practice specifically innovating ESI:

– metals/mechanical/electronics;

– transportation/communications;

– building/civil engineering.

Government policy concerning SI

There are no empirical studies of the link between the practice of surveillance and government policy. Nevertheless, several authors emphasize the role of the nation in raising awareness and its practice in corporations.

4.5.2. *The influence of corporate characteristics*

Several characteristics of the company seem to influence the type of surveillance practiced: its size, structure, competitive position, global reach and financial performance.

Size of the corporation

Contrary to recent research, older studies did not notice any influence on the size of the corporation on surveillance.

In studies at the individual level, Aguilar, as did Greenfeld, Winder and Williams, observed that there is no correlation between the size of the company and the practice of surveillance.

Diffenbach arrived at the same conclusion in terms of surveillance at corporate level. In addition, Fahey and King, and similarly Lenz and Engledow, noticed no association between company size and organizational surveillance arrangements.

However, some authors maintain that there is a fixed cost threshold for surveillance that only large corporations can afford. This affirmation is confirmed by the Ballaz study as well as the study by Bournois and Romani.

For the latter, the size of the company is a major determining factor for the practice of surveillance. Their results show that the percentage of companies not practicing Economic and Strategic Intelligence (ESI) is higher within small and medium sized companies: 39% of companies with less than 500 employees, compared to 7% of corporations with over 10,000 employees. In terms of resources, the critical threshold is 1,000 employees and approximately €0.15 billion in terms of sales.

In addition, the practice of surveillance is higher in companies belonging to a holding company than in legally autonomous companies. The authors attribute this variation to the higher vigilance required by the various activities of a holding company.

Books dedicated to the sensitive theme of surveillance (especially with intelligence) seem to have played an important role in the reputation and demystification of the function. The authors highlight the impact of the Martre report for large corporations in 1994. According to small and medium sized companies, they were late with surveillance awareness.

The influence of publications on reputation, challenges and, consequently, the practice of surveillance has already been emphasized.

The organizational structure

In the IHEDN study (2000), the traditional hierarchical organizational structure by major functions does not seem to be favorable to the practice of ESI. On the other hand, the authors notice that ESI is more important in companies organized by product, matrices or project.

Remember that Stubbart also highlighted the influence of the organizational structure, but he noted that the divisional structure was not favorable to surveillance when it was centralized.

Global reach

In several studies, companies exporting the most feel the need to practice surveillance the most.

Companies with over 40% of their sales as exports, with more than 10 foreign subsidiaries and managing global competition, practice ESI more.

Financial performance

Even though authors admit that the causes of results have multiple factors, they still maintain that companies practicing ESI derive more benefits than others. For them, it is a sign of their reactivity and a performance and modernity index: the stronger the position of companies, the higher the ESI practice.

Remember that the studies by Dollinger, Daft, Vergnaud-Shaeffer and Subramanian also highlighted the connection between corporate performance and the practice of surveillance. In all these studies, the cause and effect rate was never studied.

In conclusion, the type of surveillance practiced in organizations depends on two series of characteristics. One is linked to the nature of the corporate environment (instability, complexity, nature of competition and business sector) and the other to the company itself (size, organizational structure, competitive position, global availability and financial performance).

Chapter 5

Evaluation of the Organizational Resources of SI

Chapters 5, 6 and 7 present the variable "methods" of the research model. It has a primary descriptive goal: the methods implemented to ensure surveillance activity are reviewed. An overview of the literature in this field makes it possible to elaborate on the subject of surveillance exploration, description and the measurement model. This model is included in the main research model and constitutes a grid of surveillance activity methods for the organization.

The approaches to surveillance are mainly descriptive and prescriptive: the literature often recommends the best methods for practicing efficient surveillance. For the authors, these are simultaneously factors and indicators of surveillance effectiveness. The second objective is to extract these from the literature. As this research is exploratory at this stage, we can only raise research questions involving the effectiveness factors of surveillance methods.

Five categories of methods necessary for the surveillance activity are categorized: organizational, process, human, technical and financial methods (see Chapters 6 and 7). Each category examines the theoretical contributions and practices of corporations.

Five main elements describe the organization of surveillance: its degree of formalization, seniority, level of centralization (or decentralization), rank in the hierarchy and its network structure. A degree of formalization and seniority, a high hierarchical ranking and a dense and active network seem to be factors of surveillance effectiveness.

5.1. Formalization of the watch and SI activity

For most analysts, surveillance must be organized and formalized. The literature proposes several typologies, often based on the level of progress of the organization in terms of formalization of the surveillance activity.

5.1.1. *A certain degree of formalization of the SWI activity*

A surveillance activity can be qualified as formalized when there are written rules and procedures controlling its operation and the behavior of the elements involved. There is the example of forms that employees must fill out when they are traveling abroad. In the previous studies, formalization of the surveillance activity is studied at the individual level, but mostly at organizational level, which we are more interested in. The analysts noted the development of formalization at both levels.

In fact, Diffenbach noted that 73% of companies studied formalized their surveillance activity. The same is true for over half the companies studied by Klein and Linneman, Prebble, Rau and Reichel or by Brockhoff. Prebble for example states that 51% of managers questioned follow a formal procedure to read, summarize and distribute the information published.

The degree of formalization is very different from one country to another however. The IHEDN study has shown that formalization of intelligence was not very developed within French corporations. Only 12.4% of firms surveyed admitted having very formalized practices, i.e. written and classified for the people involved, and 68.9% considered their practices to be poorly formalized. However, these results are based on the perception of respondents and are not the result of an objective formalization measure.

The many advantages linked to formal surveillance (and the major drawbacks linked to informal surveillance) explain the rapid evolution towards formalization.

In fact, adopting an informal approach to surveillance is, for example, taking the risk of duplicating important information sources, of giving inadequate coverage to sectors being monitored, of a possible drift, in the absence of procedures aimed at preserving ethics, etc. Conversely, even though formalized surveillance seems more expensive than informal surveillance, it has important advantages. Improved targeting of information being collected may, for example, better satisfy the needs of decision makers, improve the quantity and quality of information, etc.

Table 5.1 summarizes the advantages and drawbacks of formal and informal surveillance.

ADVANTAGES OF AN INFORMAL SURVEILLANCE	DISADVANTAGES OF FORMALIZED SURVEILLANCE
Inexpensive organization and operation. But can be costly in terms of missed opportunities. Requires no specific training.	Increased organization and operation costs. Risk of perceiving the surveillance cell as espionage. Requires specific training.
ADVANTAGES OF A FORMALIZED SURVEILLANCE	**DISADVANTAGES OF INFORMAL SURVEILLANCE**
Improvement in the quality of information collected; increased reliability of timed information; closer attention from the internal network; better information supply… Information targeting according to Management and Strategy needs. More cost-effective in the long term because it is targeted, eliminates duplications; increases the probability of discovering threats or opportunities. Demand for surveillance increases at the same time as management becomes aware of the viability and value of the system. Improvement of planning and decision making. Importance of linking informal strategic information of executives to a formalized process for better usage. Possibility of respecting the confidentiality of certain data with a procedure for information access protection. Better employee mobilization.	Duplication of sources. Inadequate coverage. Risk of missing valuable information. Absence of a central evaluation cell toward which all information converges. Consequently, lack of quality control, validity and reliability of information. Absence of systematic determination of needs and priorities, consequently, information collection is random, providing too much or too little information on a subject. Lack of general or strategic vision; is not oriented toward users. Greatly depends on the will and whims of information collectors. Inadequate and random distribution of information. Possibility of ethical drift in the absence of central instructions.

Table 5.1. *Advantages and disadvantages of formal and informal surveillance (from Gilad and Gilad, 1985, and Ballaz, 1992)*

The results of empirical studies show that a large majority of managers are in favor of a more formalized surveillance activity.

The Wall study indicates that 72% of the 1,200 managers surveyed support the creation of a system for managing environmental information. The Keegan results are mixed. From the observation that there was no formal system to use the publications read by managers

– they were all reading the same magazines instead of sharing the task – the author raised the question of relevance of a formal system for using information sources. Two positions emerged. Several respondents were in favor of a formalization of source use. Others preferred an informal exchange, based on cooperative communication.

In the Gelb study where the predominance of informal surveillance was detected, executives also preferred greater formalization of the surveillance process as well as the creation of a specific group to do so. Similarly, the 153 respondents from Ghoshal and Westney's study recognized interest in the formalization of surveillance activity.

However, some analysts insist on the necessity of respecting the part played by informal surveillance. In fact, members of the company, particularly managers, can have the opportunity of collecting information during events or informal meetings. This information is not very accessible by traditional methods, but is often valuable. In addition, some independent functions can find restrictive formalization procedures difficult.

Consequently, we can question whether a certain degree of organization and formalization of the surveillance activity is a factor of surveillance effectiveness. In all studies, the degree of formalization is highly correlated to the degree of surveillance progress. Several authors proposed typologies for its characterization.

5.2. Seniority of the SWI function

The length of time for which the function has been practiced and the learning phenomenon to which it is connected are often brought up to explain the progress and the effectiveness of surveillance.

Just over 7% of the 186 companies studied by Jain practiced proactive surveillance, i.e. in phase 4, the most advanced in the typology proposed by the author. Within these 14 corporations, the function was at least five years old.

10 years later, significant progress in surveillance was observed: 25% of the 101 companies in their sample were in phase 4 (see Subramanian *et al.*). Experience as well as expertise and learning are considered as factors in the surveillance progress and effectiveness. Similarly, the authors of the IHEDN study also highlight the learning process linked to the practice of surveillance.

In conclusion, a certain degree of experience in surveillance activity by the organizational learning process involved seems to be a factor of surveillance effectiveness.

5.3. Centralization, decentralization and the number of SWI points

An opposing theory emerged early in the 1980s, involving the centralization of the surveillance activity.

For some (see Fahey and King), in an ideal continuous surveillance case, an autonomous entity responsible for surveillance must exist at the center of the corporation.

Their hypothesis is questioned by Stubbart, who supports a decentralized surveillance activity managed by the different functional departments. He is joined by several authors. For H. Lesca, for example, monitoring a multidimensional space requires the implementation of multiple antennas facing in several directions.

Each position is widely defended in academic publications. The following tables list the arguments of authors for and against each organizational arrangement.

The special surveillance unit: advantages and drawbacks

The specialized entity has a global vision enabling it to satisfy information needs of the different members of the corporation quickly. Similarly, information validations and analyses, centralized within the specialized unit, are facilitated. Duplications are decreased, avoiding a waste of corporate resources. Personnel, dedicated full time to the specialized surveillance unit, are available, motivated and trained on surveillance techniques.

Criticisms of the specialized unit involve:

– its distance from the field;

– its centralization (restricted accessibility for some employees);

– its incompatibility with the current organization;

– its instability;

– its legitimacy (some managers are skeptical of its usefulness);

– its high operation costs;

– its lack of informal information.

Decentralization of surveillance within current departmental, functional or operational units

ADVANTAGES

– The expertise of people involved in one or more surveillance fields (for example scientists in technological watch).

– The information collected responds better to the needs of managers of divisions or functional departments.

– The surveillance activity is closer to reality and immediate strategic and operational concerns.

– The integration of surveillance results in the decision process is easier.

DRAWBACKS

– There is an absence of global vision, information research is primarily done in the specialized field of the responsible function.

– Limited resources are allocated to surveillance.

– There are significant duplications.

– There is heterogenity in methods and practices linked to the surveillance process.

– There are weak relations between the different surveillance units because of the functional compartmentalization, hence there is limited circulation of information detrimental to the effectiveness of surveillance.

Faced with the advantages and drawbacks of each organizational position, the theoretical debate comparing centralization and decentralization was abandoned for a more flexible position favoring a mix of both types of organization.

This evolution was observed in the practice of corporations. It is therefore possible to find within the same company both a specific group dedicated to the surveillance of one or more environments (and/or the centralization of different watches) existing at the heart of the company, and several decentralized entities responsible for specific surveillance (legal watch, marketing watch, commercial watch, etc.).

In 1977, Terry proposed a central direction unit and functional entities. For Lesca as well, both surveillance levels must coexist. The central unit has a general vision and plays a coordinating role, whereas specific units for each division or function involve specific subjects.

In the same line, Gilad and Gilad propose a support organization; the group surveillance unit serves as watch support for operational units. It proposes training and awareness actions for employees as well as expertise and control in terms of surveillance. It can also ensure surveillance of fields not covered by the operational units.

Finally, Ghoshal and Kim favor a complete surveillance system. One of the components of the system must sense the global environmental climate in order to conceive long term plans and strategy. Another component treats specific information for more tactical and operational objectives.

Organizational steps proposed in the literature vary greatly. This diversity is present in corporate practices. From all empirical studies carried out, we can observe three types of organization:

– companies with a specialized centralized entity responsible for surveillance;

– companies that entrust the activity of surveillance to existing divisions or functional departments (the marketing or R&D department for example);

– companies that have a specialized entity as well as decentralized surveillance structures for their divisions or functions.

We notice a definite evolution toward the latter type of organization: a simultaneously centralized and decentralized surveillance.

Over the 12 companies studied by Fahey and King, only two have a specialized surveillance unit. These two companies give a high importance rating to the surveillance of the corporate environment. In addition, they justify the creation of a specialized entity by the unstable nature of their environment, which prevents management from carrying out surveillance and strategic planning operations simultaneously.

Of the 186 corporations analyzed by Jain, 30% have an autonomous surveillance unit. The companies that have adopted this organization are at the most advanced phase of surveillance established by the author. These results are confirmed by Klein and Linneman: 30% of the 445 firms in their study have a specialized unit.

In the Lenz and Engledow study, the 10 companies recognized as having the best surveillance performance have a specialized unit. These authors distinguish between the formal and operational surveillance structure. The latter groups an internal component (with the goal of soliciting and raising employee awareness to information collection) and an external component (which contracts information collection to outside firms).

A specialized surveillance structure is also found in 30% of corporations studied by Prescott and Smith and by Ballaz, and in 52% of companies analyzed by Subramanian, Fernandes and Harper.

In France, even though some authors noticed that there were not many companies with a centralized surveillance unit, the situation seems to have evolved. In fact, in the IHEDN study, a permanent unit exists in 49% of companies in the sample, and in half of the firms who have faced serious attack. In corporations with more than 50 subsidiaries, this percentage reaches 62%.

Companies in which functional departments manage surveillance activity represent 40% of the companies studied by Fahey, King and Narayanan and 47% of Jain's 186 companies. In addition, 23% of the companies studied by Jain have surveillance units for their divisions or product–market zones.

Companies having a specialized surveillance entity and decentralized structures seem to increase in numbers. In Thomas' study of nine large American corporations, the surveillance activity is centralized for the group and decentralized for operational units. It can be used in existing structures or lead to the creation of a surveillance entity.

The Jain study shows an evolution in the surveillance organization which tends to make the two forms of organizational position coexist. For the author, group surveillance involves the detection of general trends, whereas operational structures monitor specific environments. The marketing research function, for example, directs its collection toward social trends, whereas public relations are concerned with regulatory trends.

The organization of surveillance can sometimes be complex. The three major corporations analyzed by Ghoshal and Westney practice competitive surveillance on three hierarchical levels. Corporate surveillance follows competitors and offers its expertise in terms of surveillance. At a group level, the positions are varied; surveillance is centered around operational units or based on a formalized entity. Finally at the SBU (Strategic Business Unit) level, direct competitors are monitored. In addition, surveillance can be organized at the functional level. In these companies, the number of watch points can be very high.

This number of surveillance points also points to the degree of surveillance decentralization. Companies can have a single watch entity when they choose to centralize their surveillance activity, or a large number of watch units disseminated among the different divisions, functions and/or operational corporate structures. One extreme is represented by companies who give a high degree of importance to surveillance activity, and consider that surveillance is everybody's responsibility. When they put this adage in practice by individual watch awareness, training and formalization actions, they state that the number of watch points is equal to the number of employees.

The centralization and number of surveillance point choices seem to depend to a large extent on the corporate structure, as well as on its size and activity sector. In the case of large corporations, we can wonder if the existence of centralized and decentralized surveillance constitutes a factor of surveillance effectiveness.

5.4. The hierarchical connection

The literature has always recommended the positioning of highly strategic functions with the major managing executives. This recommendation is often found in the literature focusing on surveillance.

In fact, for many authors, the specialized entity situation reveals the corporation's position regarding the importance given to the surveillance function. That is why Fahey and King favor the connection of the surveillance unit to top management. Similarly, the Cartwright results suggest placing it close to managers where the importance and perceived usefulness of surveillance is the strongest – the support and implication of management is a key success factor of surveillance.

Some authors favor entrusting the main surveillance activity to existing departments with specific dispositions for this activity, such as planning, marketing and commercial, purchasing or information.

Concerning the corporate Planning Department, the interest is in entrusting surveillance to people who are closely involved in the strategic planning process, who will endeavor to use the results of surveillance in their main activity. The use of surveillance results in the strategic planning process is also the reason maintained by Lesca who, however, declares two restrictions. Planning managers are often non-specialized and their skills can be limited in terms of specific watch types such as technological, marketing or sociological, for example. In addition, the density of the planning process can obstruct the detection of alarm signals, which require flexibility and reactivity.

The Sales & Marketing Department is also well placed to be responsible for surveillance because of its permanent and favorable relations with the major players in the corporate environment, including clients, competitors, markets, etc. The research studies of Thiétart and Vivas and, more recently, Le Bon have shown the predispositions and importance of salespeople in terms of watch. This department also has definite expertise in this field because of its proven activity in Marketing Information Systems (MIS) management.

"Buyers are the eyes and ears of the company": this quote introduces the fact that the purchasing function has significant advantages in the assumption of a surveillance activity. In fact buyers, because of the nature of their job, have to monitor the environment of suppliers (products and technologies), as well as technological, competitive, commercial, political and social environments, as demonstrated by the Ballaz study among Purchasing Managers of 105 French and European companies.

The Information Department is another relevant function which could assume responsibility for the surveillance activity. Information professionals process a large volume of varied information on a daily basis. As a result of this, they have a general vision of the corporate environment which enables them to detect trends. They have an expertise for research and manipulation of information – major phases of the surveillance process. Due to of the nature of their job, they are aware of information sources and the most current research and information processing techniques. Finally, they are used to networking. All these elements are vital for surveillance activities. In addition, the information function finds many advantages in extending its job to the surveillance function. Information professionals have a more proactive attitude because of their new information analysis function. Their function is valued because they are more involved in the strategic decision process.

In the Fahey *et al.* study (1981), the task of surveillance is sometimes given to the Planning Department. Some responding companies justify this choice by the fact that the integration of surveillance results in the planning process, and strategic decision is made easier. On the other hand, the Planning Department often depends on upper management (UM); this connection indirectly gives a stronger power and credibility to the surveillance function.

In the Klein and Linneman study (1984), 70% of corporations with a specialized surveillance unit connect it to the Planning Department. The same is true for five of the 10 companies studied by Lenz and Engledow. Specialized units of the five other companies are connected to the Public Relations Department (three companies), the Marketing Department (one) and to Research & Development (one).

Companies studied by Prescott and Smith also connect their specialized surveillance unit to the planning function. The majority of companies in the Ballaz study connect the specialized unit to upper management.

The recent study by Bournois and Romani confirms these results. 55.7% of companies surveyed connect the surveillance function responsibility to upper management, 26.6% to the executive committee, 11.4% to the Strategy Manager and 6.3% to the Marketing Director. As the size of the company decreases, the connection is more toward upper management; it stands at 39.5% for corporations with over 10,000 employees, to 50% for companies between 1,000 and 10,000 employees, 55.2% for firms between 500 and 1,000 employees, and 65.3% for companies between 200 and 500 employees.

In the case of very large corporations (over 10,000 employees), the second connection structure after UM is Planning and Strategy Management (31.6%) and the Executive Committee.

Concerning the different specialized watch units, we often observe a logical connection. For example, technological watch is connected to the Research & Development Department, marketing and commercial watch to the Marketing Department, supplier watch to the Purchasing Department, etc.

Following the previous analysis, the hierarchical connection of the main surveillance function to a high (or relatively high) level seems to be a factor of surveillance effectiveness.

Any surveillance approach, whether it is formal or informal, centralized or decentralized, must operate on the information exchange and circulation model. In order to respect this rule, researchers and professionals agree on the necessity of a network organization.

5.5. Network organization

For all authors, a surveillance system is only effective if it is organized in a network: the players involved in the surveillance activity must be linked to one another through physical or virtual communication. This element is all the more important as the impact of the network organization on performance is often highlighted.

Multiplying these interpersonal relations to create intelligence networks is the advice given by D. Genelot to decision makers, with the objective of improving global performance: the intelligence of a system comes from the capacity of its elements to understand each other in order to build a coherent strategy.

The more numerous, varied and spontaneous the connections, the more reactive the system, and the better able it will be to invent behaviors adapted to an unexpected and complex environment. In an increasingly turbulent world, the company benefits in global efficiency and strategic reactivity when it operates as a network.

Two main elements seem to contribute to the effectiveness of a surveillance network: diversity and activity.

Consequently, maintaining networks also plays an important role. Before defining them and providing the results of empirical studies, the different surveillance network players will be presented.

The players in SWI networks

The network is simultaneously an instrument of acquisition, processing, distribution and use of information. It is made up of three individual profiles qualified by F. Jakobiak as observers, analysts and decision makers.

Figure 5.1 represents the three levels.

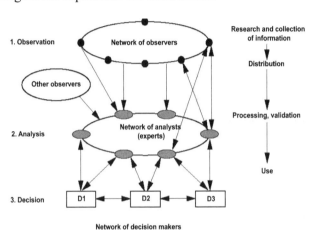

Figure 5.1. *Networks of technological watch specialists*

The observers are assimilated as information sensors, often called watchmen. By collecting information they participate in the information acquisition phase. There are two categories of observers: institutional specialists using formal, easily accessible, published background information, and other corporate observers, liable to pick up informal, largely inaccessible information, with more or less added value.

Analysts are considered experts and are involved in the information processing phase of the surveillance process. The constitution of the network of experts depends on the organization and nature of the firm, as well as the available personnel. F. Jakobiak provides the example of five families of experts: product groups (manufacturers, researchers, marketing and sales specialists), process groups (manufacturers, researchers, designers), application groups (manufacturers, researchers, marketing and sales specialists), prospective and strategy groups (researchers, marketing specialists, decision makers, strategy and planning specialists) and geographic zone groups (International Management).

Decision makers use previously processed information to make their decisions. They are involved in the operation phase of the surveillance process. Generally the least structured, this network's goal is to prepare strategic decisions from analyses and/or recommendations from experts.

In all three cases (sensors, analysts, decision makers), individuals are in turn requesters and recipients of information.

The diversity of SWI networks

The diversity of a network expresses its ability to cover various environmental fields. Individuals making up this network also have very diverse profiles.

The internal and external networks can be distinguished in Figure 5.2

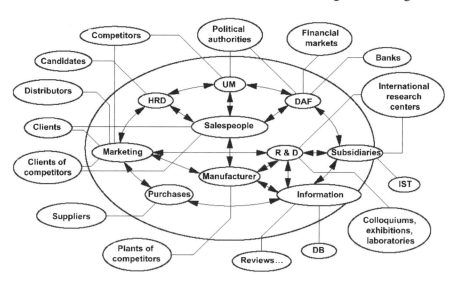

Figure 5.2. *Information network for corporate environmental surveillance (source Euréquip)*

The internal network can be made up of the employees of the different subsidiaries, divisions, functions or operational structures of the corporation. The existence of groups of internal experts is often cited in the literature as a factor of effectiveness.

The external network can be made up of a large number of partners or sources of information (clients, suppliers, competitors, research centers, public organizations, etc.).

Within a network, the distribution of information is bilateral or multilateral. Each individual – or node – transmits and receives information within a series of subnetworks. The density of the network represents the number of connections between the different nodes that it contains. The more dense a network, the higher the potential for exchanges.

The diversity of networks then seems to be a factor of surveillance effectiveness.

The activity of SWI networks

This is linked to the density of the network, and represents the number and frequency of exchanges between its different nodes. It depends on the quality of its members (active participation, motivation, competence) and the coordination quality.

In fact, a network of informers is only efficient if it operates in the exchange mode, which requires the active participation of each individual in the life of the network. By studying the relations existing within an internal communications network, four types of individuals (Allen, 1969) are identified:

– the individuals who listen but do not distribute;

– the individuals who do not listen but distribute;

– the individuals who do not listen and do not distribute;

– the individuals who listen and distribute.

Ideally, a powerful network should only have individuals of the fourth type.

To reach an accurate level of participation from each member of the network, it is important they are chosen with care, on the basis of their skills and motivations for the surveillance activity. Studies have been carried out on this theme. Le Bon, for example, studied the motivation of approximately 500 watchmen from the commercial networks of 10 companies.

The activity of networks then seems to be a factor of surveillance effectiveness.

The network survives on continuous exchanges of information. Maintaining this dynamic is necessary for the quality and continuity of the network.

The maintenance of networks

It is the responsibility of the network moderator, who can be the surveillance manager or one of the permanent surveillance team members. His mission requires a significant investment in time and energy. It consists of locating relevant individuals to constitute internal and external networks. The moderator must then establish favorable relations with each component of the network to promote a relationship of trust, to ensure long term exchanges.

He must organize regular and numerous meetings, participate in exhibitions, colloquiums, foreign missions, etc., attend locations appropriate for informal exchanges of information (coffee houses, corporate restaurants, etc.). The network coordination manager must spend at least as much time outside the office as inside.

Network effectiveness control should also be part of the coordinator's mission. He must be able to manage a database of current and possible participants, their place and their role, their fields of involvement, the information and the quality of information that they transmit, etc. By succeeding in his mission, the surveillance network coordinator works for recognition and acceptance (see Chapter 7).

In conclusion, the maintenance of networks seems to be a factor of surveillance effectiveness.

The existence of internal expert groups

The literature attaches a great importance to the existence of internal groups of experts in the surveillance activity.

It is confirmed in the IHEDN study, where 62.6% of companies practicing ESI implement internal groups of experts. The size of the company, the organizational structure and the number of attacks experienced are determining factors of the existence of these groups: 84% of companies of over 10,000 employees have internal groups of experts. This number goes down to 57.9% in the case of companies with less than 500 employees. It goes up to 88.9% for companies with foreign subsidiaries.

The traditional hierarchical organization seems to slow down the use of groups of experts. Companies using them have a modern organization by division (68.9%) or by matrix (76.6%).

Finally, 83.9% of companies use internal groups of experts when they are attacked.

In conclusion, we can wonder if the existence of internal groups of experts constitutes a factor of surveillance effectiveness.

The practice of companies

There are no empirical studies specifically dedicated to surveillance networks. The IHEDN study focuses a relatively major part of their investigation to human networks of ESI. It provides results on the existence of internal expert networks, the composition of external networks and the form and frequency of exchanges within networks.

EXTERNAL NETWORKS

The results of the study indicate quite diverse external networks. The partners of the ESI manager (ESIM) are professional associations (28.5% of respondents), consultants and engineering firms (24.8%), university research centers (21.4%) and specialized government services (20%). Associations of surveillance professionals only represent 3.3%. Among the most widely used institutional partners are chambers of commerce, Coface and ANVAR. ARIST and ADIT are the institutions with the highest levels of quality according to respondents.

At the permanent surveillance structure level: the frequency of permanent workgroup meetings is monthly on a global basis. In the larger corporations (over 10,000 employees), they occur every week or every month; the frequency of exchanges is lower in smaller companies. Permanent groups exchange more when the firms have identified sources of attacks.

At the internal groups of experts level: the modes of exchange of internal groups of experts are regular meetings based on needs (51.8%) and regular meetings (40.5%). These meetings can sometimes be extended by discussion forums using electronic messaging (7.7%).

Reuniting internal groups of experts is mostly done on the initiative of general management (GM) in 54.7% of companies. Then come ESIM (26.2% of respondents) and operational structures according to needs (13.3%). In small companies (79.3%), upper management takes the initiative of reuniting experts. ESIM is responsible for this job in 50% of companies with over 10,000 employees and 45.8% of companies with over 50 foreign subsidiaries.

When the company is national, where experts are close by, meetings are regular (56.9%). If it is a European or international company, meetings are exceptional and messaging is prevalent. The latter is used in 13.8% of companies with over 50 foreign subsidiaries.

With other internal networks: the authors observe that 47.5 % of companies organize regular meetings, 38.5 % individual meetings, 4.2% annual meetings. 9.9% of companies implement a regular distribution of documents.

The choice of organization mainly depends on the size of the company and its international dimension. 42.5% of companies with 1,000 to 10,000 employees organize regular meetings and only 15% regularly distribute documents. 51.7% of companies with about 500 employees meet regularly but 46% regularly distribute documents.

Finally, companies with several foreign subsidiaries have less regular meetings because of remoteness of the different participants, and 17.6% of them regularly distribute documents.

With external networks: to evaluate the maintenance of external networks, Bournois and Romani propose an index of the degree of openness of the ESIM. They notice that in France, surveillance happens within the company: 69.6% of ESIM spend more than two-thirds of their time in the company. The most widely used elements of the external network are shows and conferences (67.2% of respondents), professional associations (12.3%) and restaurants and cocktails (10%). Relations between ESIM and its peers are not strong. 28.1% of ESIMs have identified their counterparts within their sector without personally knowing them. Most ESIMs (42.2%) state that they have met their counterparts by coincidence. 29.7% of ESIMs initiate meetings (16.7%) or organize benchmarking (13%).

Chapter 6

Evaluation of the SI Process

Remember that the process of surveillance is a vital link between information and decision making; information is transformed during the process of surveillance in order to serve the decision process better (Figure 6.1).

Figure 6.1. *Surveillance process, vital link between information and decision*

The process of surveillance is the common central point for the majority of publications dedicated to surveillance. For different authors, it must have a certain number of essential phases to be efficient surveillance.

Six main phases have been identified by analyzing the literature:

Phase 1. The determination of information needs.

Phase 2. Information research and collection.

Phase 3. Information processing (analysis–synthesis–formatting).

Phase 2 and 3 bis. Information storage.

Phase 4. Information distribution.

Phase 5. Information use.

A brief overview of the evolution of existing models is presented, followed by the efficacy factors and variables corresponding to each phase. In conclusion, a new conceptualization of the process is proposed.

Conceptualizations of the surveillance process experienced significant progress in the 1970s and are not stable to this day.

The pioneers of surveillance have not addressed the how, or in other words the process for examining the environment or detecting weak signals. Ansoff, for example, does not propose a process for detecting weak signals, which is, according to him, the planner's job. He only states the necessity of an integration phase for weak signals detected in the process of strategic planning.

The first models appeared in the middle of the 1970s but most of the existing conceptualizations occurred in the 1980s.

Most models categorize three main phases. The terms vary by author, but the content remains the same:

– information collection;

– processing of collected information (including analysis and synthesis);

– distribution of processed information.

Two phases occur frequently, upstream and downstream, in this traditional general process. Upstream, the authors observe a phase of identification or determination of information to research. The use of the information phase is located downstream.

The use of information does not appear in the first models. The authors seem to want to build a strong barrier between the surveillance function and the strategy function. It is included in the more recent models, which deliberately bring together the surveillance process with the strategic decision process.

There are other variations. Porter recommends a classification phase, right after the data collection phase. It should be closer to the storage phase supported by Gilad, but refuted by Martinet and Ribault.

A few rare models involve an evaluation phase. Gilad and Gilad recommend an evaluation operation for the validity and credibility of data, following the information collection phase.

Wee includes a prioritizing phase for information to research, based on the degree of importance allocated following the identification phase.

The H. Lesca model is undoubtedly the most original and detailed. The author proposes a cyclical process containing targeting, tracking, selection, circulation, storage, building of meaning, distribution, access and action phases.

This quick overview of existing models of surveillance process shows that conceptualizations are not homogenous or stabilized to this day.

6.1. Phase 1: the determination of information needs

The definition of information needs is a fundamental step found in several models. It is also the subject of numerous empirical studies.

In fact, in order to be efficient, the surveillance system must respond to corporate information needs. First, the extent and direction of surveillance must be defined: should it be wide or targeted? Fields or axes of surveillance must then be prioritized, based on their importance for the company. Finally, the identification of information needs must regularly be updated.

6.1.1. *Extent and direction of surveillance*

For authors loyal to Aguilar and Ansoff's concept of scanning, the corporation must be able to detect weak signals announcing threats or opportunities. As a result of this, the environmental surveillance system must be able to scan 360° just like a radar. This all-encompassing watch responds to unidentified information needs. When the alert of an abnormal event is given, a more directed watch can be launched.

Although the interest of global and permanent watch is to reduce the risks of surprises, the overabundance of information involved is a major drawback. On the other hand, managing a 360° surveillance requires that the company faces many directions simultaneously, which demands major human and financial efforts. By being so scattered, the company risks wasting limited resources, as well as creating superficial surveillance, instead of focusing on sectors that it considers important. These limits forced the authors to propose generally sophisticated methods for managing watch efforts more accurately.

Dividing the environment into sectors to monitor is the first solution proposed.

Some authors propose different divisions. For example Lesca presents a segmentation from the standpoint of people liable to carry out actions likely to have an influence on the company. These are clients (current and potential), competitors (current and potential), authorities, research centers, social agents, collaborators, etc.

Brockhoff uses both previous approaches to propose a two-dimensional division. The zones of interest correspond to environmental sections already mentioned (technological, economic and political zones, etc.) to which he adds the socio-psychological zone (data on attitudes, images in terms of consumer behavior). Interest groups are a group of individuals or institutions who are important for the corporation. They are suppliers (of the company, competitors or clients), clients and the government. We should note however that the author only treats competitive surveillance.

Even though direction of surveillance can decrease over-information and costs, it has a major drawback: the company that decides to focus on some sectors or axes of surveillance runs the risk of being surprised by an event out of its area of surveillance, which can be fatal.

Between the drawback of an all-encompassing watch (over-information and cost) and a tightly directed watch (risk of a surprise), most authors recommend a wide scan. In order do this, they propose even more finite segmentation, and sometimes very sophisticated methodologies. Some suggest predetermining axes of surveillance within each environmental field. Lesca for example defends the targeting method. Bates recommends the division of environmental variables into relevant and critical variables to guide surveillance. Narchal proposes a methodology in three steps. The first one consists of the determination of environmental zones liable to act on the company and its market; the second step identifies descriptors and indicators of the dynamic of each zone; finally a diagram of influence of the different factors is established. Although they may constitute a real aid for the relevant division of the environment, the complexity of these different methods is their main limitation.

The extent of environmental surveillance has been analyzed in 10 empirical studies. These studies are mainly focused on the practices of American companies. The study by O'Connell *et al.* compares American and European practices; the companies studied by Ghoshal are Korean; Ballaz and Bournois present the environmental fields monitored by French firms.

Globally, the most widely monitored environment is the economic environment, which groups general economy, market, competitors, clients and suppliers; the technical and technological field follows and, in third and fourth positions, the political and social environments.

To explain the predominance of the economic environment, analysts suggest the financial nature of company objectives, such as ROI, for example. The possibility of quantification linked to the economic analysis tools can also explain this dominance. In the 1990 economic crisis, short-term elements were also invoked.

The importance of surveillance of the technological environment is explained by failures connected to technological breakthroughs, rapid development of technologies and the competitive advantage of technological advance.

On the other hand, political and social environments have not been heavily monitored, because of the problems with quantifying the variables in these fields. This has definitely changed since the 1990s. In the comparative study by O'Connell and Zimmerman, it is reported that European companies find the social environment more important than American companies do, which, however, do recognize that these fields have an impact that will increase in the future.

Empirical studies show a substantial evolution toward surveillance extended to other sectors. In 1984, Jain observed that 31% of companies did not monitor any environment. Four years later, Preble and Rau noted that over the 50 American multinational corporations studied, 90% judge the economic environment as very important, followed by competition (63%), legal (56%), political (55%) and technological (45%) environments. The Wall study also shows the interest for competitive surveillance. In the Ballaz study addressed to purchasing managers, the highest surveillance was by suppliers, which accords with the Kefalas results, which show a strong correlation between the type of information sought and the functional specification of the respondent. For close to 55% of companies, however, all environments are considered. Study results agree with author recommendations for wider environmental coverage.

Regardless of this general trend, we should note that for some companies, surveillance is not about one or several specific environments; instead it is put in place at particular times for a specific project.

In France, the recent Bournois and Romani study highlights three major sectors: the competitive environment (77.2% of companies surveyed monitor it), the marketing and client environment (75.3% of companies) and the legal and regulatory environment (61.7%). The less practiced watches, as well as the most localized, are cultural, social and environmental watch (49.2% of responses), the subcontracting, purchases and inventory watch (44.6%), major contracts, lobbying, networks of influence watch (44.4%), societal watch (44.2%), political, diplomatic, at risk countries watch (43.2%) and union, associative and medical watch (41.8%). It is unfortunate that technological watch does not appear in this study.

In the previous section, we have analyzed two types of surveillance. An all encompassing surveillance is liable to generate too much information and requires significant resources. On the other hand, surveillance that is too targeted exposes the company to a major risk, as it can experience a threat from a field that is not covered. To offset the drawbacks of both positions, the company must carry out a watch that is as wide as possible and, at the same time, targeted; targeting is the result of a deep reflection by the company on the elements to which it is most vulnerable. The results of empirical studies have shown that watch was becoming wider, confirming recommendations by the authors.

This leads us to ask whether a watch that is as wide as possible, and focused on elements identified as important by the company, is a factor of surveillance effectiveness.

6.1.2. *Field prioritizing or axes of surveillance*

Focusing watch on elements to which the company is vulnerable is an often repeated recommendation in the literature. When either resources or time are limited, it is necessary to prioritize these factors to institute surveillance priorities and measure surveillance efforts.

For example, Calori and Atamer present a model of industrial dynamics to guide watch. The model is created from expert advice, identifies 123 variables and leads to the construction of scenarios and identification of relevant variables. Each variable is defined by its degree of motricity (its impact over the other variables), and its degree of sensitivity (impact from other variables). A crossed impact matrix then classifies the variables in four categories: autonomy, sensitivity, motrices and nodal. The comparison with the degree of uncertainty and the probable impact on the company enables the identification of surveillance priorities. Priority is given to the monitoring of nodal variables. Their impact on the company is wide.

Other analysts propose prioritization methods for axes of surveillance. Classification can be made according to environmental uncertainty, its importance and impact on the company, the characteristics of the company, available time, the cost of anticipation and reaction, probabilities of occurrence of events and, finally, key success factors. The relative complexity of the different methods proposed to direct watch is also a hindrance for their use.

In a limited resource context or in a desire for efficiency and optimization, prioritization of sections and axes of surveillance seems vital to ensure the effectiveness of surveillance practiced.

6.1.3. *Updating the identification of information needs*

In the current context of a changing environment, the needs of company information constantly evolve, requiring their constant updating. This problem is summarized by R.-A. Thiétart: "the need for information varies and must be adapted to requirements formulated by decision makers. It is defined as a dynamic process which is constantly repeated and is fed with all the data from different sources that the corporation can use."

Consequently, updating of the information identification needs of the company seems to be a factor of surveillance effectiveness:

6.2. Phase 2: information research and collection

The acquisition of information can begin when the sectors and axes of surveillance are determined. This first phase of the watch process is well known by researchers and practitioners, and is widely discussed in the literature. At this level, the question of nature, diversity, quantity and quality of information sources and of information collected can be raised.

6.2.1. *Sources of information*

The research and collection of information can occur from almost unlimited sources. The following inventory presents an exhaustive list of sources of information listed in the literature since the end of the 1970s until today.

Different typologies are used:

– published/field sources, open/closed;

– general/specialized, human/material, formal/informal. The latter is the basis of the following range.

Formal sources of information

Formalized sources are in documentary, audiovisual or computer form. Relatively open and accessible, they are mainly represented by the press, books, other media (television, cinema, radio), corporate activity reports, databases and CD-ROMs, patents, standards, legal sources, studies, professional Minitel, Internet, Intranet, etc.

EXTERNAL FORMAL SOURCES

Press: this groups the different published, general or specialized, national or regional journals. Written papers are still preferred to electronic publications. It represents a source of information that is very accessible, and its cost is relatively low (annual subscription varies from €150 to €1,000). The information provided is abundant. However, we can regret its lack of confidentiality or discretion, since the information is known by a large number of individuals or companies. It is difficult to avoid redundancies between the different titles. It comes late but is faster than databases if consultation is done when published. It is not very forward looking. Finally, the presentation is particular to the journal, which requires a rearranging of information according to its centers of interest for the watchman.

Books: this includes different types of books, encyclopedias, manuals, theses, memoirs, etc. They have the same advantages as the press, but they are more detailed, with higher added value since the original information has already been analyzed by the author. On the other hand, books have the same disadvantages as the press. However, they are sometimes more forward looking.

Other media: television, cinema, and radio. They present advertising films for companies, for example, but the content is light and the information is already known. There is nevertheless an interest in press reports or documentary films from public relations which can show corporate products or installations, etc.

Databases and banks and CD-ROMs: databases contain a large volume of information at server level. There are databases which provide factual data on facts and numbers, and data file databases. Data files make it possible to:

– locate magazines, books or theses (for example, Myriade, Dissertation Abstract on disk, Doc thesis, etc.);

– obtain references of magazine articles, studies or research papers on a subject (for example, ABI Inform, Delphes, Helecon, etc.);

– access the full text of articles or research papers (for example, Business Periodical on Disk, *Le Monde, Les Échos, La Tribune*, etc.). The texts are increasingly available online;

– obtain statistical data or information on companies (for example, Datastream, France stat, Dafsa liens, Dafsa pro, Kompass, Diane, Amadeus, etc.).

Questel Orbit, Dialog and Datastar (Knight Rider) are examples of servers in the scientific and technical field.

Access to the content of databases and banks is made through the French network Transpac, international networks, the Internet, cross system queries and local hardware. Research systems are designed to interrogate databases and banks in an interactive mode.

The advantages of databases and banks are their abundance, their worldwide coverage, the time savings they provide and their low cost. The disadvantages are the lack of updated information (delay of publication and input of previously published information). To offset the obsolescence of CD-ROMs, some companies have decided to use online databanks. Interrogating databases or banks is sometimes difficult and requires the skills of a specialist. Problems may exist in obtaining full text documents, especially their illustrations.

Patents: the patent is a unique vector of information. Numerous elements make its use easier: its presentation document is done according to national and international standards and is highly homogenous; its production is centralized, its classification is international; and finally, the databases dedicated to patents are of very high quality. Very thorough statistical analyses are possible with this general organization. The statistical patent analysis for example makes it possible to identify trends in research of a country or a firm.

The publication of a patent application, with a chronological number, usually occurs 18 months after the patent is applied for. It then shows the date it was lodged, which can be compared to foreign patent requests. Anybody can access the application file. For example, in France, a patent approved by INPI (Institut National de la Propriété Intellectuelle (National Institute for Intellectual Property)) allows the right to usage monopoly and contains:

– the patent description;

– the claims (delimiting the possible range of freedom);

– the research report;

– administrative references.

Patents are a great source of information on technical and technological evolution and on competition. As with data files, the use of patent databases is done on three levels – references, summaries and full texts. Patent surveillance is quite advanced in scientific, technical and technological fields such as pharmacy, chemistry, electronics, telecommunications, etc.

The advantages of patents are mainly their wealth of information since they contain 80% of useful scientific and technical information. The drawbacks are the 18 month delay from application to registration; the necessity of having specific skills to understand very technical texts; the occasional obligation of having a text translated from Japanese, German or Swedish, etc. In addition, they do not cover all sectors (services and information technology, for example, are not covered).

Standards: as with patents, standards must be the subject of systematic and continuous surveillance, especially since they can be increasingly significant over time, for example with European harmonization policies. There are also databases involving standards. *Noriane* on the *Questel* server is an example.

Private or public studies: in general, studies involve a specific problem or a specific sector. The information is collected and processed (analyzed and synthesized). However, the potential cost is very high and they lack updates (they may not be available when needed and there is a delay from the time the problem is identified).

Legal sources: these are trade dispute courts, the land tax register, mortgage services, etc. For the USA, Porter notes several other services in the detailed appendix dedicated to information sources. They are readily accessible and are inexpensive. On the other hand, they mainly provide economic information and involve past periods.

The Internet and professional Minitel: these are now a vital source for surveillance specialists.

Financial analyst reports: the reports from financial analysts are an essential source.

INTERNAL FORMAL SOURCES

Based on Internet logic, the intranet constitutes a small revolution in the corporate world, where an increasing number of companies are implementing an internal network. Its contribution to the effectiveness of the surveillance process is already significant.

The intranet: information existing within a company is abundant and varied. Sales revenue, client files, accounting and financial documents, competitive monographic publications, internal publications (catalogs, newsletters), studies, etc. are valuable information for any employee needing information in their daily activity. Companies quickly realized the importance of applying the principle of the Internet throughout the company to group this internal information in a single area. The Intranet is a computer network enabling corporate information to freely circulate. Whereas the Internet is a public network open to the world, the Intranet is a private network for the exclusive use of the company. This can play a vital role in the effectiveness and control of the surveillance activity.

Corporate annual reports: these can easily be obtained from Financial, Communication or Public Relations Departments of corporations. Even though the information content is somewhat optimistic, it contains numbers aimed at shareholders including: year end results, the Research & Development and Innovation policy, short and long term forecasts, etc.

Table 6.1 summarizes the advantages and drawbacks of each formalized source.

FORMALIZED SOURCES	Advantages (+) and disadvantages (-)
THE PRESS (general or trade journals, national or regional)	+ very accessible + very abundant + relatively low cost (by subscription) + complete information provided - lack of confidentiality - probable redundancy between different titles - late but faster than databases if consultation occurs when published - little or no planning - presentation inherent to the journal
BOOKS (Different books, encyclopedias, memoirs, theses, etc.)	+ same as press + more in-depth information + greater added value because it is already processed by the author - same as press
OTHER MEDIA (television, cinema, radio)	- light content, information is already known + interest for public relations movies (presentation of products, installations etc.)
DATABASES, CD-ROMS	+ great abundance + worldwide coverage + time savings + low cost - lack of information "freshness" (delay of publication and capture of information already published). To offset the obsolescence of CD-ROMs, some companies are using online data banks - sometimes complex use; querying a database may require the skill of a specialist - problems in obtaining full texts especially illustrations

PATENTS	+ great wealth of information (they contain 80% of useful scientific information) - 18 month delay from the request - comprehension of the very technical text requires specialist skills and may need translation - do not cover all sectors (services and information technology for example)
PUBLIC OR PRIVATE STUDIES	+ information is already processed (analysis/synthesis) and responds to a specific problem - potentially very expensive - lack of "freshness" (not necessarily available when needed, required delay)
LEGAL SOURCES (trade dispute courts, cadastre, mortgage services, etc.)	+ easily accessible + very inexpensive - mainly provide economic information - involve past periods
MINITEL	+ source of abundant information - possibly very expensive
THE INTERNET	+ most abundant source of information - requires skills for efficient research
FINANCIAL ANALYST REPORTS	+ very high quality source (added value/raw information) + objectivity, analysis time savings
FINANCIAL ANALYST REPORTS ANNUAL REPORTS THE INTRANET	+ very high quality source (added value/raw information) + objectivity, analysis time savings + accessible - biased toward the company + the same as the Internet + low cost, reserved access, aggregation of heterogenous information, collective teamwork, access to Internet, updating, instant access, better communication...

Table 6.1. *Advantages and disadvantages of formalized sources*

Informal sources of information

Informal sources mainly transmit information that is not in concrete form, such as oral or visual information. It is mostly closed, not generally accessible, and it groups external (competitors, clients, suppliers, distributors, missions and study travels, exhibitions, shows, colloquiums, conventions, etc.) and internal sources within the company (Management, Marketing, R&D, Purchasing Departments, etc.).

The general advantage of this type of source is its relative privacy, therefore its value is compared to well known published sources.

On the other hand, the major drawback involves its accessibility. Access to information is much less passive than in the case of formal sources. The quantity and quality of information transmitted by these sources depends on the capacity and experience of the collector–investigator.

Informal external sources: the following list summarizes the different informal external sources.

– competitors;

– clients and suppliers;

– external watch and intelligence service providers;

– missions and trips;

– exhibitions and trade shows;

– colloquiums, conventions and seminars;

– professional associations, committees and unions;

– temporary personnel, interns and students;

– recruiting candidates.

Informal internal sources: there is a consensus between researchers and surveillance professionals: the majority of useful information for the decision maker is found within the company. This is where internal networks are the most useful. Some internal sources are better positioned than others to establish preferred contacts with external players and to collect valuable information:

– managers, with their often competitor counterparts;

– the Sales & Marketing Department, especially salespeople with clients and distributors;

– the Purchasing Department, with suppliers and subcontractors;

– the R&D Department; researchers are also good people to analyze in detail the technology of new competitive products, new patents, etc.;

– the Legal Department is more suitable for monitoring standards and laws, etc.;

– the Information Department processes a large volume of information, etc.

The practice of companies

Empirical studies have often attempted to find information sources that companies use most. The comparison is difficult because of the differences in typologies used and sources studied. Nevertheless, we can highlight strong trends.

Increase in the use of internal sources: up until the 1980s, information mainly came from external sources. The use of internal sources became more frequent. All the analyses show that internal and external sources are both necessary and complementary for the surveillance activity.

Predominance of human sources over other sources: human sources occupy first place in Aguilar, Keegan, O'Connel and Ghoshal studies, and seem vital in most research.

The particular importance of certain internal sources: the internal sources which can collect a specific type of information more easily are marketing and sales, in relation to clients. The sales force is the most often mentioned source in analyst studies.

Predominance in the press: the press is the most widely used formal source. On the other hand, databases were not widely used until the 1990s.

These results are confirmed by the most recent study by Bournois and Romani. In fact, periodicals are the most cited with 12.2% of responding companies, followed by conventions, colloquiums, exhibitions and trade shows (10.7%), informal information (10.3%), internal sources (8.6%), the Internet (8.2%), databanks (8.1%), annual reports (7%) and standards (6.3%). However, we can still criticize this last study which proposes informal and internal sources simultaneously, which somewhat distorts the results, because sources can be informal and internal at the same time.

To ensure the effectiveness of information collection and to avoid wasting corporate resources, which are by definition limited, it is necessary to select information sources and the most valuable information.

6.2.2. *The value of information sources*

Martinet and Ribault distinguish five criteria for assessing information sources:

1) The value of the source is its capacity to provide a high volume and variety of valuable information.

2) The performance of the source over time is assessed based on two main criteria: permanence and freshness. A source is powerful over time if, on one hand, it provides systematic and continuous information and, on the other hand, if it broadcasts fresh information or, better still, if it does so in real time. Some online databases satisfy these two criteria.

3) Reliability of the source measures its capacity to give fair and objective information, i.e. faithfully corresponding to the original information. In the case of human sources, for example, numerous biases linked to personal interpretation can modify the original information.

4) The source's discretion takes us back to the idea that the more the information is known, the less value it has. Conversely, if the company is the only one with this valuable information, it has an advantage over its competitors for a while.

5) Vulnerability of the source means that the information source may stop transmitting information. Human sources, for example, are relatively vulnerable. An employee who sends information up the ladder, possibly to the surveillance department, may stop sending information if he receives no feedback.

All these criteria show that the value of a source is actually assessed over time. An experienced user with knowledge of each source alone will be able to evaluate this value. The authors define a notation system for information sources, mainly based on reliability and validity criteria. Four grades are proposed:

– trustworthy (trade dispute court, laboratory tests, etc.);

– trustworthy but presenting risks of error or subjectivity (the press, etc.);

– unreliable source: information must be verified (informal sources, etc.);

– suspect and subjective: they must be used with caution (rumors, etc.).

The previous analysis shows that source value and information value are connected. For example, the quality of information reported from the field by salespeople depends on their perception, memory and cognitive capabilities. In fact, in order for the information transmitted to be valuable, salespeople must:

– effectively perceive environmental information;

– memorize this information;

– analyze the information to evaluate its importance.

The value of the source then has an impact on the value of information.

6.2.3. *The value of collected information*

Martinet and Ribault also proposed a notation system for information, based on its importance and usefulness. They established four grades:

– very high, vital;

– interesting;

– useful on occasion;

– useless.

It is possible to correlate the value of the source with the value of the information itself to obtain the following matrix.

Value of the source / Value of information	Suspect and subjective	Unsure	Trustworthy but risk of error or subjectivity	Trustworthy
Useless	---	--	-	+
Useful on occasion	--	-	+	++
Interesting	-	+	++	+++
High and important	+	++	+++	++++

Table 6.2. *Value of information*

For a more detailed evaluation of the information collected, we can use the relevance criteria involving the value of the information provided by the surveillance system (abundance, fineness, topicality, punctuality, form, etc.). In fact, the evaluation of the information problem can be raised with the raw information collected as well as with information provided.

To our knowledge, there are no empirical studies specifically dedicated to the value of information sources. This confirms once again that the control phase is not widely discussed in the literature, and is rarely followed in companies. The Ballaz study indicates that 70% of companies surveyed verify the information. When it is done, this verification is ensured by the watchman in 85% of cases and by the analyst in 15% of cases.

In the IHEDN study, the ESI manager and his team validate and directly verify the information sources. The ESI manager is particularly involved in the validation and verification of sources in the case of very large corporations (over 10,000 employees), the ones who export the most, in certain activity sectors (chemistry and minerals/building) and when competition is global.

In order to further improve the information research and collection phase, companies possess increasingly sophisticated watch tools. As a result of these, information acquisition is quicker and information collected is more relevant. The example of numerous search engines on the Internet is the most enlightening.

The previous section shows that the existence and quality of the research and collection phase are factors of surveillance effectiveness.

In other words, volume, diversity and quality of information sources, and the existence of control to verify value seem vital for the effectiveness of surveillance.

Compared to the research and collection phase, there is not much said in the literature about the other phases of the surveillance process, in particular the information processing phase, which is central to the activity of surveillance.

6.3. Phase 3: information processing

Researching and collecting information is not enough. The skill of the surveillance professional resides in his capacity to transform a large volume of heterogenous and fragmented data into something meaningful. With this objective, the raw information collected must be processed, i.e. analyzed, synthesized and formatted, in order to be used. It is at this level that the difference between watch and intelligence occurs. In fact, intelligence exceeds the analysis and synthesis of watch by recommending actions to the surveillance recipient.

6.3.1. *The analysis of information*

The operation of analyzing raw collected information is vital, because it attempts to make sense of an incoherent series of voluminous data. Just like elements in a puzzle, useful information, often scattered and truncated, can form a representation that is as close to reality as possible when correctly assembled.

To reach this result, different, often very popular, analysis methods are used. They come from different fields such as bibliometrics (this discipline is described below), forecasting, planning, strategic analysis, etc. The goal here is not to provide, for example, yet another interpretation of the strategic models of Porter, McKinsey or Arthur D. Little, or the method of scenarios.

Bibliometrics (or scientometrics)

This very specific method requires a more detailed explanation. Librarians were the initiators of the first rules of bibliometrics (Bradford's law, 1934). This ancient science consists of using statistical and mathematical methods to handle a large volume of information.

Today, there are over a million magazines, tens of thousands of databases and tens of millions of documents. The exponential increase of the volume of accessible information has made it necessary to use tools such as bibliometrics to structure, select and analyze large numbers of documents.

Two types of processes are possible. Traditional statistical processes enable counting and frequency operations. The analysis of patenting by company, country or field is often done this way. On the other hand, data analysis processes mainly use classification and factor analysis methods. Until recently, bibliometrics was mostly applied to scientific articles and patents.

Databases dedicated to patents are accessible and of good quality, and patent preparation documents are quite standardized. Patents therefore constitute an appropriate element for bibliometrics processing.

Even though bibliometric tools have been demonstrated in scientific and technical fields – mainly in chemistry, pharmacy or oil – their field of application remains limited. In addition, their complexity requires real skills from specialists, limiting their use.

Forecasting

Forecasting methods are generally categorized into two main families:

– statistical extrapolation methods of past trends;

– qualitative or subjective methods (in particular, expert opinions).

This is a subjective method. Based on experience, it consists of extrapolating future results from retrospective results. In the technological field, this extrapolation takes the form of sigmoid curves which represent the performance obtained, based on efforts devoted to a product or a process (investment, time, etc.). They enable the extrapolation of the evolution of a technology on a single curve, or the study of a technological breakthrough over several curves (Figures 6.2, 6.3 and 6.4).

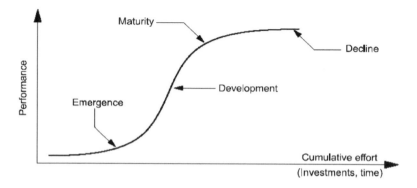

Figure 6.2. *Sigmoid curve (Foster, 1986)*

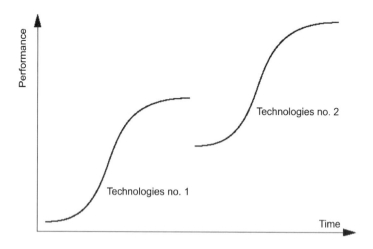

Figure 6.3. *Pair sigmoid curve example (Reyne, 1987)*

The following figure provides an example of a sigmoid curve chain in the television sector.

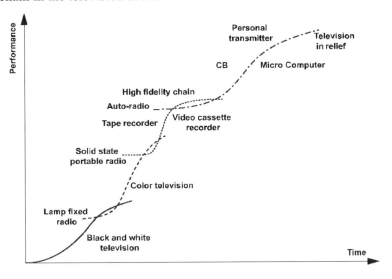

Figure 6.4. *Sigmoid curve chain: from black & white TV to TV in relief*

The danger of using these methods is that they only apply to existing technologies for which there is already a significant initial phase of a curve.

EXPERT OPINIONS

In order to be able to forecast the evolution of a phenomenon, we can rely on opinions from experts who are supposed to know it well (researchers, company salespeople or external consultants). We can consult these experts individually and aggregate their prognosis after the fact, or in groups, to create a consensus. The Delphi method combines the advantages of these two possibilities. It first consists of interrogating the experts individually, then asking the exact justifications of their forecasts. Thirdly, all the experts access all the justified forecasts. A new wave of forecasts is then created by attendees. This cycle can be done over and over again.

When growth was continuous, forecasting models could rely on past data. Then came the oil crises and permanent instability, and economic breakthroughs have shown that traditional planning methods were unsuitable. It became urgent to move from a reactive behavior to a proactive behavior. That is why the manager learned to monitor his environment, to manage uncertainty, use opportunities and transform threats. In that capacity, planning is an integral part of any surveillance, strategic watch and intelligence process.

Anticipation

Anticipation is different from forecasting. It is a generic term which defines the methods and tools for anticipating changes in the company's environment and acts for future success. In his article, "Sur la démarche prospective", Hugues de Jouvenel separates forecasting from anticipation. Whereas the goal of forecasting is predicting the future, to reveal it as if it was over and done with, anticipation helps to build it.

Three elements characterize anticipation:

– it is a multidisciplinary and systematic methodology: the problems that companies have to face are multidimensional. Anticipation makes it possible to understand them by integrating all the factors and their interrelations;

– it is a methodology which integrates the long term dimension, past and future: two types of variables coexist within a system: the variables characterized by a large degree of inertia (ecosystems, demographic changes, etc.) and variables with quicker changes (technological innovations, etc.). Only long term analysis will enable us to eliminate the period effect, and only the medium and long term alone will enable room for maneuver;

– it is a methodology which integrates breakthroughs: it does not settle for postulating the permanence of change, but tries to integrate experienced or expected breakthroughs.

The anticipation methodology includes five main steps:

1) the definition of the problem and the choice of a temporal range;

2) the development of a system and the identification of key variables liable to have an influence on the problem studied (motricity/dependence diagram);

3) the collection of data and the development of hypotheses;

4) the construction of possible future outcomes from simulation methods (scenarios and models);

5) strategic choices.

At this level, we highlight the megatrends, possible threats, advantages and drawbacks of each strategic alternative.

In the anticipation methodology, the scenario method occupies a significant place. Its objective is to develop scenarios in an uncertain environment and to highlight a progressive guideline able to control changes.

Strategic analysis models

In order to carry out their analyses, surveillance specialists can use the whole range of strategic tools for diagnosis and decision support. We may remind our reader of the LCAG model, also known as the SWOT (strengths/weaknesses, opportunities/threats) model, the three growth/market share matrices from the Boston Consulting Group (BCG), assets/attraction from McKinsey and maturity/competitive position from A. D. Little, the competitive analysis model from Porter and the two technologies/products and technology assets/attraction matrices, etc.

THE LCAG MODEL

This is one of the very first strategic analysis models. Even though it is now outdated and simplistic, its logic underlies all subsequent strategic models. The LCAG analysis, named after founding professors Learned, Christensen, Andrews and Guth, consists of confronting the company with its environment from an internal and external diagnosis. It makes it possible to evaluate the degree of adaptation of corporate skills and resources to constraints imposed by its environment.

THE BCG MATRIX

This is one of the most well known, with its "cash cow", "star", "question mark" and "dog" activities. It is organized around two strategic variables:

– the growth rate of the segment of activity analyzed;

– the relative market share of the company in this segment.

BCG's basic principle is that one of the vital objectives of the strategy is to enable an optimal allocation of resources available to the company between different strategic segments in order to obtain a better global competitive position.

There are four types of corresponding strategic recommendations:

– make a profit on cash cows;

– abandon or maintain dogs without investment;

– maintain dominant position for stars;

– double the stake or abandon question marks.

MCKINSEY'S ASSETS/ATTRACTION MATRIX

The McKinsey matrix is based on two multicriteria series:

– the strategic interest of the field of activity;

– the competitive position of the company in this field.

Unlike the BCG matrix, the analysis is done from numerous evaluation criteria of the sectors and of the competitive position.

There are three types of strategic recommendations: development, selection or withdrawal.

THE A. D. LITTLE MATRIX

This is also a multicriteria model for decision support. The two axes of the matrix are:

– the degree of maturity of the activity;

– the competitive position of the company in the field of activity.

The analysis of the degree of maturity is done from the four lifecycle phases (start up, growth, maturity and decline).

There are four types of strategic recommendations: development, withdrawal, selection or reorientation.

PORTER'S FIVE STRENGTHS – COMPETITIVE ANALYSIS MODEL

Porter highlighted five strengths which control competition within a sector. In his model, he recommends analyzing, in a detailed manner, the threat of new arrivals, the intensity of rivalry between existing competitors, the pressure felt by replacement products and the power of negotiation of clients and suppliers. This model is actually used as background to differentiate the types of watch (technological, commercial, competitive, etc.).

The following models are specifically dedicated to the analysis of technologies.

THE TECHNOLOGIES/PRODUCTS AND TECHNOLOGY ASSETS/ATTRACTION MATRICES

In his studies on technology management, Morin defines the notion of technological capital. He proposes six steps:

1) Inventory

2) Evaluation

3) Optimization

4) Enhancement

5) Surveillance

6) Protection

The technologies/products and technology assets/attraction matrices are mainly used in the first two steps. They enable the production of an inventory of corporate technological capital resources.

The first matrix (technologies/products) is a multi-input matrix, crossing the types of technologies (basic, key, emerging, etc.) with products, applications, degree of dependence, etc. Once the appropriate matrix is created, a diagnosis can be made on the strong and weak points of the company (in production, research and development, marketing, etc.) on its degree of technological dependence in each field, on available human resources, on the organization of technology management, etc. The reflection leads to a strategic analysis of the company's choices over short, medium and long terms in terms of technology management.

Two dimensions of the technological capital are specifically significant and make it possible to consider a portfolio of technologies:

1) the degree of dependence of the company on technology control;

2) the lifecycle of technologies.

The second matrix proposed by Morin, McKinsey's assets/attraction matrix, can be applied in the case of technology. The tool makes it possible to delimit four zones, therefore four types of recommendations, including:

1) "hobbyhorses", illustrating a choice of increasing investment and development;

2) withdrawal corresponding to disinvestment;

3) profitability represents the problems to solve and corresponds to a selection.

Following the inventory and evaluation of the technological capital, the methodology for strategic management of technologies consists of optimizing the corporate potential by the possible revitalizing of the underused elements of the capital. The enhancement phase maintains this optimization over time, to face the natural depreciation by renewing the technologies and/or accumulating resources. Surveillance of the environment then makes it possible to anticipate technological evolutions (threats and opportunities). The goal of the last phase is to protect technologies by launching operations of industrial properties, storage and knowledge transfer.

These different analysis tools have shown their limits in the current environmental context, but they seem to still be used in a complementary way with other methods.

Analysis methods specific to surveillance

Two analysis methods specific to surveillance are proposed in the literature. The QUEST (Quick Environmental Scanning Technique) method and the LEAP (Likelihood of Events Assessment Process) method. They are both largely inspired by traditional planning methods. Their goal is to promote the integration of environmental information in the strategic reflection process.

THE QUEST METHOD

The QUEST method presented by Nanus is based on the method of scenarios. It starts with the principle that managers have a personal point of view on future possibilities and the dynamic of environmental change. The systematic pooling of these different opinions must lead to a shared future vision of the corporate environment and to strategic alternatives. Four steps constitute the method.

The preparation step consists of gathering together around 15 managers during a workday. From an analysis of public sources, the group must provide a document on which the major trends of the environment are noted.

The second phase also occurs over a day. The attendees, with the previous analysis in hand, determine the objectives of the company, the criteria and performance indicators to retain, the probability that events occur, their probable impact on the company.

In a third phase, the coordinator produces a summary of the previous reflections, and details approximately five probable scenarios.

The last step is done in half a day. The idea is to carry out a traditional audit (strengths/weaknesses, threats/opportunities) and to define strategic options. Work teams are constituted for each strategic alternative retained.

Even though this method is easy and inexpensive, it has two drawbacks. It is based on the perception of attendees and is built from public and open sources, supposedly known by competitors.

THE LEAP METHOD

This enables forecasts when the horizon is too distant, when there is no historical information and when the environment is very unstable. In his article, Preble illustrates this method with an example applied to the social political field. As with the QUEST method, it is based on expert forecasts, and is committed to defining the probability of an event occurrence. It requires the determination of four temporal horizons (very short term, short term, medium term and long term) and the participation of experts who understand the question studied. In the first place, the experts must indicate:

– the degree of knowledge of the event judged;

– the probability of the emergence of the event at each temporal horizon;

– a comparison of the probabilities corresponding to the most probable date.

Because of the number of experts involved and its complexity, this method is difficult to implement.

The practice of companies

Empirical studies show that the analysis methods are not widely used. The method of scenarios, the method of extrapolation and the Delphi method are the most widely used. On the other hand, the most advanced companies in terms of surveillance have the largest variety of methods.

The studies addressing the problem of analysis methods generally propose a list of methods, and interrogate the responding companies on their usefulness and their actual use. In the Fahey, Jain and Klein and Linneman study, the method of scenarios is the most widely used method.

The method of scenarios is often listed in the most used methods. The extrapolation of past trends is also listed.

Concerning the forecasting of experts, the Delphi method is not so much used, according to the Diffenbach, Jain and Klein studies and Linneman, but it remains in the first place in the Preble study.

The Bournois and Romani study analyzes the planning and strategic scenario construction efforts. The majority of companies (47.2%) carry out a three year plan. Only 8.1% of companies admit not planning at all. Companies practicing intelligence carry out longer term anticipation than companies who intend only to practice intelligence.

The practice of anticipation depends on the size of the company, its activity sector, its membership or not of a group or a holding and its sales volume. Large corporations have a higher tendency to plan over five to 10 years. The greater the size of the company, the longer the temporal planning horizon. Companies in energy/water, minerals/chemistry and electronics/mechanics sectors plan over five to 10 year periods. Commerce/distribution, building/civil engineering and other manufacturing sectors plan for the medium term – three to five years. Agriculture/agri food sectors plan for the short term if they plan at all.

The autonomous company tends to plan over a very long term (5 to 10 years). According to the authors, this surprising result comes from the feeling of vulnerability linked to autonomy: these companies can only count on themselves.

There is a strong correlation between the size of the revenue and the temporal planning horizon. 26.7% of companies with revenues over €7.6 billion plan for 10 years compared to 4.3% of companies with revenues of less than €30 million.

There are many different information analysis methods. Despite this, companies only use a small number of them. The most used seem to be the method of scenarios, the extrapolation of past data and expert opinions.

6.3.2. *Information synthesis*

Synthesis is the intellectual operation of going from a mass of raw or interpreted information to a coherent and concise set. When it is aimed at a decision maker, it will help him make decisions and save time.

Neither a simple summary nor a compilation of documents, an efficient synthesis is self-sufficient. It reviews the problem and summarizes the analysis by highlighting the key elements of the subject involved. In addition, it involves the personal viewpoint of the author. In this capacity, the analysis and synthesis represent the most interesting part – but also the most risky – of the work of the watch and intelligence professional. A synthesis requires reflection, personal commitment and responsibility.

The difference between watch and intelligence emerges once again. In general, the watch manager settles for alerting the decision maker about an unexpected or probable event in the environment and may make personal commitments. The intelligence manager goes further by integrating in his synthesis actionable information or recommendations for action to the decision maker. There is not a lot written about analysis and synthesis. However, the quality of this phase is a powerful factor of surveillance effectiveness, but very difficult to assess objectively.

As with the analysis, the synthesis can be given orally, but generally it is written for the decision maker. The formatting of results emerging from the watch and intelligence activity plays an important role in the effectiveness of surveillance.

6.3.3. *Formatting of information*

Despite the increasing place of audiovisual techniques, the written word remains a powerful channel. The watch or intelligence professional must provide quality formatted products as well.

The importance of the written word

Writing is (with the help of a pencil, pen or any other means) tracing on a support (generally paper, but electronic as well) signs representing words in a given language, organized (written) with the goal of retaining or transmitting a specific message. Writing is therefore a support (we also call it a channel) making it possible for the writer to contact another person to whom the message is addressed. To illustrate the importance of the written word, Martinet and Marti recount an interesting experiment carried out by Swedish researchers.

High level scientific articles were rewritten by journalists. For them, writing was a basic tool. Expert scientific examiners had to evaluate the quality of works appearing in original or rewritten articles and the competence of their authors (their names were hidden).

The results of this study were enlightening:

– all articles from journalists were judged of better quality than the original work;

– the journalists were found to be more competent than scientists.

As in many sectors, the watch and intelligence professional must control written communication techniques perfectly to benefit from his information acquisition, analysis and synthesis work.

Despite its importance, formatting of the information broadcast by the watch and intelligence department is not described in depth in the literature.

Productions from the watch and intelligence activity

The products resulting from surveillance services occupy a significant place in our model of surveillance measure and its impact on corporate performance. A few typical products of surveillance services: the alert notice, the report of findings, competitive monographic publications, strategic watch syntheses, newsletters, press reviews, etc.

At the end of the information processing phase of the surveillance process study, the existence and quality of the analysis, synthesis and formatting of the information seem to be factors of WSI effectiveness.

The surveillance specialist, particularly of information research and collection, has the possibility of evaluating the volume, diversity and quality of sources and information collected. Concerning the processing phase, the measure can obviously only occur at the level of the user of the information involved.

Following, or in parallel with acquisition phases (phase 2) and processing of information (phase 3), a storage phase for raw or processed information must also exist. That is why we have numbered them phases 2 and 3 bis.

6.4. Phases 2 and 3 bis: storage

Storage is the operation consisting of retaining, either in inventory or in reserve, raw information collected in phase 2 (research and collection) and/or knowledge gained from phase 3 (information processing) of the surveillance process.

The availability of an inventory of raw and/or processed information enables the potential users to access the information they need at a particular moment. The surveillance entity no longer has to research or process the information requested. This phase of the surveillance process thus represents time (and cost) savings for the user and company. However, this is not the only advantage.

This operation, ignored in the literature, is important because of its direct link to a major concept: the concept of organizational memory, which is connected to the organizational learning concept.

In fact, the individual has memory, i.e. the capacity of retaining the information for later retrieval. We speak of organizational memory, because the organization is also able to acquire, process and store information.

Girod defines organizational memory as the variable group (which comes and goes) of organizational knowledge transmitted over time in the organization. Organizational memory is generally presented as an inventory of knowledge, as well as a process based on three phases: acquisition, retention/storage and restoration.

The notion of organizational memory is not new. Cyert and March mentioned it in 1958. Research on this theme was, for a long time, limited to the definition of the concept and to its role in other cognitive processes such as organizational learning. Recently, researchers set out to understand better its process and function.

The evolution of the organizational learning process followed that of organizational memory. Schrivastava, Fiol and Lyle, Lant and Ingham point out that researchers went from a behavioral vision to a more cognitive vision of the learning process. The learning process is seen as a development process of an organizational knowledge base.

Studies of memory and organizational learning process remain theoretical, notably because of the problem with processing the concepts. As with the concept of surveillance (watch and intelligence), these concepts are complex and diffused throughout the organization, which explains the problems researchers have in observing and describing their content in great detail.

Learning plays a vital role in the surveillance process, and in particular in our research.

Organizational learning can enrich and transform organizational resources and skills. Edmonson and Moingeon developed a typology of studies on organizational learning from the preferred unit of analysis and the objective of the research (descriptive or interventionist). Four types emerged:

– The first type presents the organization as the result of past learning.

– The second type considers the organization as a community of individuals who learn and blossom.

– The third type is the improvement of organizational effectiveness with the help of individuals.

– The last type has the same improvement objective, but is based on verbalization and individual learning mechanisms. The angle of approach is not the organization but the individual.

They use two fundamental concepts: observation of reality and learning process. The scale of inference shows how a person develops theories and interprets the world from the observation of reality. These theories constitute the master program to determine the decision. Learning consists of adjusting decisions to needs by modifying the master program.

Single loop learning makes it possible to return to the action and to adjust it in order to obtain the desired result. Double loop learning returns to the master program that created the action to adjust the behavior as well as the representation of the world.

Because of biases involved in the mechanisms linked to scales of inference and master program, learning can never be perfect. These biases trigger defensive routines which stop double loop learning. Argyris developed two learner organization models. Model I corresponds to an organization stuck in defensive routines where learning is in single loop. Model II goes back to double loop learning where the organization succeeded in removing defense mechanisms.

This fourth type of research is particularly interesting with studies on the improvement of surveillance effectiveness.

The information liable to be stored by the organization corresponds to events (customer order, price increase of a component, etc.), decisions (customer delivery, replacement of a component, etc.) and interpretation and decision models (why this solution was used for that problem).

The information can be stored by the intelligence department or by individuals, other internal or external devices.

Individuals retain their observations and experiences in the organization (raw facts, beliefs, representations) in this spirit.

The device connected to the structure combines definitions of functions, procedures (which define execution rules of the collection and processing work, etc.) and collective archives (reports, reviews, etc.).

Culture is a learned method for perceiving, thinking and feeling the problems transmitted to the members of the organization. It is expressed by a common language acquired during common ceremonies.

External archives retained by external organizations add to these three components of the organizational memory.

Information stored through these different elements can be researched systematically or on demand.

Organizational memory plays an important role, since information stored can contribute efficiently to the decision process. In fact, the organization stores in its memory decisions taken to solve often repetitive problems. There follows a repetition of successful behaviors and elimination of those which failed. These behaviors are expressed in procedures which avoid decision makers having to start the problem analysis and modeling phase again. Learning occurs when the organization, particularly with information processing, increases the directory of its possible responses to recurring events, or selects the best and most efficient responses; there is an increase in available knowledge in the organization.

As confirmed by R. Reix, storage of events and decisions enables efficacy gains, by reducing or removing information research and modeling processes by automating some decisions. Since it supports the possibilities of learning, organizational memory seems to be an important device for the improvement of organizational efficiency.

H. Lesca is one of the rare authors who address the question of storage based on four angles of approach: storage location, access to stored information, storage supports and the importance of the time factor in information storage.

Storage can occur within the centralized surveillance structure, or in different departments in the company. In both cases, the author recommends taking measures to facilitate access to this information.

Access to raw and processed information is an important factor of surveillance effectiveness. It partly determines the use of surveillance.

Besides the paper base still mostly used by companies, H. Lesca names two tools to retain and manage information: CAR (Computer Assisted Retrieval) systems and internal databanks.

CAR systems include three functions: information capture, memorization of texts (in the form of microfiches for example) and keyword search. Internal databanks require specialized personnel to create and use them.

Storage supports can be paper or electronic. In his study, Ballaz noticed that paper largely dominates: 89% of responding companies use it to store information.

Some authors warn against possible risk of archiving instead of storage and deliberately exclude this phase of the surveillance process. According to them, storage could turn into an archiving system. The personnel dedicated to surveillance would then spend more time managing inventory than communicating information and managing the flow of information, two vital tasks in the activity of surveillance.

In conclusion, the existence of a storage phase and the accessibility of raw and processed stored information seem to be factors of surveillance effectiveness.

6.5. Phase 4: distribution

Once the information is collected and processed, it must be circulated and distributed to potential users. The role of distribution in surveillance effectiveness is therefore obvious: information which is collected, processed, stored but not distributed is not used, which reduces surveillance effectiveness to zero.

Four main questions are raised with surveillance managers: who should receive the information? (the problems of recipient relevance and the range of distribution are implied); when and how?; by which distribution channels?; and how do we avoid slowdowns in the circulation and distribution of information?

Despite the importance of the distribution operation and the problems that it raises, it is not well documented in the literature.

6.5.1. *Recipients and the extent of distribution*

The first problem is to distribute the information to the right recipients, i.e. those interested by it and liable to use it.

Previous studies have shown that the main objective of surveillance was decision support and strategic planning. The Diffenbach study confirms that executives, upper management and the President of the company are the most frequent recipients. In addition, the author notes that they are cited more often in companies where the perceived usefulness of watch is qualified as crucial. He gives no indication on the meaning of this relation.

The Bournois and Romani results agree: for managers surveyed, ESI is a preparation system for strategic decision, in 66.7% of responses, the executive committee and upper management are the first sponsors.

In addition, syntheses produced by the experts are mostly meant for upper management (72.3%) then for the field (20.9%). In large and international corporations, the field is a more important recipient (45.8% of corporations with over 50 subsidiaries).

The extent of distribution raises the problem of information confidentiality. Surveillance managers would be more favorable to extended distribution than executives. For example Herring recommends distributing the information to all potential users. Respondents from the Ghoshal and Westney study adopt the same position.

For them, extended distribution promotes the visibility of surveillance activities, return of information and personnel awareness to environmental variables. They are opposed to their management on this point, as they prefer a more targeted distribution, especially in the case of sensitive information.

6.5.2. *The moment of distribution*

Distribution of information must happen with the correct recipient as well as at the right moment. The crucial problem comes from the temporary nature of the information, and criticisms often involve distribution of information that is too late.

In his study, Hamrefors asked respondents to evaluate the relevance of information distribution in relation to time. He obtained average results. On a seven point scale, most respondents gave a grade of five.

Lesca took into consideration this important point in the Fennec design, his tool of surveillance measurement. He proposed to include in the instrument of data collection a question on the suitability of distributed information and the frequency of possible lateness.

6.5.3. *Distribution channels*

The evolution of information technologies and communication enabled a significant widening of information distribution methods.

The distribution of the products of surveillance activity be by written, oral, electronic channels, etc. – numerous and varied. These products can be a press review, a newsletter, internal journals, mission reports, reports, information files, colloquiums, seminars, conferences, etc.

Some studies list the most widely used methods of information distribution. Globally, the written method is by far the most used. The oral method follows. It has a better impact, good visibility and instant feedback. In the Prescott and Smith study, the interest for bulletin boards and internal communication letters is low, all the more so as their use is seriously questioned. On the other hand, there is a clear preference for personal communications.

These studies highlight the fact that the electronic method is not used much, for some, it is better to start from the existing methods of distribution. In order to do this, Martinet and Ribault recommend an audit through a questionnaire and interviews to determine the sources, recipients, networks, etc. and to draw a map of information circulation.

However, a significant evolution has occurred in this field and companies now use new communication channels (messaging, the Internet, etc.) more. In the Bournois and Romani study, 46.5% of companies use electronic messaging.

6.5.4. *Slowdowns in the circulation and distribution of information*

In general, information does not circulate efficiently in a company. Power struggles, ignorance of the value of information and organizational structure are a few reasons for this recurring problem.

To avoid these slowdowns, which seriously hinder the effectiveness of the surveillance activity, the authors make some recommendations:

– managing flows of information instead of inventory. Surveillance services are not information services managing information holdings;

– spending more time distributing the products of surveillance. Only 10% of surveillance manager time is spent on distribution against 90% for collection and processing;

– taking an interest in the psychological concerns of the recipient to understand him better;

– using the advantages of the oral method.

In conclusion, the existence of a distribution phase and its quality in terms of appropriateness for the recipient and opportunity (the right person – the right moment) seem to be factors of surveillance effectiveness.

6.6. Phase 5: information use

Information has been researched, collected, processed and distributed; the recipient must now use it in his strategic decisions and actions.

This element occupies an important place in our research model. A surveillance system may be of excellent quality, but its efficiency can still be reduced to zero if it is not used. The use of surveillance products then seems to be an obvious factor of SWI effectiveness.

We must highlight that the relation between surveillance personnel and the user mainly happens at this level.

In addition, three elements seem vital in the usage phase and consequently in the effectiveness of surveillance:

– the link between surveillance and strategy functions;

– the integration of surveillance results in the strategic decision;

– the existence of recommendations for the decision maker.

6.7. Feedback

The recipient's feedback on transmitted information is recommended by many authors. It is the best way to improve the quality of information. They recommend the implementation of a feedback contract encouraging users to issue feedback on each item of information transmitted.

For Prescott and Smith, having feedback that evaluates the relevance of distributed information enables the specialist to improve the effectiveness of their function.

However, the only studies involving this subject indicate low feedback. For Ballaz, 53% of companies maintain having a feedback on transmitted information.

A study carried out by SCIP Netherlands reveals that 50% of members, surveillance professionals, regret not having feedback.

In the Bournois and Romani study, the ESI manager does not receive any feedback on the quality of his service in 53.3% of companies surveyed.

As a result of the role of feedback in the evaluation of surveillance, the existence of feedback seems to be a factor of surveillance effectiveness.

6.8. Control

From the analysis of literature, six phases are identified where the existence appears to be vital to the effectiveness of surveillance.

A phase of surveillance process control is also necessary to the effectiveness of surveillance and its impact on the performance of companies. It is rarely followed by companies, but is vital since our final objective is to propose a model of surveillance effectiveness measurement.

The control phase, which is of high quality, will only be effective if there is a feedback phase on the information distributed. That is the reason why we include this operation in the model.

The surveillance process includes the following eight phases.

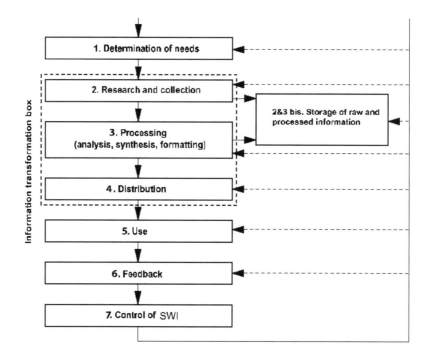

Figure 6.5. *Proposed SI process*

Chapter 5 focuses on the organizational dimension of the model. This chapter covers the evaluation of the SI process. The next step is to analyze the human, technical and financial dimensions of the model in the following chapter.

Chapter 7

Evaluation of Human, Technical and Financial Resources of SI

7.1. Human methods

The literature is rather homogenous about the factors of effectiveness related to human surveillance methods. At least five elements seem to play a major role in surveillance effectiveness: perceived importance and usefulness of surveillance, the support and involvement of upper management, the quality of the surveillance manager, the quality of the participants in the surveillance activity and the existence of a collective culture of information sharing.

7.1.1. *Perceived importance and usefulness of surveillance*

Several authors have studied the importance and usefulness of surveillance, particularly the perceptions of company managers and personnel. Diffenbach analyzes the perceived usefulness of surveillance in a small sample of American companies. He noticed that it does not vary with the size of the company, that it is perceived as especially useful for long-term planning, at corporate effectiveness level in a field and that it increases when the firms devote significant efforts to it. In his exploratory study of seven small to medium-sized companies, Marteau notes the importance given to the activity of surveillance by general managers. Cartwright works specifically on the use and perceived usefulness of surveillance in his American thesis. Noting the role of the perceived importance and usefulness of surveillance on corporate employees, she recommends placing the surveillance unit close to the highest authority.

It seems that the perceived importance and usefulness of surveillance by personnel and management is a factor of surveillance effectiveness.

7.1.2. *The support and involvement of upper management*

Upper management (UM) support and involvement are often cited as the most important factor of surveillance effectiveness. For many analysts, support from the UM is the main catalyst for surveillance. This element is even more important during implementation of the activity. O'Connel and Zimmermann note that the firms in their study who practice the most efficient surveillance are those where the support, involvement and effective participation of upper management in all phases of the surveillance process are the strongest. In these companies, surveillance is legitimate, recognized, accepted and has resources allocated to it.

In addition, 75% of people surveyed in the Jain study think that the initiative and implementation of surveillance are to the credit of UM (compared to 17% for personnel). Imitations by competitors and recommendations from consultants do not seem to carry any weight.

In reality however, few companies benefit from this support. Brenner notes it in his study. In addition, he notices a correlation between the degree of UM support and the size of the formal surveillance team, as well as the level of integration of the activity in the corporate operation.

Prescott and Smith reveal that UM support is not common, particularly in the long term. Withdrawal of UM support can then lead to frustration or discouragement among surveillance specialists.

UM involvement occurs in generally implicit ways. For many authors, the hierarchical ranking of the surveillance function to a higher level reveals the importance and support given to the activity. The bonds between the surveillance manager and UM (frequency of meetings, seat on the executive committee), the integration of SWIM recommendations in the strategic decision process, specific resource allocation, communications for implementing the products of the previous day, etc., are all part of UM support.

In the IHEDN study, the surveillance manager and UM (or the chairmanship) generally meet once a month (46.7% of companies with over 10,000 employees). They meet more often in smaller companies. The authors noted three cases involving a seat on the executive committee for the surveillance manager:

– a restrictive seat on the executive committee (51.7% of companies surveyed). According to the authors, it is the most preferred situation for the ESI Manager (ESIM): he can directly share his points of view and influence the strategic directions with a small number of players. This case generally corresponds to companies with fewer than 1,000 employees, in national markets and organized by function;

– a seat on the extended steering committee (16%);

– no seat on the steering committee (32.3%). The ESIM is then represented by his manager (strategy, commercial, etc.). This case is encountered in very large corporations.

Some authors warn about the risks related to the support of a member of the UM. In the event of the supporter's departure, the activity can be in question, reconsidered or even disbanded. We note that one of the three surveillance entities that disappeared during their study was closed after the departure of an executive who had supported it for eight years.

In conclusion, the support and involvement of management in the surveillance activity seems to represent a major factor of SWI effectiveness.

7.1.3. *The existence and quality of the SWI manager*

A surveillance manager seems essential for the majority of the authors, and the selection of this manager is vital to the effectiveness of the activity.

The literature often describes him as a five legged sheep, who must play a multifunctional role of coordinator, mediator, controller, etc. of the surveillance activity. In order to succeed, he must have solid training and experience, intellectual skills and distinct human qualities simultaneously.

In the studies, the wrong choice for manager is a major cause of surveillance ineffectiveness in a company. We observed that in two of the three surveillance failures, the surveillance manager was external to the company. Similarly, the Ghoshal study mentions the nomination of a surveillance manager who was a new graduate in several firms where the activity was a failure. In each case, the skills and credibility of the individual were seriously called into question by the personnel.

In order to be relevant, the selection of the surveillance manager seems to occur according to several criteria: his training, origin and employment history, experience and prior achievements in the organization, his power in the organization, the wealth of his personal networks, etc.

Many authors insist on the intellectual abilities and necessary human qualities of the surveillance manager, as well as from all the participants in the corporate surveillance activity. They must have an open mind, be curious, critical, have capacities of analysis and synthesis, communication skills, charisma, etc.

The IHEDN study gives us valuable information on the sex, employment history and training of the ESIM from the 1,200 companies in the survey.

In the sample studied, the ESIM is male in 94% of companies. He was internally recruited in 90.5% of the companies. The future ESIMs are executives who occupy technical, commercial or information technology jobs. On the other hand, the evolution of ESIM careers takes them to senior management positions. The education level is quite high (MBAs on average) and mainly an engineering degree (45% of the firms). Managers seem more in demand than economists. French companies historically prefer engineers (47.3%), whereas management specialists are favored by companies in the rest of the world (36.4%). In American companies, we find more self-taught people.

With regard to the required skills of the ESIM, we can cite the research results of Prescott. The researcher identified seven key skills of the ESIM:

1) the capacity to define and understand customer requirements;

2) the capacity to build a methodology of collection and processing of multi-source information;

3) analysis;

4) statistical and data analysis;

5) the capacity to come to conclusions;

6) the capacity to communicate his results to decision makers;

7) the capacity to retrieve a customer evaluation.

Here again, we note the importance of the evaluation of the surveillance activity.

In conclusion, the existence and qualities of the SWI Manager (SWIM) seem to be factors of surveillance effectiveness. In terms of qualities for the SWIM, they are his training, experience and skills as well as his human qualities.

7.1.4. *The quality of the other SWI players*

These are specialized people responsible for surveillance, and managed by the surveillance manager. They can also be employees with a part time surveillance activity in addition to their main job.

The role of the permanent team, and of other members of internal surveillance networks in the effectiveness of the surveillance activity, is largely highlighted in the literature. As a result of this, training, experience and human qualities are the main recruitment criteria.

With regard to the choice of the candidates for surveillance positions, we find all the same requirements as for the surveillance manager above. However, certain works highlight the need for diversified profiles depending on the phase of the surveillance process involved. For example, in the case of information research, specialists in new information technologies will be required. The phase of information processing (analysis and synthesis) will be the job of the analyst.

Awareness and motivation of the participants are paramount factors of effectiveness. In his work on the attitude of salespeople involving surveillance, Le Bon verified the three following assumptions:

1) the intention of a watch effort from salespeople is all the stronger as their attitude towards this mission is favorable;

2) salespeople are less motivated if they perceive the ambiguity of their role;

3) they are all the more motivated if they are recognized for this activity.

To improve the motivation of salespeople, the author recommends a reward systems for ESI efforts of employees.

In reality, the efforts of participants in surveillance are insufficiently rewarded. Only 11.1% of the companies in the IHEDN study thought of a reward system for employees. This percentage is higher (22%) in smaller companies (less than €30 million in revenue). There is a reward system for employees in 20.9% of companies who experienced several major attacks. Companies organized by division or by product are the most advanced in the practice of rewards for employees (17.6%) because of the need to defend products in the field.

One of the most often cited slowdowns in employee motivation, and thus in surveillance effectiveness, involves the time dedicated to surveillance. There are numerous cases where the surveillance activity gets stacked on top of a main activity.

To motivate employees, many authors recommend education and awareness training for employees, whether specialized or not. They must first involve the stakes and results of surveillance, and apply them using any channel available (mail, Internet, seminars, reports, etc.).

Several consultants proposed training and awareness products for surveillance, and this market is still thriving. Innovation 128, for example, proposes Infomaster. In summary, it groups all high ranking corporate executives (Research & Development Management, Marketing Management, UM, etc.), making them aware of the value of information, training them in techniques of information collection and processing, assisting them in defining their information requirements and in identifying the most interesting sources for creating a collective plan of action for developing the surveillance function in the company.

However, certain authors warn against risks of frustration resulting from awareness campaigns, which can be perceived as attempts at influencing the culture of the organization. They come back to the importance of UM support.

In the IHEDN study, employee awareness is low. Only 6.7% of French managers who practice ESI estimate that their employees are well or completely aware of the challenges. The export share of the revenue seems to be a good indicator of the degree of awareness. This percentage goes down to 0.6% for companies who intend to implement a surveillance activity.

In conclusion, qualities of surveillance managers seem to be fundamental in surveillance effectiveness. As previously mentioned, these are their training, experience, skills and especially their human qualities.

In spite of the crucial role that human resources play in the effectiveness of surveillance, the links between human resource management and economic and strategic intelligence are not explained in sufficient detail. However, these are the men and women in the company, vectors of information, who can improve the quality of the process (Bournois and Romani). They also have an influence on the culture of their company.

7.1.5. *A collective culture of information*

For most authors, surveillance is a state of mind and everybody's business, according to the formulae repeated many times by F. Lainée. The existence of a collective culture of information is an important catalyst of surveillance effectiveness.

In fact, the activity is based on sharing, exchanging and circulating information within different networks. It will be all the more effective as it will occur in a favorable context, where information is no longer seen as a tool of power. This cultural problem is linked to the nationality of the company, it happens less in Japan than in France, for example. The authors of the Martre report actually considered a steep hill ahead in trying to change habits and behaviors. According to them, the role of government is important in this regard.

On the other hand, collection, classification, synthesis and communication of data exceed the capabilities of a single person, if we want the process to be effective. In fact, surveillance is a collective job involving all employees in the company in various degrees.

According to Bournois and Romani, a strong corporate culture would support the involvement of employees in the surveillance activity. Referring to the identity of the company and the organizational environment, the corporate culture is often characterized by the degree of confidence of employees toward management, bureaucratic intensity of corporate operation, capacity to be innovative, the pride of being a member of the company and employee commitment to future projects. In their study, 89.6% of managers estimate that their corporate culture is strong. When the company is a leader in the field, this percentage goes up to 96%. There again, the results do not come from an objective measurement, respondents are the managers, the risk of bias is thus significant.

The existence of collective information sharing seems to be a major factor in surveillance effectiveness.

Following the analysis of human surveillance methods, the following factors are elements of surveillance effectiveness:

– perceived importance and usefulness of upper management;

– perceived importance and usefulness by personnel;

– support and involvement of upper management (UM);

– quality of the surveillance manager (training, experience, skills and human qualities);

– quality of the other participants in the surveillance activity (the same as above);

– a collective information sharing culture.

7.2. Technical methods

Treating technical methods used in the surveillance activity requires specific and advanced skills in terms of information technology. Without getting too technical, this section analyzes the literature devoted to this topic.

The range of tools useful for environmental surveillance keeps growing, primarily because of the extremely fast evolution of communication and information technologies. Their contributions to the effectiveness of the research, collection and information distribution phases no longer need to be proven, and the products expected for the information processing phases are extremely promising. Using and controlling the available tools is undoubtedly a factor of surveillance effectiveness.

A brief overview of the most widely known tools used in surveillance activity is given. In fact, this list will evolve, and some of these elements will eventually become obsolete.

7.2.1. *Information research collection tools*

These seem infinite, especially on the Web where there are more than a million sites and several billion pages. The following table presents a few of the most well known research tools.

Tools	Examples	Notes
Online directories	Nomad, MSN, Voilà, Yahoo, etc.	Very efficient for people pressed for time who already know the category to search from
Simple search engines	Altavista, Hotbot, Lycos, etc.	There are a lot of them. The most popular are the best
Meta-search engines	Metacrawler, Inference, Mamma	Very powerful: power, speed, simplicity
Online encyclopedias and dictionaries	Britannica Online, Encarta, Infoplcase, Onelook, MSN, Expedia, etc.	Some are not free
Online libraries	Alapage, Amazon, etc.	Interesting for building an online bibliography
Leading search engine	Google	Probably the most commonly used search engine

Table 7.1. *Example of information research and collection tools*

Search engines known to be intelligent appear regularly. In France, the INPI is very prolific on the matter. L'Institut National de la Propriété Industrielle (the National Institute for Industrial Property) launched *Plutarque*, an Internet portal. This facilitates the search for information on industrial property using an intelligent search engine. This will make it possible to find French or foreign data on patents in all languages. It will propose searches for logos, trademarks and reproductions of drawings and models starting from an image. The stake is important for the INPI. The portal will give access to 40 million French and foreign patents, 800,000 logos from French, community or international trademarks and over 5 million diagrams from patents. The INPI mainly wants to set up subscription-based information and watch services by user-personalized email.

There is also an enormous volume of databases, both online and on CD-ROM, which are widely used by surveillance specialists.

Many companies propose research tools. The LexiQuest company markets *LexiQuest Guide*, which enables research using natural language and facilitates the immediate delivery of the desired documents.

The results of the empirical studies show a progressive rise of the Internet's power. In the French companies surveyed by Bournois and Romani, the Internet is not yet a monopolistic source of information. Only 6.7% of companies state that they obtain more than 30% of their information through the Internet. For 69.6% of companies, the Internet provides less than 15% of information.

The use of the Internet seems dependant on the size of the company, its revenue, competitive environment and organization. The Internet is used more in larger companies and in companies with worldwide competition. The use is stronger in organizations divisional by product (11.1% of companies retrieve more than 30% of information) and by project matrix (10.4% retrieve more than 30% of information).

7.2.2. *Tools for information processing*

Still in their first stages, they are marked out to revolutionize the analysis and synthesis of an enormous mass of information. Their main interest is connecting scattered and varied information in order to comprehend it.

LexiQuest proposes the *LexiQuest Mine* tool, for example, which analyzes large volumes of documents to extract the key information and build charts of data showing the main concepts and the links between them. Their *LexiQuest Categorize* tool analyzes, organizes and automatically assigns documents to a taxonomy, classification plan, predefined or personalized standard, while analyzing and understanding the content and context of a large volume of documents. There are also tools for analyzing quantitative information (SPSS, for example), and qualitative data (content analysis by SPHINX, for example).

7.2.3. *Tools for information storage*

Storage of raw or processed data is one of the phases of surveillance, done by a growing number of organizations. In this field, the possibilities are also expected to grow.

Idealist, from the Cadic company, stores information in the form of files, with a selection that is done by keyword.

7.2.4. *Tools for information distribution and communication*

The communication methods used in networks can be multiform. There are three distinct possibilities. The oral method is used during formal or informal meetings, the paper method goes back to the design of written reports, standardized or not, the electronic method covers the teleprocessing networks (telephone, fax, teletel) and the mother of all networks: the Internet network. This network is increasingly being used through the services that it provides: messaging (email), newsgroups, information research, etc. It constitutes a sure method of developing corporate communication.

Information and Communication Technologies (ICT) made it significantly easier and faster to exchange information within surveillance networks. A real evolution has recently taken place in favor of the use of email at the expense of oral and written methods.

In French companies, 46.5% of companies surveyed use an internal email system. 32% favor the oral method and 21.5% transmit information on paper (form, 14.8%, or plain paper, 6.7%).

According to the authors, the mode of information flow is influenced by the complexity of the organizations and the innovative nature of their management. In companies with more than 10,000 employees, the percentage of firms using email accounts for 70%. This figure goes up to 81.5% for companies with more than 50 foreign subsidiaries. This method is used more when competition is worldwide (59.5%). Then the oral method follows when competition is European or national (respectively 32 and 31.5%), and paper when competition is national (28.5%). The traditional organization seems to be resistant to using ICT. On the other hand, the divisional by product and by project matrix organization uses email more (54.8% and 59.6%).

Concerning the tools used for information flow in external networks, informal ones dominate. The oral method accounts for 50.2% of answers compared to the paper medium (form: 5.8%, plain paper: 23.7%) and email (20.3%). The determining factor here is the export revenue. In companies with a strong export volume, email accounts for 35.3% of answers.

Bournois and Romani wanted to know if software to manage networks was present in companies. They note that mapping is used by 17.1% of the firms (see technical factors of effectiveness).

7.2.5. *The intranet*

The stakes of the intranet are nothing less than massive gains of competitiveness, and still not enough companies are aware of it. Half of the 100 largest Americans companies already have their network. On the other hand, in 1996, only 28% of French companies with over 1,000 employees had developed an intranet. This percentage was 4% for firms of fewer than 200 employees. Some pioneer companies went into it without question. At Essilor, when a customer asked for optical specifications of Varilux – varifocal lenses for spectacles – it took some time to find the accurate information in catalogs. Today, all this information is accessible instantaneously from each salesperson's laptop. However, not all companies use the potential of these new means of communication fully, settling for email or internal directory functions, and yet, there are many advantages of the intranet:

Low cost: the internal network makes it possible to manage internal flows of corporate information with minimal costs, effort and delays. In fact, a basic system costs a few thousand Euros. It only requires computer terminals connected by cable or by phone and the design of an intranet page, like any service provider on the Web.

Simple access: as simple, user friendly and attractive as the Internet, the intranet is accessible to each company employee, provided that he or she has access to a computer.

Quick access to information: the acquisition of information is instantaneous, without any constraint of space, time and hierarchy.

The possibility of determining the information need: the intranet makes it possible to provide internal corporate information to employees based on their needs. With the help of its system of interrogation in simple language, each user is able to define his requests for access to needed information.

Reserved access: each type of information has a generally limited access based on its sensitive and confidential character. For example, executives may be the only ones authorized to access certain strategic information. Each employee can have access to their own pay slip, etc.

Aggregation and analysis of heterogeneous data: each user is able to incorporate and analyze scattered and various information. He can individually carry out his watch under the best conditions, and contribute to the global watch of the company by distributing high added value information.

Updated information: the permanent updating of internal information is made possible with the help of the intranet. The updating of monographs, for example, can be done directly on intranet pages. The delays in formatting, publication and distribution inherent to the paper medium disappear.

Collective work: intranet facilitates communication and communal tasks between individuals who are geographically remote. Exchanges between experts are favored and quicker which increases the volume and the quality of available information with high added value.

Information sharing: similarly, for an organization with sites that are very distant from one another, the intranet is the ideal solution. Each site or subsidiary can constantly consult and provide information very inexpensively. This method avoids organizing meetings, which can be difficult because of the limited availability of managers and potentially high traveling expenses.

Communication: the intranet eliminates hierarchical compartmentalization and barriers. The different functions of the company communicate freely between each other, and each employee can communicate directly with the higher levels of his choice. On the other side of the Atlantic, for example, each Microsoft employee can send a simple email to Bill Gates, the owner of the firm.

Access to the Internet: the user can access the Internet without jeopardizing the safety of the informational content of his company's intranet. He can thus consult internal and external databases without any problem.

Easier information distribution: with the help of the intranet, it is now possible to distribute information to all employees. In certain cases, such as an attack from a competitor or a new law, etc., this possibility can prove to be vital for the company, which then becomes more reactive. However, as in any new system, mistakes can occur. That is how the employees of Marks & Spencer learned by email of their company's intentions to close stores and dismiss employees, which generated instant reactions from employees, as well as from the press and authorities.

Economics: we have seen it; the intranet prevents potentially huge costs in the distribution of paper media, first by the publication itself, but also by the cost in time and work. It also makes it possible to obtain a return on IT investment.

Two main elements emerge from this quick overview of technical methods for the surveillance activity: the list of these tools is infinite and in constant evolution, and the factors of effectiveness corresponding to these methods are related to the human effectiveness factors which have already been addressed. The effectiveness of technical tools depends on their intrinsic qualities as well as the capabilities and experience of specialists in information dedicated to surveillance, who are also able to evaluate the effectiveness of each tool.

Following the analysis of technical methods, the quantity, diversity and quality of the tools used in the practice of surveillance (information research, collection, processing, storage, communication and distribution) seem to be a factor of surveillance efficiency.

7.3. Financial resources

Financial resources have an important place in our model since they are part of the calculation of the surveillance efficiency activity (efficiency ratio). Three main elements arise from analyzing the literature. Firstly, it is a sensitive subject from which only a few numbers are available. Secondly, the importance of the sum dedicated to surveillance does not seem to be a factor of surveillance effectiveness. Thirdly, having a minimum budget, adequate for surveillance requirements for the company, and especially a budget specific to surveillance seems to be a factor of effectiveness which is confirmed by recent studies.

7.3.1. *A budget for SWI needs*

Mention of the budget for the surveillance activity and its distribution is almost absent in the literature, probably because of the sensitive nature of the topic. In any case, the cost of handling information is high. It consists of three main factors: human methods (workforce), technical methods (computer tools, office automation equipment, printing, etc.) and information holdings (books, subscriptions, etc.).

In term of workforce, we have some figures from empirical studies. Generally, the number of members of the surveillance team is proportional to the size of the company. The entity of IBM surveillance includes 25 people at head office and 35 people overseas, Royal Dutch Shell surveillance has 30 and General Motors 42. In the Lenz and Engledow study, the structures of monitoring range from one to seven members. Seven of the 12 companies studied have, at most, two people dedicated to the activity of surveillance, including one part-time. In the Prescott study, the team includes three full-time people, one part-time and a secretary.

Figures involving the payroll are rare. However, the IHEDN study of 1,200 French companies gives us interesting information on the age and compensation of the surveillance manager. The average salary of an ESIM is €73,000. Revenue, international dimension, sector of activity, financial results and the age of the manager explain the variations observed. Globally, compensation for ESIMs is more important in larger companies, in organizations with more than 50 subsidiaries, in building/civil engineering sectors and when there are profits. Regarding the correlation between compensation and the age of the ESIM, 11.5% of people over 50 years old receive compensation of over €153,000. In fact, UM can combine several functions, including the ESI function, and ESIMs reach higher levels of compensation.

Prescott and Smith obtained the average annual budget of the surveillance activity of the 95 companies studied. It is $550,000. However, the author notes important variations from $15,000 to $6.5 million. The most important accounts are payroll (46%), research contracts (23%) and hardware (14%). In addition, he notes that 59 companies out of the 95 studied have a budget allocated to surveillance.

With regard to technical costs, the figures are rare. American companies exported more than $66 billion of information processing technologies in 1993.

Some authors tried to give orders of magnitude to evaluate the cost of a surveillance activity. The Martre report for example, evaluates the cost at €9 per manager per day, the cost of a daily online press review. Martinet and Marti announce that 46% of the studies of service providers cost less than €8,000, 42% between €8,000 and €38,000 and 12% more than €38,000. These authors quote Alaterre who estimates the costs associated with books, subscriptions, CD-ROMs, consultation of data banks, etc. An information file can cost from €3,000 to €7,000 according to him. However, these figures are estimates; they evolve quickly and should be considered with care.

The level of the budget allocated to the activity does not seem to be a factor of surveillance effectiveness. Large financial resources are not inevitably necessary to carry out efficient surveillance. The results of the study carried out by Jain agree, by considering that the lack of financial resources is not a major problem. However, a basic budget is recommended. The percentage of 1% of revenue is found in many publications. It is often compared to 1.5% of the revenue that Japanese companies dedicate to their surveillance.

7.3.2. *The existence of a budget specific to SWI*

Having a specific surveillance activity budget seems to be a factor of effectiveness. An efficient surveillance activity requires specific, regular and continuous resource allocation. An appropriate budget has two major advantages: autonomy of management in relation to other functions and increased legitimacy of the surveillance manager.

The existence of a budget suitable for the activity exists in 50% of companies known as international, 44.6% in export companies, 27.6% in technical companies and 19.3% in national companies.

In conclusion, the following elements are factors of surveillance effectiveness:

– the existence of an appropriate surveillance budget;

– the appropriateness of the surveillance budget for the needs of the company.

7.4. Conclusion

Five dimensions corresponding to surveillance methods were analyzed.

The model of exploration, description and measurement of the methods implemented in the surveillance activity is represented in Figure 7.1.

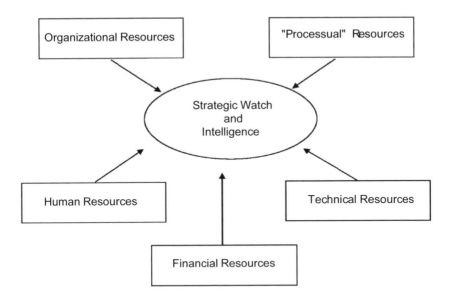

Figure 7.1. *Model of exploration, description and measure of surveillance methods*

Chapter 8

SI Measurement Tools for SI Managers

This chapter focuses on the measuring instrument corresponding to the technical evaluation of SI methods. This tool is mainly aimed at SI managers who wish to control the operation of their system. It leads to an evaluation grid and a first control panel for SI.

The idea will be to compare the two evaluation instruments to propose, in the end, a scorecard based on SI effectiveness indicators and its impact on global performance.

The questionnaires created contain descriptive and evaluation questions. Descriptive questions enable us to make an inventory of what exists. Evaluation questions will serve as a basis for the design of a control panel.

The notation system associated with the evaluation questions is simple. It is inspired by the traditional methodology used in marketing. Each response corresponds to a grade of zero to four. The total grade obtained represents the level of effectiveness reached for each of the objects evaluated.

Preface on the study level and terminology

Before applying the measuring instrument, it is imperative that we detail the level of the study and the terminology used in the company and in the questionnaire.

Several SI entities can be evaluated: a central SI entity, a decentralized SI entity, a group of decentralized SI entities, a group of corporate SI entities, etc.

The following image gives an example of these different levels:

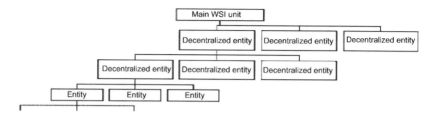

In the questionnaire preface, the following questions explain the level of the study:

Level of SI study?

The central SI entity	❏
The decentralized SI entity	❏
A group of decentralized SI entities	❏
The corporate SI activities	❏
Other:	

The following two-dimensional table locates the different SI entities of the company as well as their "clients". It may highlight the group that we want to study more closely.

What are the different corporate SI entities and their "clients"?

Situation of SI activities \ Client	UM	R&D	Mktg	Sales	Purchasing	Fin.	Strat.	HR	Legal	Information	Other
UM	❑	❑	❑	❑	❑	❑	❑	❑	❑	❑	❑
R & D	❑	❑	❑	❑	❑	❑	❑	❑	❑	❑	❑
Mktg	❑	❑	❑	❑	❑	❑	❑	❑	❑	❑	❑
Sales	❑	❑	❑	❑	❑	❑	❑	❑	❑	❑	❑
Purchasing	❑	❑	❑	❑	❑	❑	❑	❑	❑	❑	❑
Fin.	❑	❑	❑	❑	❑	❑	❑	❑	❑	❑	❑
Strat.	❑	❑	❑	❑	❑	❑	❑	❑	❑	❑	❑
HR	❑	❑	❑	❑	❑	❑	❑	❑	❑	❑	❑
Legal	❑	❑	❑	❑	❑	❑	❑	❑	❑	❑	❑
Information	❑	❑	❑	❑	❑	❑	❑	❑	❑	❑	❑
Other	❑	❑	❑	❑	❑	❑	❑	❑	❑	❑	❑

Concerning terminology, several cases may occur: the company may use the term "watch", even though it practices intelligence, it can use "intelligence" when it "only" practices watch, it can use both terms and make a clear distinction between the two functions or it can use its own terminology.

The introduction to the questionnaire explains that the term "surveillance" is a generic term representing watch and/or intelligence. The responding company is invited to replace surveillance or its equivalent, the SWI acronym, with the term(s) that it usually uses. For example, it may use SW to evaluate its Strategic Watch function or SI to measure the most advanced form of surveillance, its Strategic Intelligence function. SI is used in the rest of this chapter.

The following question explains the terminology used:

What is the most often used terminology to designate the SI activity of the company?

Surveillance ❑	Watch ❑	Intelligence ❑	Other:

This is the terminology used in the rest of the questionnaire.

8.1. Organizational methods

The organization of SI includes five descriptive variables: formalization, seniority, the degree of centralization and the number of SI points, hierarchical ranking and organization network structure.

The empirical survey confirmed the organizational effectiveness factors identified from the analysis in the literature: a certain level of formalization and seniority, a high hierarchical ranking and a dense and active network are vital for an efficient SI.

8.1.1. *The degree of formalization of SI*

The formalization degree expresses the level of organization and structure of methods implemented for SI.

Beyond a certain threshold in quantity and complexity of procedures, the formalization degree slows down effectiveness, as SI managers spend more time managing procedures than effectively monitoring their environment. In addition, a certain degree of informal intelligence without constraints seems necessary. A happy medium must be found in the formalization of the SI activity.

To evaluate the degree of formalization of the SI activity, most analysts only considered the perceptions of respondents. It is in fact interesting to ask the opinion of the manager surveyed on the formalization degree of the activity:

In your opinion, what is the degree of formalization of SI practiced?

Informal only	❑
Not very formalized	❑
Somewhat formalized	❑
Formalized	❑
Very formalized	❑

In order to have a more objective measure, however, this degree should be assessed after the global evaluation of SI methods at the end of the questionnaire. In addition, from the moment we choose to proceed with an evaluation for a quality assessment, a "normative" approach seems vital.

For most of the experts surveyed during the validation test of factors of SI effectiveness, "a certain degree of formalization" is necessary in order for the activity to be efficient. However, how can we define this *certain degree of formalization*?

It can be defined from the SI process implemented which best represents the formalization of the activity. For example, the existence of an information research and collection operation is not enough to declare that the minimum degree of formalization is reached. In this case, we could be in the presence of a simple information activity instead of a watch or *a fortiori* intelligence activity: the information analysis and distribution phases are also necessary. The existence of information research, collection, analysis and distribution operations is the premise to agree on a minimum formalization level.

However, this level is insufficient. A sufficient formalization level also corresponds to the existence of feedback on the information distributed, which may give evidence to the use of this information and a minimum SI control.

Then, we encounter a first problem in the notation of this criterion. In fact, a *very formalized* SI is not necessarily more efficient than *formalized* or *somewhat formalized* SI. Knowing the degree of formalization is useful, but we must also know if it is sufficient. In order to find out if the *certain degree of formalization* necessary to the effectiveness of SI is reached, we have to make the notation in the following scale:

Is the degree of formalization of SI:

0.	Completely insufficient	❏
1.	Insufficient	❏
2.	Almost sufficient	❏
3.	Sufficient	❏
4.	Completely sufficient	❏
Grade:		

In this way, an SI including research, collection, analysis, distribution and feedback phases will have a *completely sufficient* level of formalization and will get a maximum grade of four points.

8.1.2. Seniority of the SI function

SI activity control requires time and a long learning process. The quality of SI methods (quality of research and collection of information, for example) improves with practice and time (a certain level of maturity and effectiveness is reached from five years of seniority).

We must remain cautious in interpreting this indicator. The SI system of company A will not necessarily be more effective than the SI in company B merely because it is older. The degree of seniority is simply one of the indications of the level of SI progress in the company (presuming that the company provides the necessary efforts to improve its practice).

As a result of this, a notation problem is also raised in the case of SI function seniority. A four point grade is given if the five year threshold is reached, while being conscious of the fact that a 10 year SI, for example, is not necessarily more effective than a five year one. On the other hand, an SI with over five years of seniority (four points) will presumably be more effective than an SI with two to four years of seniority (three points), which is more effective than an SI with one to two years of seniority (two points), etc.

In the questionnaire, the following question evaluates the seniority of the intelligence activity:

What is the seniority of the intelligence function within the company?

0	No surveillance	❏	1	Less than one year	❏
2	Between one and two years	❏	3	Between two and four years	❏
4	Five years and older	❏		Note:	

8.1.3. *SI organization*

The organization of SI, its centralization or decentralization and, in this case, the number of SI points are all elements which greatly depend on the organization of the corporation. Consequently, they do not constitute factors of SI effectiveness. The best agreement must be found between the SI organization and the company's organization.

The following questions describe the type of organization, the number of SI points and SI functions.

A. THE SI ORGANIZATION: CENTRALIZED AND/OR DECENTRALIZED

What is the type of SI organization of the company as a whole?

Centralized only (a single entity is responsible for SI in the company)	❏
Decentralized only (several entities, spread over the company, are responsible for SI)	❏
Centralized and decentralized (a central structure and several entities are responsible for IS)	❏
An organization by SI project	❏
Other:	

B. THE NUMBER OF SI ENTITIES

How many entities responsible for SI are there in the company?

Only one	❏
Between two and five	❏
Between six and nine	❏
Between 10 and 20	❏
Over 20	❏

C. FUNCTIONS OF SI ENTITIES

1. The functions of the (possible) centralized SI entity

If there is a centralized SI entity, what are its functions? Is it responsible for:

– the SI itself ❏
– centralizing the products of the different SIs in the company ❏
– leading the different SIs in the company ❏
– leading the SI networks in the company ❏
– controlling SI ❏
– supporting SI (methods, tools, etc.) ❏
– Other:

2. The functions of decentralized SI entities

What are the functions of the decentralized SI entities? Are they responsible for:

– the SIs themselves ❏

– decentralizing the products of other SIs ❏

– leading different SIs ❏

– leading SI networks ❏

– controlling SI ❏

– supporting SI (methods, tools, etc.) ❏

– Other:

8.1.4. *The hierarchical ranking*

A "fairly high" hierarchical ranking is clearly a factor of SI effectiveness. It indirectly reveals the importance and support that upper management gives to SI, and improves the importance and usefulness of SI perceived by employees, two other factors of IS effectiveness.

It is necessary to specify the level and function of hierarchical ranking of the centralized entity and decentralized entities studied:

A. THE LEVEL OF HIERARCHICAL RANKING OF THE (POSSIBLY) CENTRALIZED SI ENTITY

What is the level of hierarchical ranking of the (possible) centralized SI entity?

0. N–5	❏	1. N–4	❏	2. N–3	❏
3. N–2	❏	4. N or N–1	❏	Note:	

N represents the highest hierarchical level (President and CEO or Upper Management).

B. THE LEVEL OF HIERARCHICAL RANKING OF THE ENTITY STUDIED

What is the level of hierarchical ranking of the entity studied, in relation to higher management?

0. N–5	❏	1. N–4	❏	2. N–3	❏
3. N–2	❏	4. N or N–1	❏	Note:	

C. THE RANKING FUNCTION OF THE (POSSIBLY) CENTRALIZED ENTITY

Another question should define the nature of the ranking function (General Manager, Strategy Management, etc.) and its coherence with the nature of the SI practiced. Even though it may be logical to connect a technological SI to technical management, it is not wise to link a SI group to level other than General Manager or Strategy Management.

What is the ranking function of the centralized SI entity?

Upper Management	❏	Strategy	❏
Research & Development	❏	Human Resources	❏
Marketing	❏	Legal	❏
Sales	❏	Information	❏
Purchasing	❏	Subsidiaries	❏
Finance	❏	Other:	

D. THE RANKING FUNCTION OF THE ENTITY STUDIED

What is the ranking function of the SI entity studied?

Upper Management	❏	Strategy	❏
Research & Development	❏	Human Resources	❏
Marketing	❏	Legal	❏
Sales	❏	Information	❏
Purchasing	❏	Subsidiaries	❏
Other:			

8.1.5. *The existence of a network organization*

The intelligence activity is mainly based on information exchange. A network organization is therefore vital to its effectiveness.

The corresponding question is as follows:

Is the SI networked?

(In networked surveillance, people involved in the system exchange information amongst each other through different means of communication).

0. No ❏	4. Yes ❏	Note:

Diversity, activity and maintenance of SI networks are also factors of SI effectiveness.

A. THE DIVERSITY OF NETWORKS

Check the boxes corresponding to the profiles belonging to the internal SI network.

Upper Management	❏	Strategy	❏
Research & Development	❏	Human Resources	❏
Marketing	❏	Legal	❏
Sales	❏	Information	❏
Purchases	❏	Subsidiaries	❏
Finance	❏	Other:	

Name the members of external SI networks? (check the corresponding boxes).

	Never	Rarely	Sometimes	Often	Always
Research centers, Universities	❏	❏	❏	❏	❏
Administration; specialized government departments	❏	❏	❏	❏	❏
Professional associations of the activity sector	❏	❏	❏	❏	❏
Consultants, engineering departments, information providers	❏	❏	❏	❏	❏
Other	❏	❏	❏	❏	❏

The scale from *never* to *always* may not be suitable. Extremes that may be too "radical" can be replaced by "very rarely" and "very often" respectively. Another solution can be to go to a seven point scale presenting more choices.

However, the ideal is to be able to define the frequencies corresponding to these items exactly (for example: annual for rarely, weekly for often).

This comment will be verified in the rest of the questionnaire for each frequency scale used.

The respondent can then base his responses on this inventory to indicate the degree of diversity and note if it is correct, for more precision:

From the elements in the previous responses, evaluate the degree of diversity of SI networks:

0.	Very low	❏	1.	Low	❏	2.	Average	❏
3.	High	❏	4.	Very high	❏	Grade:		

Is this degree:

0.	Very bad	❏	1.	Bad	❏	2.	Average	❏
3.	Good	❏	4.	Very good	❏	Grade:		

Only one notation can be copied to the evaluation grid.

B. THE ACTIVITY OF NETWORKS

What is the frequency of exchanges between the different members of internal SI networks? (Different communications: meetings, discussions, etc.)

Daily	❏	Weekly	❏
Monthly	❏	Annually	❏
Less frequent	❏		

What is the frequency of exchanges between internal and external network members?

Daily	❏	Weekly	❏
Monthly	❏	Annually	❏
Less frequent	❏		

Over the entire internal SI network, what is the percentage of people really active in SI?

Less than 10%	❏	Between 40 and 60%	❏
Between 10 and 20%	❏	Over 60%	❏
Between 20 and 40%	❏		

From the elements in the previous responses, indicate the degree of activity of SI networks

0.	No activity	❏	1.	Low	❏	2.	Average	❏
3.	High	❏	4.	Very high	❏	Grade:		

Is this degree:

0. Very bad	❏	1. Bad	❏	2. Average	❏
3. Good	❏	4. Very good	❏	Grade:	

C. NETWORK MAINTENANCE

What are the coordination methods of internal SI networks?

Meetings	❏	Presentations	❏
Distribution of material	❏	Other:	

What are the maintenance methods of external SI networks?

Attend shows	❏	Attend conferences	❏
Restaurants, cocktails	❏	Join associations	❏
Other:	❏		

What is the level of maintenance of SI networks?

0.	No maintenance	❏	1.	Not well maintained	❏
2.	Maintained	❏	3.	Well maintained	❏
4.	Very well maintained	❏	Grade:		

D. THE EXISTENCE OF GROUPS OF EXPERTS

The existence of groups of experts with expertise in terms of analysis and synthesis are vital, and identified as a factor of SI effectiveness.

Are there internal groups of experts in the SI activity?

0. No	❏	4. Yes	❏	Grade:

8.2. Resources for the intelligence process

Evaluating the frequency of one or another phase of the SI process is not wise. For example, the existence of a phase of determination of information needs is necessary to improve the effectiveness of SI, but if it is frequent, this does not make it more efficient.

We must find out if this frequency is appropriate (not too low and not too high). It is more advantageous to note the existence of the phase, consider its frequency as a descriptive complement and make an additional notation of the level of this frequency in the following scale:

0. Very bad	❏	1. Bad	❏	2. Average	❏
3. Good	❏	4. Very good	❏	Grade:	

8.2.1. *Phase 1. The determination of information needs*

In the first phase of the SI process, the determination of information needs, the range, direction, prioritization and updating of the SI must be addressed.

To be efficient, SI must be both sufficiently broad and targeted, oriented toward SI axes classified by order of priority and regularly updated.

A. EXISTENCE

Is there a phase of determination of information needs?

0. No	❏	4. Yes	❏	Grade:

What is its frequency?

Never	❏	Rarely	❏	Sometimes	❏
Often	❏	Always	❏		

Is the level of this frequency:

0. Very bad	❏	1. Bad	❏	2. Average	❏
3. Good	❏	4. Very good	❏	Grade:	

B. SI COVERAGE

What environmental fields are monitored?

Monitored environments	No	Yes
Competitive environment	❏	❏
Technological environment (technical and scientific environment)	❏	❏
Marketing and sales environment (economic environment, suppliers, clients, markets)	❏	❏
Legal and regulatory environment	❏	❏
Socio-cultural environment	❏	❏
Financial environment (stock exchange, shareholder, etc.)	❏	❏
Other:	❏	❏

In order to determine the most or least monitored environments, it is necessary to ask the respondent to classify:

For each of these environmental fields monitored (checked box), indicate a ranking number from the most monitored (number 1) to the least monitored (number 1, 2, 3, etc.)

Monitored environments		Rank no.
Competitive environment	❏	
Technological environment (technical and scientific environment)	❏	
Marketing and sales environment (economic environment, suppliers, clients, markets)	❏	
Legal and regulatory environment	❏	
Socio-cultural environment	❏	
Financial environment (stock exchange, shareholder etc.)	❏	
Other:	❏	

Another solution is to use a frequency scale:

Monitored environments	Never	Rarely	Sometimes	Often	Always
Competitive environment	❏	❏	❏	❏	❏
Technological environment (technical and scientific environment)	❏	❏	❏	❏	❏
Marketing and sales environment (economic environment, suppliers, clients, markets)	❏	❏	❏	❏	❏
Legal and regulatory environment	❏	❏	❏	❏	❏
Socio-cultural environment and PEST	❏	❏	❏	❏	❏
Financial environment (stock exchange, shareholder etc.)	❏	❏	❏	❏	❏
Other:	❏	❏	❏	❏	❏

Indicate the SI coverage:

one field	❏	two fields	❏	three fields	❏
four fields	❏	more than than four fields			❏

Is the level of this coverage:

0. Very bad	❏	1. Bad	❏	2. Average	❏
3. Good	❏	4. Very good	❏	Grade:	

C. THE DIRECTION OF SI

In each monitored field, are there predetermined axes?

No	❏	Yes	❏

In all monitored fields, what is the average number of axes monitored?

None	❏	Between 1 and 3 axes	❏
Between 4 and 5 axes	❏	Between 5 and 10 axes	❏
More than 10 axes	❏		

There has to be a distinction between SI carried out over well identified axes and that carried out without specific targets. To have an idea of the percentage of one or the other possibility, the following question can be asked:

In your opinion, what is the targeted SI/non-targeted SI ratio? (in terms of time for example):

0/100	❏	20/80	❏	40/60	❏	50/50	❏
60/40	❏	80/20	❏	100/0	❏		

D. PRIORITIZATION OF SI AXES

Is there prioritization of SI fields (from highest priority to lowest priority)?

0. No	❏	4. Yes	❏	Grade:

E. UPDATING OF INFORMATION NEEDS DETERMINATION

Is there updating of SI fields (from highest priority to lowest priority)?

0. No	❏	4. Yes	❏	Grade:

Explain this frequency:

Daily	❏	weekly	❏	Monthly	❏
Annually	❏	Not often	❏		

What is important is mostly to find out if this updating frequency is sufficient:

Is the level of this frequency:

0. Very bad	❏	1. Bad	❏	2. Average	❏
3. Good	❏	4. Very good	❏	Grade:	

The user's opinion, given in the second questionnaire, is also necessary to confirm the Strategic Intelligence Manager (SIM) notation.

8.2.2. *Information research and collection phase*

In the second phase of the SI process, the information research and collection phase, information sources and the information itself are involved; volume, diversity, quality and control are factors of SI effectiveness.

A. EXISTENCE

Is there an information research and collection phase?

0. No	❏	4. Yes	❏	Grade:

Explain its frequency:

Never	❏	Rarely	❏	Sometimes	❏
Often	❏	Always	❏		

Is the level of this frequency:

0. Very bad	❏	1. Bad	❏	2. Average	❏
3. Good	❏	4. Very good	❏	Grade:	

B. INFORMATION SOURCES

What sources of information are used? Explain their usage frequency.

External formal sources	Never	Rarely	Sometimes	Often	Always
Economic periodicals	❏	❏	❏	❏	❏
Trade press	❏	❏	❏	❏	❏
Books (general non-fiction, encyclopedias, theses, etc.)	❏	❏	❏	❏	❏
Other media (television, cinema, radio)	❏	❏	❏	❏	❏
Data bases and banks, CD-ROMs	❏	❏	❏	❏	❏
Patents	❏	❏	❏	❏	❏
Standards	❏	❏	❏	❏	❏
Private or public studies	❏	❏	❏	❏	❏
Legal sources (chambers of commerce, trade dispute courts, cadastre, mortgages, etc.)	❏	❏	❏	❏	❏
Professional Minitel	❏	❏	❏	❏	❏
The Internet	❏	❏	❏	❏	❏
Other:	❏	❏	❏	❏	❏

Internal formal sources	Never	Rarely	Sometimes	Often	Always
Annual report	❏	❏	❏	❏	❏
The intranet	❏	❏	❏	❏	❏
Other	❏	❏	❏	❏	❏

External informal sources	Never	Rarely	Sometimes	Often	Always
Competitors	❏	❏	❏	❏	❏
Clients	❏	❏	❏	❏	❏
Suppliers	❏	❏	❏	❏	❏
Missions and trips	❏	❏	❏	❏	❏
Exhibitions, shows, trade shows	❏	❏	❏	❏	❏
Colloquiums, conventions, seminars	❏	❏	❏	❏	❏
Professional associations	❏	❏	❏	❏	❏
Temporary personnel, interns, students	❏	❏	❏	❏	❏
Recruitment candidates	❏	❏	❏	❏	❏
External providers in watch and intelligence (firms, consultants)	❏	❏	❏	❏	❏
Research centers, universities	❏	❏	❏	❏	❏
Financial analysts	❏	❏	❏	❏	❏
Other:	❏	❏	❏	❏	❏

Internal informal sources	Never	Rarely	Sometimes	Often	Always
Upper Management	❏	❏	❏	❏	❏
Marketing department	❏	❏	❏	❏	❏
Sales (Salespeople)	❏	❏	❏	❏	❏
Purchasing	❏	❏	❏	❏	❏
Research and Development	❏	❏	❏	❏	❏
Legal	❏	❏	❏	❏	❏
Information	❏	❏	❏	❏	❏
Other:	❏	❏	❏	❏	❏

The questions involving information sources were built from a dual criteria typology (formal/informal, internal/external) which seems to complicate the respondent's job. The ambiguity connected to the criterion of source formalization mandates that the respondent only propose one typology based on the location of sources in relation to the company, i.e. on the internal/external dichotomy.

1. THE QUANTITY OF SOURCES OF INFORMATION

Based on the previous elements, evaluate the quantity of sources of information used:

0. Very low	❏	1. Low	❏	2. Average	❏
3. High	❏	4. Very high	❏	Grade:	

2. THE DIVERSITY OF SOURCES OF INFORMATION

Based on the previous elements, evaluate the diversity of sources of information used:

0. Very low	❏	1. Low	❏	2. Average	❏
3. High	❏	4. Very high	❏	Grade:	

3. THE QUALITY OF SOURCES OF INFORMATION

Globally, evaluate the quality of sources of information used:

0. Very low	❏	1. Low	❏	2. Average	❏
3. Good	❏	4. Excellent	❏	Grade:	

4. THE EVALUATION OF SOURCES OF INFORMATION

a. EXISTENCE

Is there an evaluation procedure for sources of information?

0. No	❏	4. Yes	❏	Grade:

Explain its frequency

Never	❏	Rarely	❏	Sometimes	❏
Often	❏	Always	❏		

b. CRITERIA OF EVALUATION

From which element(s) is the evaluation of the source done?

	Never	Rarely	Sometimes	Often	Always
On its reliability (secure)	❏	❏	❏	❏	❏
On its wealth	❏	❏	❏	❏	❏
On its performance over time	❏	❏	❏	❏	❏
On its vulnerability	❏	❏	❏	❏	❏
On its discretion (its scarcity)	❏	❏	❏	❏	❏
Its freshness	❏	❏	❏	❏	❏
Its delay	❏	❏	❏	❏	❏
Other:	❏	❏	❏	❏	❏

It is difficult to explain the frequency corresponding to each evaluation criterion proposed. That is why we can simply check the boxes relative to each criterion evaluated. For a detailed evaluation, the frequency scale makes it possible to visualize the criteria on which we should improve.

c. THE EVALUATOR

When the verification is completed, it is done:

	Never	Rarely	Sometimes	Often	Always
By the initial collector (i.e. the person who collected the information)	❏	❏	❏	❏	❏
By an internal expert	❏	❏	❏	❏	❏
By a member of the internal network	❏	❏	❏	❏	❏
By one of the members of the SI entity	❏	❏	❏	❏	❏
By the SI manager	❏	❏	❏	❏	❏
Other:	❏	❏	❏	❏	❏

C. COLLECTED INFORMATION

1. THE VOLUME OF INFORMATION COLLECTED

Evaluate the volume of information collected:

0. Very low	❏	1. Low	❏	2. Average	❏
3. High	❏	4. Very high	❏	Grade:	

2. THE DIVERSITY OF INFORMATION COLLECTED

Evaluate the diversity of information collected:

0. Very low	❏	1. Low	❏	2. Average	❏
3. High	❏	4. Very high	❏	Grade:	

3. THE QUALITY OF INFORMATION COLLECTED

Globally, evaluate the quality of information collected:

0. Very low	❏	1. Low	❏	2. Average	❏
3. Good	❏	4. Excellent	❏	Grade:	

4. THE EVALUATION OF INFORMATION COLLECTED

a. EXISTENCE

Is there an evaluation procedure for information collected?

0. No	❏	4. Yes	❏	Grade:

Explain its frequency

Never	❏	Rarely	❏	Sometimes	❏
Often	❏	Always	❏		

b. CRITERIA OF EVALUATION

From which element(s) is the verification of the source done?

	Never	Rarely	Sometimes	Often	Always
On its validity (is it real?)	❏	❏	❏	❏	❏
On its relevance	❏	❏	❏	❏	❏
On its discretion (its scarcity)	❏	❏	❏	❏	❏
On its importance, usefulness	❏	❏	❏	❏	❏
Other:	❏	❏	❏	❏	❏

c. The evaluator

When the verification is completed, it is done:

	Never	Rarely	Sometimes	Often	Always
By the initial collector (i.e. the person who collected the information)	❏	❏	❏	❏	❏
By an internal expert	❏	❏	❏	❏	❏
By a member of the internal network	❏	❏	❏	❏	❏
By one of the members of the SI entity	❏	❏	❏	❏	❏
By the SI manager	❏	❏	❏	❏	❏

The recipient users may notice an error in the distributed information. They then return the information. In this regard, their feedback is also part of the quality of information

8.2.3. *Information processing phase*

The information processing phase is vital. At this level, the analysis methods used, the planning horizon, major players and the types of SI productions provided can be studied. This part of the study is the time to verify if we have watch or intelligence.

A. Existence

Is there an analysis and synthesis phase of information collected?

0. No	❏	4. Yes	❏	Grade:

Explain its frequency:

Never	❏	Rarely	❏	Sometimes	❏
Often	❏	Always	❏		

Is the level of this frequency:

0. Very low	❏	1. Low	❏	2. Average	❏
3. Good	❏	4. Very good	❏	Grade:	

Is there a formatting phase for the information processed?

0. No	❏	4. Yes	❏	Grade:

Explain its frequency:

Never	❏	Rarely	❏	Sometimes	❏
Often	❏	Always	❏		

Is the level of this frequency:

0. Very low	❏	1. Low	❏	2. Average	❏
3. Good	❏	4. Very good	❏	Grade:	

B. THE ANALYSIS METHODS USED

What methods of analysis are used?

	Never	Rarely	Sometimes	Often	Always
Bibliometrics	❏	❏	❏	❏	❏
Past data extrapolation	❏	❏	❏	❏	❏
Expert opinions (Delphi type)	❏	❏	❏	❏	❏
Method of scenarios	❏	❏	❏	❏	❏
Strategic analysis methods (SWOT, BCG, etc.)	❏	❏	❏	❏	❏
Specific SI methods	❏	❏	❏	❏	❏
Segmentations, factor analyses	❏	❏	❏	❏	❏
Other	❏	❏	❏	❏	❏

C. HORIZON OF PLANNING CARRIED OUT

Indicate the temporal horizon of planning carried out in the company:

No planning	❏	1 year	❏	3 years	❏
5 years	❏	10 years	❏		

D. THE PLAYERS

Who carries out the analysis and synthesis of information?

	Never	Rarely	Sometimes	Often	Always
The initial collector (i.e. the person who collected the information)	❏	❏	❏	❏	❏
An internal expert	❏	❏	❏	❏	❏
Members of the SI entity	❏	❏	❏	❏	❏
The SI manager	❏	❏	❏	❏	❏

Who carries out the formatting of the processed information?

	Never	Rarely	Sometimes	Often	Always
The initial collector (i.e. the person who collected the information)	❏	❏	❏	❏	❏
An internal expert	❏	❏	❏	❏	❏
Members of the SI entity	❏	❏	❏	❏	❏
The SI manager	❏	❏	❏	❏	❏

E. OUTPUT

1. NATURE

Name the types of product from the SI department

	Never	Rarely	Sometimes	Often	Always
Press reviews	❏	❏	❏	❏	❏
Competitive monographic publications	❏	❏	❏	❏	❏
Monographic publications on specific terms	❏	❏	❏	❏	❏
Newsletters	❏	❏	❏	❏	❏
Alerts	❏	❏	❏	❏	❏
Report of findings	❏	❏	❏	❏	❏
Syntheses	❏	❏	❏	❏	❏
Databases	❏	❏	❏	❏	❏
Competitive financial results	❏	❏	❏	❏	❏
Survey results	❏	❏	❏	❏	❏
Other:	❏	❏	❏	❏	❏

2. FREQUENCY OF UPDATES

Indicate the frequency of updates of products from the SI entity:

Every day	❏	Every week	❏	Every month	❏
Every year	❏	Less frequently	❏		

The scope of the question involving updates is not suitable for all products. For those done when the updating is justified, for example, there is no corresponding method. In addition, since updates are variable, it is therefore necessary to repeat the question for each product. The following table explains the updates of the different products. It may be interesting for SIM to also note if the frequency is sufficient or insufficient.

	Frequency of updates	Insufficient	Sufficient
Press reviews		❏	❏
Competitive monographic publications **Monographic publications on specific terms**		❏	❏
Newsletters		❏	❏
Alerts **Report of findings**		❏	❏
Syntheses		❏	❏
Databases **Competitive financial results**		❏	❏
Survey results		❏	❏
Other:		❏	❏

F. WATCH OR INTELLIGENCE?

Do the products of surveillance include recommendations for the recipient?

Never	❏	Rarely	❏	Sometimes	❏
Often	❏	Always	❏		

The goal of this question is to verify if the company "stops" at the watch, or if it goes farther by practicing intelligence.

8.2.4. *Storage phase*

The storage phase is important because it is involved in the construction of the organizational memory, and opens the possibility of using background information and evolutionary analyses.

Questions of storage documents (hard copy or e-copy) and accessibility can be raised at this level. Access to stored information, even if controlled, is an obvious factor of effectiveness. An inaccessible SI is not used, therefore inefficient.

A. EXISTENCE

Is there a storage phase for the information collected?

0. No	❏	4. Yes	❏	Grade:

Explain its frequency:

Never	❏	Rarely	❏	Sometimes	❏
Often	❏	Always	❏		

Is the level of this frequency:

0. Very low	❏	1. Low	❏	2. Average	❏
3. Good	❏	4. Very good	❏	Grade:	

Is there a storage phase for the information processed?

0. No	❏	4. Yes	❏	Grade:

Explain its frequency:

Never	❏	Rarely	❏	Sometimes	❏
Often	❏	Always	❏		

Is the level of this frequency:

0. Very low	❏	1. Low	❏	2. Average	❏
3. Good	❏	4. Very good	❏	Grade:	

B. STORAGE DOCUMENTS

What storage documents are used?

Paper	❏	Electronic	❏	Other:

C. ACCESS TO STORED INFORMATION

What is the degree of ease of access to stored information (raw and processed)?

0. No access	❏	1. Difficult	❏	2. Average	❏
3. Easy	❏	4. Very easy	❏	Grade:	

8.2.5. *Distribution phase*

The distribution phase addresses the recipients (or SI clients), the coverage, methods and, especially, the quality of distribution. In order to be efficient, SI output must be distributed to the right recipients at the right times.

A. EXISTENCE

Is there a distribution phase for the information processed?

0. No	❏	4. Yes	❏	Grade:

Explain its frequency:

Never	❏	Rarely	❏	Sometimes	❏
Often	❏	Always	❏		

Is the level of this frequency:

0. Very low	❏	1. Low	❏	2. Average	❏
3. Good	❏	4. Very good	❏	Grade:	

B. DISTRIBUTION RECIPIENTS

Name the recipients of products from the SI department

	Never	Rarely	Sometimes	Often	Always
Upper Management (of the company)	❏	❏	❏	❏	❏
Strategy	❏	❏	❏	❏	❏
Marketing	❏	❏	❏	❏	❏
Sales (Salespeople)	❏	❏	❏	❏	❏
Purchasing	❏	❏	❏	❏	❏
Research & Development	❏	❏	❏	❏	❏
Finance	❏	❏	❏	❏	❏
Human Resources	❏	❏	❏	❏	❏
Legal	❏	❏	❏	❏	❏
Information	❏	❏	❏	❏	❏
Other:	❏	❏	❏	❏	❏

C. DISTRIBUTION COVERAGE

What is the coverage of distribution?

Very restricted	❏	Restricted	❏	Average	❏
Wide	❏	Very wide	❏		

D. QUALITY OF DISTRIBUTION

In your opinion, what is the quality of distribution in terms of appropriateness for the recipient?

0.	Largely insufficient	❏	1.	Insufficient	❏
2.	Average	❏	3.	Good	❏
4.	Very good	❏	Grade:		

In general, distribution is done:

0. Late	❏	4. On time	❏	Grade:

In your opinion, what is the quality of distribution in terms of time of distribution?

0.	Largely insufficient	❏	1.	Insufficient	❏
2.	Average	❏	3.	Good	❏
4.	Very good	❏	Grade:		

E. DISTRIBUTION METHODS

What methods of distribution are used?

Paper	❏	Electronic	❏
Oral	❏	Other:	

It is possible to associate a frequency scale to this question.

What methods of distribution are used?

	Never	Rarely	Sometimes	Often	Always
Paper	❏	❏	❏	❏	❏
Electronic	❏	❏	❏	❏	❏
Oral presentations, projections, meetings	❏	❏	❏	❏	❏
Other:	❏	❏	❏	❏	❏

8.2.6. *SI use phase*

Using SI is fundamental. SI may well function and be under the best conditions possible, but if it is not used, it will not be effective.

This theme is found in both questionnaires (for the manager and user of SI). Using SI and the connection between SIM and the SIU are factors of SI effectiveness.

A. USING SI

Is information from SI used in strategic decision making?

Never	❏	Rarely	❏	Sometimes	❏
Often	❏	Always	❏		

Measuring the use of SI is very difficult. The *Intelligence Manager* may not know if the products of SI are used in the strategic decision of the recipient. In addition, information resulting from the intelligence activity is not always used in strategic decisions. Other elements occur in the decision process, such as personal knowledge of the market, financial elements and subjective perception of managers. SWI is not only used for supporting decisions. The anticipation of threats and opportunities and the improvement of general knowledge of the corporate environment are other examples of objectives that it must serve.

B. THE SI–STRATEGY CONNECTION

Is there a link between the SI manager (SIM) and the SI user (SIU)?

0. No	❏	4. Yes	❏	Grade:

What is the frequency of exchanges between the SIM and SIU?

Every day	❏	Every week	❏	Every month	❏
Every year	❏	Less frequently	❏		

Understanding the different uses of the products of SI by recipients is therefore very useful information for the SI manager that only a feedback phase can provide.

8.2.7. *Feedback phase*

The feedback phase is important on many levels. It verifies the use and usefulness of SI, its correct distribution, quality, etc.

A. EXISTENCE

Is there a feedback (return) phase for the distributed information?

0. No	❏	4. Yes	❏	Grade:

Explain this frequency:

Never	❏	Rarely	❏	Sometimes	❏
Often	❏	Always	❏		

Is the level of this frequency:

0. Very bad	❏	1. Bad	❏	2. Average	❏
3. Good	❏	4. Very good	❏	Grade:	

B. NATURE OF THE FEEDBACK

When there is a return, recipient comments include:

	Never	Rarely	Sometimes	Often	Always
On the usefulness of information received	❏	❏	❏	❏	❏
On the relevance of the recipient	❏	❏	❏	❏	❏
On the use of information received	❏	❏	❏	❏	❏
Other:	❏	❏	❏	❏	❏

8.2.8. *SI evaluation and control phase*

A. EXISTENCE

Is there an SI evaluation and control phase?

0. No	❏	4. Yes	❏	Grade:

Explain this frequency:

Never	❏	Rarely	❏	Sometimes	❏
Often	❏	Always	❏		

Is the level of this frequency:

0. Very bad	❑	1. Bad	❑	2. Average	❑
3. Good	❑	4. Very good	❑	Grade:	

Is there an SI control panel?

0. No	❑	4. Yes	❑	Grade:

8.3. Human methods

The perceived importance and usefulness of SI by the personnel and management, the support for it, the existence and skills of the SI managers as well as a collective culture of information sharing are all factors of human SI effectiveness.

8.3.1. *Perception of SI by personnel and management*

The SIM may have an opinion and/or use survey results on these variables to evaluate them.

What is the level of perceived importance and usefulness of SI by personnel?

0. Very low	❑	1. Low	❑	2. Average	❑
3. High	❑	4. Very high	❑	Grade:	

What is the level of perceived importance and usefulness of SI by management?

0. Very low	❑	1. Low	❑	2. Average	❑
3. High	❑	4. Very high	❑	Grade:	

8.3.2. *Support and involvement of upper management*

An objective evaluation is also difficult to obtain at this level. The SIM's inclusion in the executive committee and the hierarchical position of SI are indicators of the level of management involvement.

Is the Strategic Watch Intelligence Manager (SWIM) a member of the Executive Committee?

0. No	❏	4. Yes	❏	Grade:

What is the degree of support from management for SI activity?

0. Non-existent	❏	1. Low	❏	2. Average	❏
3. Strong	❏	4. Very strong	❏	Note:	

8.3.3. *The existence of the SI manager*

Is there an SI manager?

0. No	❏	4. Yes	❏	Grade:

8.3.4. *SIM attributes*

A. ATTRIBUTES LINKED TO TRAINING, EXPERIENCE AND SKILLS

1. THE ORIGIN OF SIM

What is the origin of the SWIM?

Internal recruiting	❏	External recruiting	❏

2. SIM TRAINING

What training does the SIM have?

Humanities	❏	Economy	❏	Management	❏
Engineering	❏	Other:			

What level of training does the SIM have?

0. None	❏	1. High school graduate	❏
2. College graduate	❏	3. Undergraduate studies	❏
4. Master's	❏	Grade:	

3. The experience of SIM

What is the level of professional seniority of the SIM (total active time life?

0. Less than 2 years	❏	1. From 2 to 4 years	❏
2. From 5 to 10 years	❏	3. From 11 to 20 years	❏
4. Over 20 years	❏	Grade:	

4. SIM skills

	0	1	2	3	4	
What aptitudes does the SIM have for:	Very Low	Low	Average	High	Very High	**Note**
Understanding information needs	❏	❏	❏	❏	❏	
Researching and collecting information	❏	❏	❏	❏	❏	
Analyzing and synthesizing information	❏	❏	❏	❏	❏	
Formatting information Produce recommendations	❏	❏	❏	❏	❏	
Communicating	❏	❏	❏	❏	❏	
Other	❏	❏	❏	❏	❏	

It is obviously tricky to directly ask these questions on skills and human qualities of corporate intelligence professionals, usually involving the Human Resources department. In addition, self-evaluation would have very little credibility. A compromise must be found to evaluate this important component of the questionnaire.

It is possible to replace the terms low/high by insufficient/good in the scale of the question. After the evaluation of each skill, the following global question may be asked:

Based on the training, experience and skills of the SWIM, globally evaluate the quality of the SIM:

0.	Largely insufficient	❏	1.	Insufficient	❏
2.	Average	❏	3.	Good	❏
4.	Very good	❏	Grade:		

B. Human qualities of the SIM

Curiosity and open-mindedness are two of the many qualities that an SI manager must possess. The respondent is invited to list them and to complete the list.

What are the human qualities of the SIM? (Check the corresponding boxes and complete)

Curiosity	❏	Open-mindedness	❏	Other:

Based on the elements in the previous response, globally evaluate the human qualities of the SWIM:

0.	Largely insufficient	❏	1.	Insufficient	❏
2.	Average	❏	3.	Good	❏
4.	Very good	❏	Grade:		

8.3.5. *The quality of SI professionals*

The same methodology can apply to each SI professional.

A. Attributes linked to training, experience and skills

1. The origin

What is the origin of the members of the SI networks?

Internal recruiting	❏	External recruiting	❏

2. Training

What training does the SI professional have?

Humanities	❏	Economy	❏	Management	❏
Engineering	❏	Other:			

What level of training does the SI professional have?

0. None	❏	1. High school graduate	❏
2. College graduate	❏	3. Undergraduate studies	❏
4. Master's	❏	Grade:	

3. EXPERIENCE

What is the training seniority of the SI professional?

0. Less than 2 years	❏	1. From 2 to 4 years	❏
2. From 5 to 10 years	❏	3. From 11 to 20 years	❏
4. Over 20 years	❏	Note:	

4. SKILLS OF SI PROFESSIONALS

	0	1	2	3	4	
Globally, what are the aptitudes of the members of the SI network for:	Very Low	Low	Average	High	Very High	Grade
Understanding information needs	❏	❏	❏	❏	❏	
Researching and collecting information	❏	❏	❏	❏	❏	
Analyzing and synthesizing information	❏	❏	❏	❏	❏	
Formatting information	❏	❏	❏	❏	❏	
Produce recommendations	❏	❏	❏	❏	❏	
Communicating	❏	❏	❏	❏	❏	
Other:	❏	❏	❏	❏	❏	

The SIM may, here again, have problems evaluating his own team. He may, for example, give a global evaluation and/or indicate strong/weak points of each member on each quality listed.

B. HUMAN QUALITIES OF SI PROFESSIONALS

Awareness and motivation are two of the qualities that SI professionals must possess. The respondent is also invited to complete the list.

What are the human qualities of the intelligence professionals? (Check the corresponding boxes and complete)

Awareness	❏	Motivation	❏	Other:

What degree of awareness to SI networks do SI participants have?

0. No awareness	❏	1. Low	❏	2. Average	❏
3. High	❏	4. Very high	❏		

What is the degree of motivation of SI network members?

0. Very low	❏	1. Low	❏	2. Average	❏
3. High	❏	4. Very high	❏	Grade:	

Based on the elements in the previous response, globally evaluate the human qualities of the SI professionals:

0.	Largely insufficient	❏	1.	Insufficient	❏
2.	Average	❏	3.	Good	❏
4.	Very good	❏	Grade:		

The questions concerning the SIM and the SI professionals may be extended to other members of the SI networks evaluated.

8.3.6. *Culture of the corporation*

The position of the SIM gives him the possibility of verifying that the information circulates correctly in the company.

Does your company have a collective culture of information sharing? Is it:

0. Very low	❏	1. Low	❏	2. Average	❏
3. High	❏	4. Very high	❏	Grade:	

8.4. Technical methods

The diversity and quality of technical tools used in the practice of SI are vital for its effectiveness.

8.4.1. *The nature of technical tools used*

A. INFORMATION RESEARCH AND COLLECTION TOOLS

What tools are used in information research and collection?

	Never	Rarely	Sometimes	Often	Always
Internet	❑	❑	❑	❑	❑
Online databases	❑	❑	❑	❑	❑
CD ROM	❑	❑	❑	❑	❑
Intranet	❑	❑	❑	❑	❑
Other:	❑	❑	❑	❑	❑

What Internet search engines are used the most?

....

B. INFORMATION PROCESSING TOOLS

What information processing tools are used?

	Never	Rarely	Sometimes	Often	Always
Quantitative data analysis software:	❑	❑	❑	❑	❑
Qualitative data analysis software:	❑	❑	❑	❑	❑
Other:	❑	❑	❑	❑	❑

C. INFORMATION STORAGE TOOLS

What information storage tools are used?

	Never	Rarely	Sometimes	Often	Always
Manually	❑	❑	❑	❑	❑
Software packages	❑	❑	❑	❑	❑
Other:	❑	❑	❑	❑	❑

D. INFORMATION DISTRIBUTION AND COMMUNICATION TOOLS

What tools are used for information distribution and communication?

	Never	Rarely	Sometimes	Often	Always
Paper	❑	❑	❑	❑	❑
Orally	❑	❑	❑	❑	❑
Email	❑	❑	❑	❑	❑
Other:	❑	❑	❑	❑	❑

8.4.2. *The diversity of the technical tools used*

Based on the elements in the previous response, evaluate the diversity of tools used:

0. Very low	❑	1. Low	❑	2. Average	❑
3. High	❑	4. Very high	❑	Note:	

8.4.3. *The quality of technical tools used*

Based on the elements in the previous response, evaluate the quality of the tools used:

0.	Largely insufficient	❏	1.	Insufficient	❏
2.	Average	❏	3.	Good	❏
4.	Very good	❏	Grade:		

8.5. Financial methods

Two factors of effectiveness clearly appear for financial SI methods: the characteristic of the SI budget and its appropriateness to the needs of the company.

8.5.1. *The SI budget*

Is there a budget for SI in your company?

0. No	❏	4. Yes	❏	Note:

What is the amount of this specific budget?

....

In the following table, indicate the annual budget amounts corresponding to the workforce, technical equipment, information resources, etc. dedicated to SI:

Workforce	❏	Technical	❏
Information	❏	Other expense accounts	❏

8.5.2. *Budget appropriateness to the needs of SI*

In relation to SI needs, indicate the level of appropriateness of the budget:

0. Very low	❏	1. Low	❏	2. Average	❏
3. Good	❏	4. Excellent	❏	Note:	

8.6. The SI context

The section dedicated to the SI context can be found either in the questionnaire aimed at the SI manager or in the one for the SI user. It may also be interesting to include it in both for comparison. Its goal is to describe the environment and characteristics of the company.

8.6.1. *Corporate environment*

The goal for the first part of this section is to define the degree of instability, complexity and competitive intensity of the corporate environment. The more unstable, complex and competitive the environment, the higher the importance of implementing or practicing efficient SI.

A. INSTABILITY OF THE ENVIRONMENT

Globally, the environment in which the company is evolving is:

Very stable	❏	Stable	❏	Somewhat stable	❏
Unstable	❏	Very unstable	❏		

(In a very unstable environment, changes occur more frequently)

B. COMPLEXITY OF THE ENVIRONMENT

Globally, the environment in which the company evolves is:

Very simple	❏	Simple	❏	Somewhat simple	❏
Complex	❏	Very complex	❏		

(In a very complex environment, players and exchanges are abundant)

C. COMPETITIVE INTENSITY

Globally, the environment in which the company evolves is:

Not competitive	❏	Not very competitive	❏
Somewhat competitive	❏	Competitive	❏
Very competitive	❏		

(In a very competitive environment, there are many competitors and they engage in fierce battles)

Is the competition:

Regional	❏	National	❏
European	❏	Worldwide	❏

Evaluate the competitive aggressiveness:

0. Very low	❏	1. Low	❏	2. Average	❏
3. High	❏	4. Very high	❏	Grade:	

D. THE SECTOR OF ACTIVITY

What is the main sector of activity of the company?

....

In this sector of activity, it is:

The leader	❏
One of the three main competitors	❏
One of the five main competitors	❏
One of the ten main competitors	❏
Other:	❏

8.6.2. *Corporate characteristics*

The implementation and practice of SI also depends on characteristics of the company such as its size, its organizational structure, its level of international openness and its resources.

A. THE SIZE OF THE COMPANY

What is the total workforce of the company?

....

What is the revenue of the company?

....

B. THE ORGANIZATIONAL STRUCTURE

What is the organizational structure of the company?

Traditional, by function	❏
Divisional by geographical zone or group of countries	❏
Divisional by product	❏
By matrix or project	❏

C. INTERNATIONAL OPENNESS

The company is:

An autonomous company	❏
The subsidiary of a French group or company	❏
The subsidiary of a foreign group or company	❏

In the latter case, in what country is the head office:

....

What is its export revenue percentage?

From 0 to 20%	❏	From 20 to 40%	❏
From 40 to 60%	❏	From 60 to 80%	❏
From 80 to 100%	❏		

D. THE RESULTS

Evaluate the financial results of the company in the last three years (choose one per year)

Significant losses (higher than 5% of Revenue)	❏
Losses (less than 5% of Revenue)	❏
Profits (between 0 and 5% of Revenue)	❏
Significant profits (between 5 and 10% of Revenue)	❏
Very significant profits (higher than 10% of Revenue)	❏

The main results of the questionnaire can be copied into the following evaluation grid. With this tool, the SIM can evaluate the performance of the methods implemented in SI by adding the total points obtained in each element evaluated.

This evaluation grid will enable him to build an SI control panel (SICP) from a limited number of indicators that he will have carefully chosen to follow an SI operation.

Evaluation grid of SI methods

ORGANIZATIONAL METHODS					
SI Organization	0	1	2	3	4
1. A certain degree of SI formalization					
2. A certain degree of SI seniority					
3. High or somewhat high hierarchical ranking of SI					
4. A network organizational structure					
5. Diversity of SI networks					
6. Activity of SI networks					
7. Maintenance of SI network					
8. The existence of internal groups of experts					
Total					

PROCESSUAL METHODS					
SI Process	0	1	2	3	4
1. The existence phase of determination of information needs					
2. The existence of SI that is wide enough and target at the same time					
3. Prioritization of SI axes					
4. Updating of information needs					
5. The existence of a phase of information research and collection					
6. Quantity of information sources					
7. Diversity of information sources					
8. Quality of information sources					
9. The existence of an evaluation of information sources					
10. Volume of information					
11. Diversity of information					
12. Quality of information					
13. The existence of information evaluation					
14. The existence of a phase of information analysis and synthesis					
15. The existence of a phase of information formatting					
16. The existence of a phase of collected and processed information storage					
17. Accessibility of stored information					
18. The existence of a phase of information distribution					
19. Appropriateness to recipients					
20. Distribution opportunity					
21. The use of SI products in strategic decision					
22. The existence of a connection between Intelligence and Strategy functions (user)					
23. The existence of a phase of distributed information feedback					
24. The existence of a phase of SI evaluation and control					
Total					

HUMAN METHODS					
Human Resources	0	1	2	3	4
1. The perceived importance and usefulness by the personnel					
2. The perceived importance and usefulness by management					
3. Support and involvement of upper management					
4. The existence of an SI manager (SIM)					
5. Qualities of the SIM linked to his history (training, skill, experience, etc.)					
6. "Human" qualities of the SIM (curiosity, ability to convince, etc.)					
7. Qualities of SI professionals linked to their history (training, skill, experience, etc)					
8. "Human" qualities of SI professionals (curiosity, motivation, etc.)					
9. The existence of a collective information sharing culture					
Total					

TECHNICAL METHODS					
Technical Resources	0	1	2	3	4
1. Diversity of technical tools used in SI					
2. Quality of technical tools used in SI					
Total					

FINANCIAL METHODS					
Finanical Resources	0	1	2	3	4
1. The existence of a budget dedicated to SI					
2. The existence of an appropriate budget for corporate SI objectives					
Total					

Grand total	

Chapter 9

Measurement Tools
for SI Users

This chapter deals with the three other objects of model measurement: the product (information), the use, and SI results (including its impact on corporate performance). It leads to the development of a measuring tool for these three objects, aimed at SI users, particularly executives and strategy managers. This tool will help develop a control panel for controlling both corporate intelligence and performance.

9.1. SI product and services

At user satisfaction level, the measurement corresponds to the quality of information and functions provided by the SI system.

As with the preceding questionnaire, a grade is given for each evaluation question.

9.1.1. *Level of user satisfaction on information quality*

In terms of quality of information, the result relates to completeness, absence of noise, precision, respect of time constraints (timeliness/topicality), reliability, form and accessibility of the information.

Globally, what is your degree of satisfaction on the next dimensions of information quality provided by the SI entity that you use in the company?

Completeness of information:

0. Not satisfied at all	❏	1. Not satisfied	❏
2. Somewhat satisfied	❏	3. Satisfied	❏
4. Very satisfied	❏	Note:	

The degree of useful information (i.e. absence of noise, absence of useless information):

0. Not satisfied at all	❏	1. Not satisfied	❏
2. Somewhat satisfied	❏	3. Satisfied	❏
4. Very satisfied	❏	Note:	

Information precision:

0. Not satisfied at all	❏	1. Not satisfied	❏
2. Somewhat satisfied	❏	3. Satisfied	❏
4. Very satisfied	❏	Note:	

RESPECT FOR TIME CONSTRAINTS

Delay of information distribution (i.e. obtaining information at the appropriate time):

0. Not satisfied at all	❏	1. Not satisfied	❏
2. Somewhat satisfied	❏	3. Satisfied	❏
4. Very satisfied	❏	Note:	

The degree of information topicality (i.e. freshness):

0. Not satisfied at all	❏	1. Not satisfied	❏
2. Somewhat satisfied	❏	3. Satisfied	❏
4. Very satisfied	❏	Note:	

Information reliability:

0. Not satisfied at all	❏	1. Not satisfied	❏
2. Somewhat satisfied	❏	3. Satisfied	❏
4. Very satisfied	❏	Note:	

The form of the information (i.e. information formatting):

0. Not satisfied at all	❏	1. Not satisfied	❏
2. Somewhat satisfied	❏	3. Satisfied	❏
4. Very satisfied	❏	Note:	

Information accessibility:

0. Not satisfied at all	❏	1. Not satisfied	❏
2. Somewhat satisfied	❏	3. Satisfied	❏
4. Very satisfied	❏	Note:	

9.1.2. *The degree of user satisfaction on the quality of services offered*

A. ALLOCATED FUNCTIONS AND THE IMPORTANCE GIVEN TO EACH SI FUNCTION

Each company can assign specific functions to SW or SI as the case may be. They range from the anticipation of threats and opportunities (anticipatory function) to the implementation of an action (proactive function 2) and the main analysis and synthesis functions of the information collected (analytical and synthetic function). The user can give a general degree of importance to these various functions.

What functions are attributed to SI? (check the corresponding box at the beginning of the line).

What importance do you give each function? Answer on a scale from 0: not important at all to 4: very important.

	0	1	2	3	4
❏ 1. Anticipatory function (anticipating environmental threats/opportunities)	0	1	2	3	4
❏ 2. The identification function of your information needs	0	1	2	3	4
❏ 3. The basic information function (providing raw information)	0	1	2	3	4
❏ 4. The analytical function (analyzing information)	0	1	2	3	4
❏ 5. The synthetic function (synthesizing information)	0	1	2	3	4
❏ 6. The information formatting function (formatting information)	0	1	2	3	4
❏ 7. Coordination and communication function (coordinating and communicating information)	0	1	2	3	4
❏ 8. The protective function (protect against obsolescence of know-how, techniques, technologies, etc.)	0	1	2	3	4
❏ 9. The "security" function (protecting against acts of abuse)	0	1	2	3	4
❏ 10. Coordinating function (coordinating decisions and operations)	0	1	2	3	4
❏ 11. Proactive 1 function (make recommendations)	0	1	2	3	4
❏ 12. Proactive 2 function (implementing actions)	0	1	2	3	4
Other:	0	1	2	3	4

B. The degree of satisfaction for functions used

Which functions provided by the SI entity do you use? (check the box at the beginning of the line) For each function provided, what is your degree of satisfaction? (check the corresponding box)

❑ *1. The anticipatory function of SI (the anticipation of threats and/or opportunities of the environment):*

0. Not satisfied at all	❑	1. Not satisfied	❑
2. Somewhat satisfied	❑	3. Satisfied	❑
4. Very satisfied	❑	Note:	

❑ *2. The identification function of your information requirements (identification of your information requirements):*

0. Not satisfied at all	❑	1. Not satisfied	❑
2. Somewhat satisfied	❑	3. Satisfied	❑
4. Very satisfied	❑	Note:	

❑ *3. The basic information function (distribution of raw information):*

0. Not satisfied at all	❑	1. Not satisfied	❑
2. Somewhat satisfied	❑	3. Satisfied	❑
4. Very satisfied	❑	Note:	

❑ *4. The analytical function (analysis of information):*

0. Not satisfied at all	❑	1. Not satisfied	❑
2. Somewhat satisfied	❑	3. Satisfied	❑
4. Very satisfied	❑	Note:	

❑ *5. The synthetic function (synthesis of information):*

0. Not satisfied at all	❑	1. Not satisfied	❑
2. Somewhat satisfied	❑	3. Satisfied	❑
4. Very satisfied	❑	Note:	

❑ *6. The information formatting function (formatting information):*

0. Not satisfied at all	❑	1. Not satisfied	❑
2. Somewhat satisfied	❑	3. Satisfied	❑
4. Very satisfied	❑	Note:	

❑ *7. The coordination and communication function (the coordination and communication of information):*

0. Not satisfied at all	❑	1. Not satisfied	❑
2. Somewhat satisfied	❑	3. Satisfied	❑
4. Very satisfied	❑	Note:	

❑ *8. The protective function (protection against obsolescence of know how, techniques, technologies, etc.):*

0. Not satisfied at all	❑	1. Not satisfied	❑
2. Somewhat satisfied	❑	3. Satisfied	❑
4. Very satisfied	❑	Note:	

❑ *9. The security function (protection against abusive acts for example):*

0. Not satisfied at all	❑	1. Not satisfied	❑
2. Somewhat satisfied	❑	3. Satisfied	❑
4. Very satisfied	❑	Note:	

❑ *10. The coordinating function (coordination):*

0. Not satisfied at all	❑	1. Not satisfied	❑
2. Somewhat satisfied	❑	3. Satisfied	❑
4. Very satisfied	❑	Note:	

❑ *11. Proactive function 1 (making recommendations):*

0. Not satisfied at all	❑	1. Not satisfied	❑
2. Somewhat satisfied	❑	3. Satisfied	❑
4. Very satisfied	❑	Note:	

❑ *12. Proactive function 2 (implementing actions):*

0. Not satisfied at all	❑	1. Not satisfied	❑
2. Somewhat satisfied	❑	3. Satisfied	❑
4. Very satisfied	❑	Note:	

It is interesting to compare the importance given by an SI user to the various missions of intelligence, and his level of satisfaction for each. This intersection indicates that *it is necessary to be good where it counts* (see Detrie, 2001). Figure 9.1 is an example.

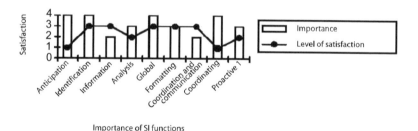

Importance of SI functions

Figure 9.1. *Crossing, importance and satisfaction of SI functions (example)*

The differences between the importance given to the various functions and the satisfaction obtained by each one can clearly be seen. In this example, we note right away the important gap between the anticipatory function and the coordinating function. Expectations and required efforts are predominant on these two levels.

Satisfaction in identification and synthesis functions is good, but must be improved in relation to the level of importance given. It is also very close to the case of analytical and proactive 1 functions.

Basic information function and coordinating and communication function grades exceed the levels of importance indicated, and indirectly, the expectation levels of both points.

Lastly, the grades are exactly the same with SI formatting.

9.2. Using SI

As indicated within the context of the measurement instrument for SI managers, its use is a vital phase in the SI process. SI users are the only ones able to really evaluate the use of SI however.

In this phase, the intelligence–strategy connection and the integration of SI results in the strategic decision are powerful factors of effectiveness.

The measurement of general SI satisfaction can then be completed by measurements relating to the use and frequency of IS solicitation. If the products of SI used can be examined on the intranet, systematic measures of the rate of usage and intensity of the use will be easier.

Some questions concerning the products of SI and the phase of use of the questionnaire intended for SIM can be asked again here.

9.2.1. *Products of SI used*

Indicate your usage frequency of SI service products:

	Infrequently	Annual	Monthly	Weekly	Daily
Press reviews	❏	❏	❏	❏	❏
Competitive monographic publications	❏	❏	❏	❏	❏
Monographic publications on specific topics	❏	❏	❏	❏	❏
Newsletters	❏	❏	❏	❏	❏
Alert notes	❏	❏	❏	❏	❏
Report of findings	❏	❏	❏	❏	❏
Syntheses	❏	❏	❏	❏	❏
Survey results	❏	❏	❏	❏	❏
Other:	❏	❏	❏	❏	❏

9.2.2. *Watch or intelligence?*

Do the products of SI contain recommendations for the recipient?

Never	❏	Rarely	❏	Sometimes	❏
Often	❏	Always	❏		

The goal of this question is to verify if the company exceeds the watch activity, and effectively practices intelligence.

The next question is more precise:

Among products of SI that you use, how many contain recommendations for the recipient?

0%	❏	Between 0 and 20%	❏
Between 20 and 40%	❏	Between 40 and 60%	❏
More than 60%	❏		

9.2.3. *The connection between intelligence and strategy*

What is the frequency of exchanges (face to face, phone, emails, etc.) between IS manager(s) and the user (i.e. yourself)?

Not often	❏	Daily	❏	Weekly	❏
Monthly	❏	Annually	❏		

In your opinion, the level of this frequency is:

0. Very bad	❏	1. Bad	❏	2. Average	❏
3. Good	❏	4. Very good	❏	Note:	

9.2.4. *The level of SI integration in the strategic decision*

Globally, what is the influence of SI outputs (i.e. results, products) in your strategic decisions?

Less than 10%	❏	Between 10 and 30%	❏
Between 30 and 50%	❏	Between 50 and 70%	❏
More than 70%	❏		

In your opinion, the level of integration of SI results in the strategic decision process is:

0. Very bad	❏	1. Bad	❏	2. Average	❏
3. Good	❏	4. Very good	❏	Note:	

9.2.5. *General satisfaction with the SI department*

What is your general level of satisfaction with the SI department?

0. Not satisfied at all	❏	1. Not satisfied	❏
2. Somewhat satisfied	❏	3. Satisfied	❏
4. Very satisfied	❏	Note:	

9.2.6. *The rate of use and level of SI solicitation*

In your opinion, what is the rate of SI product use? (number of users/workforce involved)

Less than 10%	❏	Between 10 and 20%	❏
Between 20 and 40%	❏	Between 40 and 60%	❏
More than 60%	❏		

What is the frequency of your use of SI service:

Not often	❏	Daily	❏	weekly	❏
Monthly	❏	Annually	❏		

Is the level of frequency:

0. Very bad	❏	1. Bad	❏	2. Average	❏
3. Good	❏	4. Very good	❏	Note:	

9.3. SI results: the intelligence–performance control panel

The measure involving this major model object mainly consists of evaluating the effectiveness of the SI itself, its impact on the performance of the organization, and its efficiency.

At this level, we propose to design and use a prospective combined intelligence–performance control panel, from the prospective control panel created by Kaplan and Norton in 1992.

The evaluation of SI effectiveness and its impact on corporate performance is only possible if, and only if, clear objectives, preferably quantified, are given to SI, and if they are aligned with the performance objectives of the organization. If these conditions are not observed, only qualitative, thus subjective, findings can be given by users on results obtained by SI. The rare studies addressing this topic only provide elements of this nature.

SI must, indeed, serve the strategic objectives of the company. To evaluate its effectiveness and impact, it is mandatory to connect intelligence, strategy and performance within a double prospective control panel.

9.3.1. *The measure of SI effectiveness*

The actual measure of SI effectiveness comes down to comparing the results obtained with initial objectives set. It requires a preliminary definition specific to the objectives of intelligence.

A. REACHING THE THREE FUNDAMENTAL SI OBJECTIVES

SI must satisfy three main objectives: anticipating the threats and opportunities of the corporate environment, satisfying the requirements in information for the user and creating strategic decision support.

1. Importance given to the three general SI objectives

As discussed previously, finding out the importance given to these three major SI objectives and the satisfaction of the user in the corresponding results is interesting.

What importance do you give the three following objectives, generally assigned to SI:

	Not at all important	Not very important	Somewhat important	Important	Very important
Anticipating threats & opportunities of the environment	❑	❑	❑	❑	❑
Satisfying information needs of the user	❑	❑	❑	❑	❑
Decision support	❑	❑	❑	❑	❑

2. Reaching the objective of anticipating threats and opportunities:

What is your degree of satisfaction in SI results that you use in terms of threats and opportunities detection?

0. Not satisfied at all	❑	1. Not satisfied	❑
2. Somewhat satisfied	❑	3. Satisfied	❑
4. Very satisfied	❑	Note:	

Can you give concrete examples of threats and/or opportunities detected by SI which you use:

....

It can be useful to have periodic lists (every year for example) of threats and opportunities detected by SI activity that a manager and/or SI user can update regularly.

3. Reaching the objective of information requirement satisfaction:

What is the importance of your information needs in the different environments of the company?

	Infrequently	Annual	Monthly	Weekly	Daily
Press reviews	❏	❏	❏	❏	❏
Competitive monographic publications	❏	❏	❏	❏	❏
Monographic publications on specific topics	❏	❏	❏	❏	❏
Newsletters	❏	❏	❏	❏	❏
Alert notes	❏	❏	❏	❏	❏
Report of findings	❏	❏	❏	❏	❏
Syntheses	❏	❏	❏	❏	❏
Survey results	❏	❏	❏	❏	❏
Other:	❏	❏	❏	❏	❏

Does the SI that you use satisfy your information needs? Indicate this level of satisfaction.

0. Not satisfied at all	❏	1. Not satisfied	❏
2. Somewhat satisfied	❏	3. Satisfied	❏
4. Very satisfied	❏	Note:	

This question can be global or used in each environment involved.

4. Reaching the decision support objective

From the information obtained with the SI, what type of decisions have you made?

	Never	1 time	2-5 times	5-10 times	More than 10 times
Project launching	❏	❏	❏	❏	❏
Project stop	❏	❏	❏	❏	❏
Project reorientation	❏	❏	❏	❏	❏
New product launch	❏	❏	❏	❏	❏
Penetration in new markets	❏	❏	❏	❏	❏
Choice of new technologies/techniques	❏	❏	❏	❏	❏
Partnership	❏	❏	❏	❏	❏
License agreement	❏	❏	❏	❏	❏
Diversification	❏	❏	❏	❏	❏
Acquisitions	❏	❏	❏	❏	❏
Alliance	❏	❏	❏	❏	❏
Joint-venture	❏	❏	❏	❏	❏
Other:	❏	❏	❏	❏	❏

In this table, the frequencies and items suggested can obviously be adapted to each company.

Indicate your level of satisfaction on decision support provided by the SI which you use:

0. Not satisfied at all	❏	1. Not satisfied	❏
2. Somewhat satisfied	❏	3. Satisfied	❏
4. Very satisfied	❏	Note:	

B. Other identified results, contributions and benefits

Even if the quantitative evaluation is not possible, notably because the objectives were not clearly defined, a qualitative evaluation is, however, possible.

What other results, contributions or benefits from the SI activity have you identified?

Better reactivity	❏
Better crisis management	❏
Better adaptation capacity	❏
Better knowledge of the global corporate environment (competitors, markets, clients, etc.)	❏
Better understanding of plans and actions of competitors	❏
Better communication in the company	❏
Wider open-mindedness in the company	❏
Better strategic choices (less risks of making decision mistakes)	❏
More convenient strategic decisions	❏
Better strategies (innovation successes, diversifications, alliances, etc.)	❏
Better protection of the company	❏
Better coordination in decisions and operations	❏
Better corporate environmental control	❏
Other:	❏

Has the SI activity generated concrete results?

Yes	❏	No	❏

Can you cite concrete results directly or strongly related to the activity of SI?

....

9.3.2. *The evaluation of SI activity impact on corporate performance*

The logic of the Prospective Control Panel (PCP) developed by Kaplan and Norton in 1992 is involved at the level of the questionnaire.

Before presenting the questions relating to the impact of SI on organizational performance and intelligence–performance control panel, we point out the principle of the PCP.

A. THE INTELLIGENCE–PERFOMANCE CONTROL PANEL

a. The Prospective Control Panel (Kaplan and Norton, 1992)

On the basis of the inadequacy report of traditional systems of performance measurement to the current requirements of continuous improvement and innovation of companies, Kaplan and Norton proposed a PCP – a set of measures presenting managers with a quick but complete overview of their business.

This PCP takes into account financial measures, which are the reflection of actions already taken, and operational measures involving client satisfaction, internal processes, innovations and training, which actually involve the performance to come.

The PCP transforms corporate strategic objectives into a coherent series of performance measurements.

Contrary to traditional evaluation systems, which are generally supervised by financial experts, the PCP requires the involvement of top executives, who have a more complete vision of the company and its priorities. Whereas control was at the heart of traditional financial systems, the strategy and the vision are emphasized in the PCP.

In addition, it is a management system able to cause radical changes in critical elements such as products, processes, customers and markets.

Figure 9.2 presents the four PCP axes using the four questions, and proposes answers.

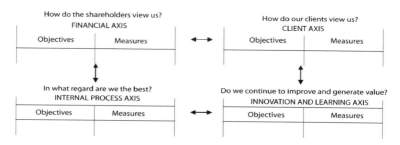

Figure 9.2. *The PCP of Kaplan and Norton*

The following table summarizes the many advantages of the PCP.

THE ADVANTAGES OF THE PROSPECTIVE CONTROL PANEL

By limiting the volume of data required, it avoids overabundance of information and forces the manager to only store the most critical information.

It combines into a single document some very different and important elements for the company.

It is a guard against "under-optimization". The fact of simultaneously taking into account all the most important operational measurements makes it possible to ensure that improvements carried out on one side are not a hindrance to the other.

It helps managers understand many correlations by combining many axes.

It is an integral part of strategy.

The PCP indicators are in direct line with the strategic objectives of the company and its needs for competitiveness.

It helps to concentrate on the strategic vision of the company.

It represents the present and the future of the firm at the same time.

It enables a balance between external and internal indicators.

It is a definition tool for priorities and their communication.

It connects long-term strategy and immediate action.

It reports the progress of the company in its long term plans.

The PCP is not a copy that can be transferred to all companies. Each unit of the company can personalize theirs according to their mission, strategy, technology and culture.

This element of involving management in the development of performance measures is interesting within the context of SI and its impact on performance.

b. The intelligence–performance control panel

There used to be a major barrier to SI effectiveness: the absence of a permanent link between surveillance and strategy. Many problems stemmed from this main dysfunction which caused many barriers to the effectiveness of SI. They are mainly problems:

– in obtaining a return on the use of transmitted information;

– in measuring the effects of SI;

– in defining information needs for executive users;

– in directing information research toward relevant axes;

– in obtaining the support of upper management;

– in communicating the importance and usefulness of SI;

– in motivating the SI specialists, etc.

However, undoubtedly the most serious consequence is the lack of SI use.

We propose aligning SI objectives with corporate strategy objectives with the help of a double intelligence–performance PCP. This table offsets these problems while forcing executives and SI specialists to work towards the same goal. The major advantage of this step is therefore to enable sharing of the vision and strategic objectives of the corporation. It provides research axes for SI specialists, making it possible to provide more useful information to the decision makers and better evaluate the impact of SI on performance.

On the financial axis, the objectives and measurements remain the same. Including them in CP of the SI makes it possible to set the major goals of the company in the minds of the SI players, and helps in making them a reality. In the customer axis, the SI can be oriented towards the watch and intelligence of customers, suppliers, patents, etc., and provide recommendations to improve the rate of new products, punctuality of deliveries, partnerships, etc.

Also, to specifically evaluate the volume of information or recommendations resulting from intelligence and used in the strategic decision, it is imperative to have a measurement and a control of SI. Before the constitution of the intelligence–performance control panel, questions about the impact of SI on corporate performance and the possible indicators of performance related to the activity of SI will be useful.

B. IMPACT RESULTS

In your opinion, what is the impact of SI activity on the performance of your company?

	0. Not at all important	1. Not very important	2. Somewhat important	3. Important	4. Very important
The improvement of your financial performance	❏	❏	❏	❏	❏
The improvement of your competitive position	❏	❏	❏	❏	❏
Cost savings	❏	❏	❏	❏	❏
Budgetary economy	❏	❏	❏	❏	❏
Time savings	❏	❏	❏	❏	❏
Improvement of innovaiton	❏	❏	❏	❏	❏
Increase of your market share	❏	❏	❏	❏	❏
Contribution of new markets	❏	❏	❏	❏	❏
Higher sales volume	❏	❏	❏	❏	❏
Other:	❏	❏	❏	❏	❏

C. EXAMPLE OF IMPACT INDICATORS OF SI ON CORPORATE PERFORMANCE

According to the objectives assigned to SI, which would be the indicator(s) of performance that would best reflect the impact of SI practiced in your company (even if it only involves one contribution)?

FINANCIAL AXIS

Revenue (R)	❏	EVA, RAOI, EBITDA	❏
ROA	❏	Financial results	❏
Operation results/net	❏	Cash flow	❏
Profitability	❏	Return on investment	❏
Export rate	❏	Proposed dividend	❏
Growth of sales, market shares	❏	Other:	❏

CLIENT AXIS

Index of customer satisfaction	❏	New clients	❏
Classification by clients	❏	New markets	❏
Timeliness of deliveries	❏	Other:	❏

INNOVATION AND LEARNING AXIS

Number of new products designed/developed/launched	❏
Product quality	❏
Success rate for new product launch	❏
Production lifecycle	❏
Percentage of new products in the revenue	❏
Improvement rate	❏
New product time to market	❏
Other:	❏

PROCESS AXIS

Unit cost	❏
Performance	❏
Life cycle	❏
Production methods, comparison with competition	❏
Other:	❏

9.3.3. *The measure of efficiency*

The measure of efficiency is also part of the evaluation of results (see the measurement model). The efficiency compares the results obtained with committed financial methods. It is a measure of productivity and profitability. The questions referring to SI costs in the SIM tool are asked once more. They involve the budget corresponding to payroll, technical equipment, various information holdings, etc.

Indicate in the following table the amounts from annual budgets corresponding to workforce, technical equipment and information resources, etc. devoted to SI:

Workforce budget: ....

Technical budget: ....

Information budget: ....

Others expense accounts: ....

The idea then is to compare expenses with actual results and to follow this evolution. This concept of profitability means that the maximum results must be obtained with the minimum expenditures.

9.3.4. *Other user perceptions*

It can be interesting to take advantage of this audit to reveal perceptions of the SI user on the global effectiveness of the IS practiced in the company, in terms of the intelligence–performance link and the importance given to the SI.

A. GLOBAL SI EFFECTIVENESS

SI effectiveness is defined here as the set objectives/results obtained, in the most objective way possible; strategic watch and/or intelligence practiced in your company is:

0. Not efficient at all	❏	1. Not efficient	❏
2. Somewhat efficient	❏	3. Efficient	❏
4. Very efficient	❏		

B. THE SIGNIFICANCE OF THE INTELLIGENCE–PERFORMANCE CONNECTION

Provide your level of agreement with the two following statements: an efficient SI improves global corporate performance:

0. Do not agree at all	❏	3. Somewhat agree	❏
1. Do not agree	❏	4. Totally agree	❏
2. No opinion	❏		

The performance of the organization makes it possible to invest in strategic watch and/or intelligence:

0. Do not agree at all	❏	1. Do not agree	❏
2. No opinion	❏	3. Somewhat agree	❏
4. Totally agree	❏		

C. THE IMPORTANCE GIVEN TO SI

What importance do you give SI?

0. No importance at all	❏	1. Not very important	❏
2. Somewhat important	❏	3. Important	❏
4. Very important	❏		

As in the case of the questionnaire addressed to the SIM, it is possible to produce the following summary evaluation grids:

I. EVALUATION GRID OF SI PRODUCTS AND SERVICES

SATISFACTION ON THE QUALITY OF INFORMATION PROVIDED BY SI					
	0	1	2	3	4
1. Completeness					
2. Level of useful information					
3. Accuracy					
4. Delay of distribution					
5. Level of topicality					
6. Reliability					
7. Form					
8. Accessibility					
Total					

SATISFACTION ON FUNCTIONS ATTRIBUTED TO SI					
	0	1	2	3	4
1. Anticipating					
2. Identification					
3. Informative					
4. Analytical					
5. Global					
6. Formatting					
7. Coordination and communication					
8. Protective					
9. Security					
10. Coordinating					
11. Proactive no. 1					
12. Proactive no. 2					
Total					

II. EVALUATION GRID OF SI USE

EVALUATION OF SI USE					
	0	1	2	3	4
1. Intelligence – Strategy link					
2. Level of SI integration in the decision 3. General SI satisfaction					
4. Rate of usage					
5. Frequency of solicitation					
Total					

III. EVALUATION GRID OF SI RESULTS

EVALUATION OF THE SI DEGREE					
	0	1	2	3	4
Satisfaction on the level of objectives 1. Satisfaction on reaching the objective of threat and opportunity anticipation					
2. Satisfaction on information needs					
3. Satisfaction on reaching the objective of decision support					
Total					

Other identified results, contributions and benefit	❏
Better reactivity	❏
Better crises management	❏
Better capacity of adaptation	❏
Better knowledge of global corporate environment	❏
Better understanding of plans and actions of competitors	❏
Better communication in the company	❏
Better strategic choices (less risks in making decision mistakes)	❏
More convenient strategic decisions	❏
Better strategies (innovation, diversification successes, of alliances, etc.)	❏
Better protection of the company	❏
Better coordination with decisions and operations	❏
Other:	❏

Concrete examples

....

....

....

EVALUATION OF THE IMPACT OF SI ON PERFORMANCE	0	1	2	3	4
Improvement of financial performance					
Improvement of competitive position					
Cost savings					
Budgetary economy					
Time savings					
Improvement of innovation					
Increase in market share					
Contribution to new markets					
More sales					
Other:					
Total					

IMPACT INDICATORS OF SI ON PERFORMANCE

(a few indicators to retain from the list only)

FINANCIAL AXIS		T	T+X
Sales revenue (SR)	❑		
ROA	❑		
Operation result/net	❑		
Profitability	❑		
Export rate	❑		
EVA, RAOI, EBITDA	❑		
Financial results (loss or profits)	❑		
Cash flow	❑		
Capital performance	❑		
Proposed dividend	❑		
Sales and market share increase	❑		
Other:	❑		
CLIENT AXIS	❑	T	T+X
Customer satisfaction index	❑		
Classification by clients	❑		
Timeliness of deliveries	❑		
New customers	❑		
New markets	❑		
INNOVATION AND LEARNING AXIS	❑	T	T+X
Number of new products designed/developed/launched	❑		
Success rate of new product launch	❑		
Percentage of new products in SR	❑		
Delay to market new products	❑		
Quality of products	❑		
Production lifecycle	❑		
Improvement rate	❑		
PROCESS AXIS	❑	T	T+X
Production methods, comparison with competition	❑		
Life cycle	❑		
Unit cost	❑		
Performance	❑		
Other:			

Global effectiveness evaluation	0	1	2	3	4

Efficiency measure	0	1	2	3	4

9.4. Conclusion

By comparing the two measuring tools (one dedicated to SI methods for SI managers, and one dedicated to products, use and results of SI, for executive users), we have a global tool for evaluating SI performance. The results of the questionnaires make it possible to build an SI specific control panel from a limited number of indicators, chosen according to four criteria (methods, products, use and results).

This control panel is shown in Figure 9.3.

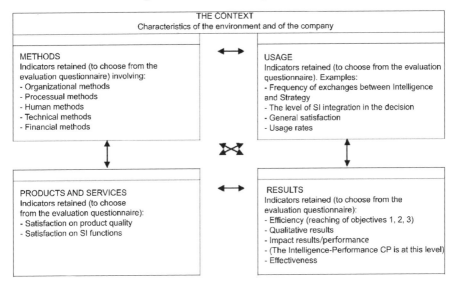

Figure 9.3. *SI control panel*

Conclusion

The tools proposed in this book make it possible to set up and continuously improve SI effectiveness and its impact on the performance of companies, by evaluating five components of SI:

– its context;

– its resources (organizational, "processual" SI, human, technical and financial);

– its products and services;

– its use;

– its results (including its impact on performance).

Managers who wish to have an efficient SI system should follow at least four fundamental rules:

– Set up a strategic watch and/or intelligence (SWI) measurement and control system at the start of the activity.

Measurement and control are normally designed to support organizational learning and progress in the organization (Reix). As for the corporate SWI system, the challenge is significant, since its objective is to improve its effectiveness, efficiency and impact on the performance of the organization.

In addition, it is important to consider, right from the start, the combination of resources, with the help of simple questions: What is SWI for? (effectiveness) and how do we implement it? (efficiency). Three fundamental rules have to be respected for an effective SI:

– Support the SWI activity.

The support and involvement of management and all the elements which make it visible (high hierarchical ranking, integration in the strategic decision, allocation of financial resource, etc.) are indeed powerful factors of SWI effectiveness.

– Positioning human resources at the heart of improvement policy of SWI effectiveness.

Training, experience, capabilities and qualities of SWI personnel are indisputable guarantees of SWI effectiveness. It is these human elements which allow, for example, quality SWI networks and products, and consequently a high usage ratio and tangible results.

– Endeavoring to evaluate the impact of the SWI activity on corporate performance.

Evaluating SWI results, in particular the impact on performance, is stimulating for all the players involved. As a result of this, SWI managers and users must evaluate the SWI results in strategic decisions. It is also necessary to choose various indicators of performance which are in contact with SWI activities and the strategic objectives of the company that they must serve.

Topicality constantly shows that a company with an effective SI system has a major competitive advantage. Its vision is clearer, its decisions more confident and its performance will be better.

Bibliography

AAKER D. A., "Organizing a strategic information scanning system", *California Management Review*, Vol. 25, n°2, January 1983, 76–83.

ABEGGLEN J. C., STALK G. Jr., *Kaïsha – The Japanese Corporation*, Basic Books Inc., 1985.

AFNOR, *Qualité et systèmes de management ISO 9000*, AFNOR Publications, 2001.

AGGARWAL V., ALLAN P., LACHAT D. (Anastasie Sablier), *Le renseignement stratégique d'entreprise*, L'Harmattan, 1997.

AGUILAR F.-J., *Scanning the Business Environment*, Macmillan, 1967.

ALARY-GRALL L., "Comment maîtriser l'information stratégique" Report, *Cahier Industries*, n°14, February 1996.

ALLAIN-DUPRE P., DUHARD N., *Les armes secrètes de la décision – La gestion de l'information au service de la performance économique*, Gualino, 1997.

ALLAIRE Y., "Coping with strategic uncertainty", *Sloan Management Review*, Vol. 20, n°3, 7–10, Spring 1989.

ALLEN T. J., COHEN S.I., "Information flow in research and development laboratories", *Administrative Science Quarterly*, March 1969.

ALLOUCHE J., SCHMIDT G., *Les outils de la décision stratégique*, Vol. 1 – *Before 1980*, Vol. 2 – *Since 1980*, Repères collection, Editions La Découverte, 1995.

ANDRIEU O., *Comment trouver l'information sur Internet*, Eyrolles, 1998.

ANSOFF I, *Corporate Strategy*, McGraw-Hill, 1965.

ANSOFF I., *Stratégie du développement de l'entreprise*, Hommes et Techniques, 1968.

ANSOFF I., *Strategic Management*, Macmillan, 1979.

ANSOFF I., "Managing strategic surprise by response to weak signals", *California Management Review*, Vol. 23, n°2, Winter 1975, 21–33.

ANSOFF I., "Strategic issue management", *Strategic Management Journal*, Vol. 1, n°2, April June 1980, 131–48.

ANSOFF I., *Implanting Strategic Management*, Free Press, 1984.

ANSOFF I., *The New Corporate Strategy*, John Wiley & Sons, 1988.

ANSOFF I., DECLERC R. P., HAYES R. L., *From Strategic Planning to Strategic Management*, John Wiley & Sons, 1979.

ANTOINE J., "Un nouveau métier pour les hommes de marketing: la veille prospective et ses applications stratégiques", *Revue française du Marketing*, n°139, 1992/4, 5–30.

APQC (American Productivity & Quality Center), *The Benchmarking Management Guide*, Productivity Press, 1993.

ARAM J. D., COWEN S. C., "The Director's role in planning: what information do they need?", *Long Range Planning*, Vol. 19, n°96, April 1986, 117–24.

ARIST (Agence Régionale d'Information scientifique et Technique), *Veille industrielle: le guide*, ACFCI, Collection l'Intelligence Economique Pratique, 1996.

ARRO E., DEMERY A., PANFELY P., PRESCOTT J., (eds), *Competitive and Business Intelligence: Leveraging Information for Action*, Competitive and Business Intelligence Best-Practice Report, American Productivity and Quality Center, January, 1997.

ARTUS P., CDC Ixis Capital Markets, "Comment ne pas suivre l'exemple du Japon", *Le Figaro Economie*, April 13, 2001.

ASSADI D., *Intelligence économique sur Internet: études de marché et veille concurrentielle*, Publi-Union, 1998.

ASSADI D., DEMEUNYNK, J.-Y., "Internet: un véritable outil de veille et d'études", *Marketing Magazine*, n°20, April 1997.

ATAMER T., CALORI R., LAURENT P., "Dynamique des marchés et veille stratégique – Méthodologie", Working Paper from Institut de Recherche de l'Entreprise, Série *Management Stratégique de l'Information*, Groupe Ecole Supérieure de Commerce de Lyon, January 1987.

ATHENA, "L'Intelligence économique", *La Documentation française*, n°5, 1998, 135–88.

ATTANASIO R., "The multiple benefits of competitor intelligence", *Journal of Business Strategy*, May–June 1988, 16–19.

ATTAWAY M. C., "A review of issues related to gathering and assessing competitive intelligence", *American Business Review*, January 1998, 25–35.

AUBERT M., "La veille technologique en recherche et développement dans l'industrie pharmaceutique", *Documentaliste, Sciences de l'information*, 1995, Vol. 32, n°3, 1995, 176–8,

AUBERT N., GAULEJAC (de) V., *Le coût de l'excellence*, Editions du Seuil, October 1991.

AUDET J., "La veille stratégique chez les PME de haute technologie: une étude de cas par comparaisons inter-sites", Communication at the *10th Conference of AIMS*, Laval University, Quebec, June 13–15, 2001.

AUSTER E., CHOO C. W., "How senior managers acquire and use information in environmental scanning", *Information Processing & Management*, Vol. 30, n°5, 1994, 607–18.

BABBAR S., RAI A., "Competitive intelligence for international business", *Long Range Planning*, Vol. 26, n°3, June 1993, 103–13.

BABINET C., *Le devoir de vigilance*, Denoël, 1992.

BAIRD L., *Managing Performance*, John Wiley & Sons, 1986.

BALLAZ, B., "Le processus de veille stratégique examiné du point de vue des directions d'achat: présentation des résultats d'une enquête réalisée auprès d'une centaine d'entreprises industrielles", *Working Paper* n° 92-04, Centre d'Etudes et de Recherches Appliquées à la Gestion, Ecole Supérieure des Affaires de Grenoble, 1992.

BALLAZ B., LESCA H., "Le processus de veille stratégique: l'examen de quelques questions importantes", *Working Paper* n°92-05, Centre d'Etudes et de Recherches Appliquées à la Gestion, Ecole Supérieure des Affaires de Grenoble, 1992.

BALLERY E., *Le nouveau référentiel*, EFQM, 1999.

BALM G., *Evaluer et améliorer ses performances, le Benchmarking*, AFNOR, 1994.

BARDIN L., *L'analyse de contenu*, PUF, 9th edn., May 1998.

BARROUX D., "Le Japon est à nouveau en récession", *Les Echos*, December 10, 2001.

BAUDET M-B., "L'IE est un outil stratégique encore mal perçu par les entreprises", *Le Monde*, Wednesday November 27, 1996.

BAUMARD P., *Stratégie et surveillance des environnements concurrentiels*, Masson, 1991.

BEAL R. M;, "Competing effectively: environmental scanning, competitive strategy, and organizational performance in small manufacturing firms", *Journal of Small Business, Management*, Vol. 38, n°1, 2000, 27–47.

BEAUFILS P., DALAN M., GUERIN C., LOUKIL R., MAHE T., GIROU G., Dossier "Veille Technologique", *Industries et Techniques*, n°789, January 1998, 42–57.

BELOT L., Dossier "Intelligence Economique", *Le Monde*, December 12, 1998.

BERNARD C-Y., *Le management par la qualité totale, l'excellence en efficacité et en efficience opérationnelles*, AFNOR, 2000.

BERTALANFFY L., *Théorie générale des systèmes*, Dunod, 1973.

BESSON B. ,POSSIN J.-C., *Du renseignement à l'intelligence économique: Détecter les menaces et les opportunités pour l'entreprise*, Dunod, 1996.

BLOCH A., *Intelligence économique*, Economica, 2 edn., 1999.

BOURNOIS F., ROMANI P.-J., *L'intelligence économique et stratégique dans les entreprises françaises*, Economica, 2000.

BOWER J. L., CHRISTENSEN C. M., "Disruptive technologies: catching the wave", *Harvard Business Review*, January–February, 1995.

BROCKHOFF K., "Competitor Technology Intelligence in German Companies", *Industrial Marketing Management*, Vol. 20, n° 2, May 1991, 91–8.

BROHOLM P., "Formal scanning of the organizational environment: addressing the limitations", *Wharton School of Pennsylvania, Social Systems Science Program*, 1982.

BRUFFAERTS J., BOUCHARD B., *Veille et intelligence économique. De la stratégie à la communication de l'information*, Information Documentation Presse, 1996.

BURACK E. H., MATHYS N. J., "Environmental scanning improves strategic planning", *Personnal Administrator*, n° 34/4, April 1989, 82–7.

CADUC P., "L'intelligence économique: un nouvel enjeu pour l'état et les entreprises", *Défense,* n°74, December 1996, 44–6.

CALORI R., "Designing a business scanning system", *Long Range Planning,* Vol. 22, n°113, February 1989, 69–82.

CALORI R., ATAMER T., LAURENT P., "Dynamique des Marchés et Veille Stratégique", *Revue d'Economie Industrielle,* n°46, 4th term 1988, 55–71.

CAMP R. C., *Benchmarking: The Search for Industry Best Practices that Lead to Superior Performance,* ASQC Quality Press, 1989.

CAMPBEL A., "On the Nature of Organizational Effectiveness", in P. S. GOODMAN and J. M. PENNINGS (eds.), *New Perspectives on Organizational Effectiveness,* Jossey Bass, 1977.

Centre d'Etude et de Prospective Stratégique (CEPS), Deloitte & Touche, *Pratiques et attentes des entreprises en matière d'intelligence économique,* CEPS/Deloitte & Touche, 1998.

CORVELLEC A., ARRIS F., *La veille technologique et concurrentielle au et sur le Japon,* Centre de Documentation Industrielle et Direction des Industries et Services du CFCE, Les Éditions du CFCE (Centre Français de Commerce Extérieur), 1991.

CORVELLEC A., BAZILLE B. *Intelligence économique et concurrentielle aux Etats-Unis,* Centre de Documentation Industrielle du CFCE, Les Editions du CFCE, 1991.

CHABERT, P., "L'intelligence économique balbutie. Le concept se répand plus vite que la pratique", *Les Echos,* Wednesday May 2, 2001.

Chambres de Commerce et d'Industrie, *Intelligence économique – Un engagement stratégique,* Analyses et Propositions, Livres Blanc collection from Chambres de Commerce et d'Industrie, Assemblée des Chambres de Commerce et d'Industrie, 1997.

CHRISTENSEN C. R., ANDREWS K. R, BOWER J.L., *Business Policy: Text and Cases,* R. Irwin, 1973.

CLELAND D. J., KING W. R., "Competitive business intelligence systems", *Business Horizons,* December, 1975, 19–28 .

CLELAND D. J., KING W. R., "Information for more effective strategic planning", *Long Range Planning,* Vol. 10, 1977, 59–64.

CLEVELAND H., "Information as a resource", *The Futurist,* December 1982, 34–9.

Collectif, "Veille technologique et politique de brevets", *Travaux de la Commission Riboud du Xième Plan,* 1986.

Collectif du Commissariat Général au Plan, *Information et compétitivité,* group presided over by René MAYER, Documentation française, 1990.

Collectif, "XIème plan: la performance globale, meilleure mesure de la compétitivité des entreprises", *Liaisons Sociales,* Série Documents, n°12–93, February 10, 1993.

Collectif du Commissariat Général du Plan, group presided over by Henri MARTRE, *Intelligence économique et stratégie des entreprises,* La Documentation française, 1994.

Collectif, *Revue d'Intelligence Économique,* n°1, March 1997.

Collectif, *Les nouveaux tableaux de bord pour piloter l'entreprise: Systèmes d'information, nouvelles technologies et mesure de la performance*, Paris, 1997.

Compétitivité française, work of the commission presided over by J. GANDOIS, P. D. G. de PECHINEY, in preparation for the 11th program (1993–7), 1992.

CROZIER M. and FRIEDBERG E., *L'acteur et le système*, Le Seuil, 1975.

CULNAN M. J., "Environmental scanning: the effect of task complexity and source accessibility on information gathering behavior", *Decision Sciences*, Vol. 14, n°2, April 1983, 194–206.

CYERT R. M. and MARCH J. G., *A Behavioral Theory of the Firm*, Prentice Hall, 1963.

DAFT R. L., SORMUNEN J., PARKS D., "Chief executive scanning, environmental characteristics and company performance: an empirical study", *Strategic Management Journal*, Vol. 9, n°2, March–April 1988, 123–39.

De JOUVENEL H., "Sur la démarche prospective: un bref guide méthodologique", *Futuribles*, n°179, September 1993, 51–72.

De JOUVENEL H., "La veille et le bruit", *Vigie-Faits, Idées et Tendances porteurs d'avenir*, Quarterly bulletin from Futuribles International, n°20, October–December 1996.

De LA VILLARMOIS O. "Le concept de performance et sa mesure: un état de l'art", *XIVèmes Journées Nationales des I.A.E, Nantes*, Vol. 2, 1998, pp 199–216.

De MARICOURT R. *et al.*, *Marketing Européen: Stratégies et actions*, Publi-Union, 1997.

DENNING B. W., "Strategic environmental appraisal", *Long Range Planning*, Vol. 6, n°1, March 1973, 22–7.

DENZIN N. K., LINCOLN Y. S. (eds), *Handbook of Qualitative Research*, Sage Publications, 1994.

DESVALS H., DOU H., *La veille technologique, l'information scientifique, technique et industrielle*, Dunod, 1992.

DIFFENBACH J., "Corporate environmental analysis in large U. S. corporations", *Long Range Planning*, Vol. 16, n°3, 1983, 107–16.

DOTY H., GLICK W. H., HUBER C. P., "Fit, equifinality and organizational effectiveness: a test of two configurational theories", *Academy of Management Journal*, Vol. 36, n°6, 1993, 1196–250.

DOU H., *Veille technologique et compétitivité – l'intelligence économique au service du développement industriel*, Dunod, 1995.

DRUCKER P. F., "L'information dont les dirigeants ont vraiment besoin", in *Les systèmes de mesure de la performance,* Harvard Business Review, Editions d'Organisation, 1999.

DUNCAN R., "Characteristics of organisational environments and perceived environment uncertainty", *Administrative Science Quaterly*, 17, 3, 313–27.

EISENHARDT K. M., "Building theories from case study research", *Academy of Management Review*, Vol. 14, n°4, 1989, 532–50.

EISENHARDT K. M., "Has strategy changed?", *Sloan Management Review*, Winter 2002.

EL SAWY O. A., "Personal information systems for strategic scanning in turbulent environments:can the CEO go on line", *Management Information Systems Quarterly*, March 1985, 53–60.

ENGLEDOW J. L., LENZ R. T., "Whatever happened to environmental analysis?", *Long Range Planning*, Vol. 18, n°2, April 1985, 93–106.

ESTRIN T. L., "The roles of information providers in decision making", *Journal of General Management*, Vol. 15, n°3, Spring 1990, 80–95.

FAHEY L., KING W. R. "Environmental scanning in corporate planning", *Business Horizons*, August 1977, 61–71.

FAHEY L., KING W. R., NARAYANAN V. K., "Environmental scanning and forecasting in strategic planning – the state of the art", *Long Range Planning*, Vol. 14, February 1981, 32–9.

FARH J. L., HOFFMAN R. C., HEGARTY W. H. "Assessing environmental scanning at the subunit level: a multitrait – multimethod analysis", *Decision Sciences*, Vol. 15, n°2, Spring 1984, 197–220.

FORSTER R., *L'innovation: avantage à l'attaquant*, InterEditions, 1986.

FOUCAULT M., *Surveiller et Punir*, Gallimard, 1975.

FULD L. M., *Competitor Intelligence: How to Get it How to Use It*, John Wiley & Sons, 1985.

GHOSHAL S., Environmental scanning, PhD Thesis, MIT, Sloan School of Management, 1985.

GHOSHAL S., "Environmental scanning in Korean firms", *Journal of International Business Studies*, Spring 1988, 69–86.

GHOSHAL S., KIM S. K., "Building effective intelligence systems for competitive advantage", *Sloan Management Review*, Vol. 28, n°1, Fall 1986, 49–58.

GHOSHAL S., WESTNEY E., "Organizing competitor analysis systems", *Strategic Management Journal*, 12, 1991, 17–31.

GIBBONS P. T., The integration of formal and personalized competitive intelligence: a comparative analysis of organisational responses to Europe, PhD Thesis, University of Pittsburg, 1992.

GILAD T., GILAD B., "Business intelligence: the quiet revolution", *Sloan Management Review*, Vol. 27, n°4, Summer 1986, 53–61.

GILAD B., GILAD T., *The Business Intelligence System: a New Tool for Competitive Advantage*, Amacon, 1988.

GILAD B., GORDON G., SUDIT E., "Identifying gaps and blind spots in competitive intelligence", *Long Range Planning*, Vol. 26, n°6, December 1993, 107–13.

GIROD M., "La Mémoire organisationnelle", *Revue Française de Gestion*, n°105, September–October 1995.

GLASER B., STRAUSS A., *The Discovery of Grounded Theory: Strategies for Qualitative Research*, Hawthorne, Aldine de Gruyter, 1967.

GODET M., "Veille prospective et flexibilité stratégique", *Futuribles*, n°91, 1985, 3–10.

GODET M., *Manuel de Prospective Stratégique*. Vol. 1: *Une discipline intellectuelle* – Vol. 2: *L'art et la méthode*, Dunod, 2nd edn., 2001.

GODIWALLA Y. M., MEINHART W. A. & WARDE W. D., "Environmental scanning – does it help the chief executive?", *Long Range Planning*, Vol. 13, n°5, October 1980, 87–99.

GOGUE J-M., *Management de la qualité*, Economica, 2nd edn., 1997.

GRAWITZ M., *Méthodes en sciences sociales*, 10th edn., Dalloz, 1996.

GUTH J-P., "La veille de l'entreprise ; un service qui n'a pas de prix !", *Le Progrès Technique*, n°2, 1987, 9–12. Article used in "La veille technologique, les conditions de la réussite", *Problèmes Economiques*, n°2,054, December 23, 1987.

HAMBRICK D. C., Environmental scanning, organizational strategy and executives' roles: a study in three industries, unpublished PhD Thesis, Pennsylvania State University, 1979.

HAMBRICK D. C., "Environment, strategy and power within top management teams", *Administrative Science Quaterly*, n°26, 1981, 253–76.

HAMBRICK D. C., "Specialization of environmental scanning activities among upper level executives". *Journal of Management Studies*, Vol. 18, n°3, 1981, 299–320.

HAMBRICK D. C., "Environmental scanning and organizational strategy", *Strategic Management Journal*, Vol. 3, 1982, 159–74.

HAMEL G., PRAHALAD C. K., "Strategic intent", *Harvard Business Review*, n°3, May–June 1989, 63–76.

HAMEL G., PRAHALAD C. K., "Core competence of the organization", *Harvard Business Review*, May 1999, 79–91.

HARBULOT C., *Techniques offensives et guerre économique*, Aditech, 1990.

HARBULOT C., *La machine de guerre économique: Etats-Unis, Japon, Europe*, Economica, 1994.

HARVARD BUSINESS REVIEW, *Les systèmes de mesure de la performance*, Editions d'Organisation, 1999.

HENDRICK L., "Competitive intelligence", *Business & Economic Review*, Vol. 42, n°4, July September 1996, 7–10.

HERRING J. P., "Building a business intelligence system", *Journal of Business Strategy*, May–June 1988, 4–9.

HERRING P., "Senior management must champion business intelligence programs", *Journal of Business Strategy*, September–October 1991, 48–52.

HERRING J., "Intelligence to enhance american companies' competitiveness: the government's role and obligation", *Competitive Intelligence Review*, Vol. 5, n°3, Fall 1994, 12–16.

HERRING J. P., *Measuring the Effectiveness of Competitive Intelligence: Assessing and communications CI's Value to Your Organisation*, SCIP Publications, 1999,

HUBERMAN M, MILES B., *Qualitative Data Analysis: A Source of New Methods*, Sage Publications, 1984.

HUNT C., ZARTARIAN V., *Le Renseignement stratégique au service de votre entreprise*, Editions First, 1990.

HUSSEY D., JENSTER P., *Competitor Intelligence: Turning Analysis into Success*, John Wiley & Sons, 1999.

JAIN S. C., "Environmental scanning in US corporations", *Long Range Planning*, Vol. 17, n°2, April 1984, 117–28.

JAKOBIAK F., *Maîtriser l'information critique*, Editions d'Organisation, 1988.

JAKOBIAK F., *L'intelligence économique en pratique*, Editions d'Organisation, 1998.

KAHANER L., "Competitive intelligence pays off on the home front", *Information Week*, Manhasset, September 25, 2000.

KAPLAN R. S., NORTON D. P., "Mettre en pratique le tableau de bord prospectif", in *Les systèmes de mesure de la performance*, Editions d'Organisation, 1999.

KAPLAN R. S., NORTON D. P., "Le tableau de bord prospectif: un système de pilotage de la performance", in *Les systèmes de mesure de la performance*, Editions d'Organisation, 1999.

KAPLAN R. S., NORTON D. P., "Le tableau de bord prospectif, outil de management stratégique", in *Les systèmes de mesure de la performance*, Editions d'Organisation, 1999.

KEEGAN J., Scanning the international business environment, unpublished dissertation, Harvard Business School, June 1967.

KEEGAN W. J., "Multinational scanning: a study of the information sources utilized by headquarters executives in multinational companies", *Administrative Science Quaterly*, Vol. 19, n°3, September 1974, 411–21.

KEFALAS A., SCHODERBEK P.P., "Scanning the business environment – some empirical results", *Decision Sciences*, Vol. 4, n°4, January 1973, 63–74.

KLEIN H. E., LINNEMAN R. E., "Environment assessment: an international study of corporate practice", *Journal of Business Strategy*, Vol. 5, n°1, Summer 1984, 66–75.

LA VILLARMOIS O. "Le concept de performance et sa mesure: un état de l'art", *XIVèmes Journées Nationales des I.A.E, Nantes*, Vol. 2, 1998, 199–216.

LAINEE F., "La veille technologique: comment devenir professionnel ?", *Annales des mines, Gérer et Comprendre*, September 1991, 14–25.

LANCESSEUR B., D'AVOUT F., TOURNIER J., NOISETTE T., M. Q., "Dossier Intelligence Economique", *Les Echos*, Wednesday January 31, 1996.

LASSERRE P., "Gathering and interpreting strategic intelligence in Asia Pacific", *Long Range Planning*, Vol. 26, n°3, 1993.

LAWRENCE P, LORSCH J., *Developing Organization: Diagnosis and Action*, Addison Wesley, 1969.

LEARNED E. P., CHRISTENSEN C. R., ANDREWS K. R., GUTH W. D., *Business Policy: Text and Cases*, R. Irwin, 1965.

LENDREVIE J., LINDON D., *Mercator*, 5th edn., Dalloz, 1996.

LENZ R. T., ENGLEDOW J. L., "Environmental analysis units and strategic decision making: a field study of selected 'leading-edge' corporations", *Strategic Management Journal*, Vol. 7, n°1, January–February 1986, 69–89.

LESCA E., "Systèmes d'information de l'entreprise ouverts sur son environnement", *Research Paper* n°8307, CERAG, Grenoble, June 1983.

LESCA H., *Système d'information pour le management stratégique de l'entreprise*, McGraw Hill, 1986.

LESCA H., "Fennec: logiciel expert pour l'évaluation de la veille stratégique dans les PME –PMI", *Direction et Gestion des Entreprises*, n°132–3, December 1991, 9–15.

LEVET J.-L., "Intelligence économique et stratégie des entreprises: pour un management de l'intelligence économique", *Revue d'Intelligence Économique*, n°5, October 1999, 50–67.

LUNH H., "A business intelligence system", *IBM Journal*, October 1958.

MARCH G.-J., *Décisions et organisation*, Editions d'Organisation, 1982.

MARTEAU G., "Scanning de l'environnement de l'entreprise: discours et réalités", *Working Paper* n°8502, CERAG, Grenoble, July 1984.

MARTEAU G., "La fonction surveillance de l'environnement dans la PMI ouverte sur l'extérieur et engagée dans des technologies de pointe", *Research Paper* n°8512, CERAG, Grenoble, June 1985.

MARTINET B., MARTI Y.-M., *L'intelligence économique, les yeux et les oreilles de l'entreprise*, Editions d'Organisation, 1995. 2nd edn.: *L'intelligence économique – Comment donner de la valeur concurrentielle à l'information*, 2001.

MARTINET B., RIBAULT J.-M., *La veille technologique, concurrentielle et commerciale*, Editions d'Organisation, 2nd edn., 1989.

MATHE J-C., CHAGUE V., "L'intention stratégique et les divers types de performance de l'entreprise", *Revue Française de Gestion*, January–February 1999, 39–49.

MINTZBERG H., *Le management*, Editions d'Organisation, 1998.

MONTGOMERY D. B., WEINBERG C. B., "Toward strategic intelligence systems", *Journal of Marketing*, Vol. 43, Fall 1979, 41–52.

MORGAT P., "L'information est R.O.I.", *Veille Magazine*, April 1997, 9–11.

MORIN E. M., SAVOIE A., BEAUDIN G., *L'efficacité de l'organisation. Théories, représentations et mesures*, Gaëtan Morin, 1994.

NARCHAL R. M., KITTAPA K., BHATTACHARYA P., "An environmental scanning system for business planning", *Long Range Planning*, Vol. 20/6, n°106, December 1987, 96–105.

NONAKA I, TAKEUCHI H., *La connaissance créatrice*, De Boeck University, 1997.

OHINATA Y., "Benchmarking: the Japanese experience", *Long Range Planning*, Vol. 27, n°4, 48–53, 1994.

O'REILLY C. A., "Variation in decision makers' use of information sources: the impact of quality and accessibility of information", *Academy of Management Journal*, Vol. 25, n°1,December 1982, 756–71.

OUATTARA A., "Les obstacles au recueil des données: les solutions adoptées par les entre prises ivoiriennes", *Revue française du Marketing*, 1992, 7784.

OURY J.-P., *Economie politique de la vigilance*, Calmann-Lévy, 1983.

PARASURAMAN, ZEITHAML V. A., BERRY L., "SERVQUAL, A multiple item scale for measuring customer perceptions of service quality", *Journal of Retailing*, 64, 137, 1988.

PETTIFER D., "Measuring the Performance of the Corporate Centre", *Long Range Planning*, Vol. 31, n°5, October 1998, 783–85.

PFEFFER J. & SALANCIK G-R., *The external control of organization – A resource perspective*, Harper & Row, 1978.

PORTER M., *Competitive Strategy*, Free Press, 1980.

PRAHALAD C. K., HAMEL G., "The core competence of the corporation", *Harvard Business Review*, May–June 1990, 79–91.

PREBLE J. F., "Future Forecasting with LEAP", *Long Range Planning*, Vol. 15, n°4, August 1982, 64–9.

PREBLE J. F., RAU P. A., REICHEL A., "The environmental scanning practices of U.S. multinationals in the late 1980's", *Management International Review*, Vol. 28, 4–13, 1988.

PRESCOTT J. E., "The Evolution of Competitive Intelligence", in *Rethinking Strategic Management*, HUSSEY D. (ed.), John Wiley & Sons, 1995.

PRESCOTT J. E., "A Manager's Guide To The Ethics Of Competitive Intelligence", in *Competitive Intelligence: Where Are The Ethical Limits?*, *Ethics in Economics*, n° 3 & 4, 1998.

PRESCOTT J. E., "Competitive Intelligence: Lessons from the Trenches", *Competitive Intelligence Review*, Vol. 12, n°2, second quarter 2001, 5–19.

PRESCOTT J. E., GIBBONS T., "Parallel competitive intelligence process in organization", *International Journal Technology Management*, Vol. 11, n°1, 1996.

PRESCOTT J. E., GIBBONS T., *Global Perspectives on Competitive Intelligence*, Society of Competitive Intelligence Professionals, 1993.

PRESCOTT J. E., MILLER S. H., *Proven Strategies in Competitive Intelligence: Lessons from the Trenches*, SCIP, John Wiley & Sons, 2001.

PRESCOTT J. E., SMITH D. C., "The largest survey of "leading edge" competitor intelligence managers", *Planning Review*, Vol. 17, May–June 1989, 6–16.

RACINE M., BESSON B., BOYELDIEU D'AUVIGNY M., "Le référentiel d'intelligence économique du Ministère de l'Intérieur", Ministère de l'Intérieur, May 2000.

RAMBAUD N., "Intelligence économique & Internet", *MOCI report*, n°1338, 21 May, 1998, 69–75.

RAMBAUD N., "Les structures d'aides et de conseil", Dossier "Comment maîtriser l'information stratégique", *Les Echos Industries*, n°14, February 1996, 19–21.

REINHARDT W. A., "An early warning system for strategic planning", *Long Range Planning*, Vol. 17, n°5, October 1984; 25–34.

REIX R., "Le système d'information: une réalité vivante", *Revue française de Gestion*, November–December 1983, 6–8.

REIX R., *Système d'information et management des organisations*, Vuibert, 2nd edn., 1998.

REVELLI C., *Intelligence stratégique sur Internet: comment développer efficacement des activités de veille et de recherche sur les réseaux? Moteurs de recherche, réseaux d'experts, agents intelligents*, Dunod, 1998.

REYNE M., *Le développement de l'entreprise par la veille technico-économique*, Hermes Science, 1990.

RIBAULT J.-M., MARTINET B., LEBIDOIS D., *Le management des technologies*, Editions d'Organisation, 1991.

RIVELINE C., "Nouvelles approches des processus de décision", *Futuribles*, n°72, December 1983.

ROIRON L, LESCA H., "Enquête sur la veille stratégique dans les entreprises britanniques", *Technologies Internationales*, n°32, March 97, 40–3.

ROLAND M., "Le benchmarking: l'art de copier les meilleurs", *La Tribune*, November 4, 1992.

ROMAGNI P., WILD V., *L'intelligence économique au service de l'entreprise: ou l'information comme outil de gestion*, Les Presses du Management, 1998.

ROUACH D., *La Veille Technologique et l'Intelligence Economique, Que sais-je ?*, PUF, 2nd edn., 1999.

ROUSH G. B. "A program for sharing corporate intelligence", *Journal of Business Strategy*, January–February 1991, 4–7.

RUSSELL S., PRINCE M. J., "Environmental scanning for social services", *Long Range Planning*, Vol. 25, n°5, October 1992, 106–13.

SAMMON W. L., KURLAND M. A., SPITANIC R., *Business Competitor Intelligence: Methods for Collecting Organizing and Using Information*, John Wiley & Sons, 1984.

SAWKA K. A., "Demystifying business intelligence", *Management Review*, Vol. 85, n°10, October 1996, 47–51.

SAWYER O., "Environmental uncertainty and environmental scanning activities of nigerian manufacturing executives: a comparative analysis", *Strategic Management Journal*, Vol. 14, n°4, May 1993, 287–99.

SCIP, *2000/01 Competitive Intelligence Professionals Salary Survey Report and Reference Guide on Analyst Job Descriptions*, SCIP Publications, 2000/2001.

SENGE P. M., *The Fifth Discipline*, Century Business, 1990.

SERIEYX H., *La nouvelle excellence*, Maxima, 2000.

SEURAT R., ROUGEOT J., "Intelligence Service et Marketing des Projets Industriels", *Revue française du Marketing*, n°127–8, 1990/2–3, 39–50.

SEURAT S., *La coévolution créatrice, réseau de vigilance et d'intelligence*, Rivages, 1987.

SIMON H., *Administrative Behavior*, Macmillan, 1947.

SIMON H., *The New Science of Management Decision*, Harper & Row, 1st edn., 1960. Revised edition: Prentice Hall, 1977.

SIMON H., *Le nouveau management*, Economica, 1980.

SIMON H., *Administration et processus de décision*, Economica, 1983.

STOFFELS J. D., "Environmental scanning for futur success", *Managerial Planning*, November–December 1982, 4–12.

STRAUSS A., CORBIN J., *Basics of Qualitative Research. Grounded Theory – Procedures and Techniques*, Sage Publications, 1990.

STUBBART C.,"Are environmental scanning units effective?", *Long Range Planning*, Vol. 15, n°3, June 1982, 139–45.

SUBRAMANIAN R., FERNANDES N., HARPER E., "Environmental scanning in U.S. companies: their nature and their relationship to performance", *Management International Review*, Vol. 33, 1993/3, 271–86.

SUN TZU, *L'art de la guerre*, Flammarion, 1972.

TABATONI P. & JARNIOU P., *Les systèmes de gestion – Politiques et structures*, PUF, 1971.

THIETART R.-A. *et al.*, *Méthodes de recherche en management*, Dunod, 1999.

THIETART R.-A., VIVAS R., "Strategic intelligence activity: the management of the sales force as a source of strategic information", *Strategic Management Journal*, Vol. 2, n°1, January–March 1981, 15–25.

VELLA C.M., McGONAGLE J. J., *Protecting your Company against Competitive Intelligence*, Geenwood, 1998.

VERGNAUD-SCHAEFFER M.-P., "Veille de l'entreprise et performance: une approche pour les PME/PMI", *Direction et Gestion des Entreprises*, n°143, September–October 1993.

VILLAIN J., *L'entreprise aux aguets*, Masson, 1989.

WESTNEY E., GHOSHAL S., "Building a competitor intelligence organization adding value in an information function", in ALLEN T. and SCOTT MORTON M S (eds), *Information Technology and the Corporation of the 1990s*, Oxford University Press, 1994.

WILENSKY H., *Organizational Intelligence: Knowledge and Policy in Government and Industry*, Basic Books, 1967.

YIN R., *Case Study Research: Design and Methods*, Sage Publications, 1991.

ZEITHAML V. A., PARASURAMAN, BERRY L., *Delivering Quality Service: Balancing Customer Perceptions and Expectations*, Free Press, 1990.

ZMUD R., "An empirical investigation of the dimensionality of the concept of information", *Decisions Sciences*, 9, 1978, 187–95.

Index